"Professionals will debate the techniques, and economists will debate the payback, but no one will debate Jeff Wilson's pluck in attacking his own Deep Energy Retrofit—all the while living with his family in the house! *The Greened House Effect* is a good overview of the DER field and a great argument for moving out while you do the work! Jeff must have a very patient wife!"

> **STEVE THOMAS**, former host of PBS's *This Old House*
> and Planet Green's *Renovation Nation*

"I live on an island. There are 17,000 existing buildings here. Each will be brought into the 21st century, at some point, or be summarily discarded—demolished, dumped, and replaced. The Deep Energy Retrofit method is the key to restoring our existing housing stock. At South Mountain Company we practice this approach. Jeff Wilson does, too, and he has written a comprehensive and robust introduction to the subject that balances practical instructions with design, engineering, and social/environmental context. *The Greened House Effect* is very informative. And it's a good read, too."

> **JOHN ABRAMS**, president and CEO,
> South Mountain Company, Inc., author of *Companies We Keep*

"Jeff Wilson has provided an extraordinary service to all of us who are struggling to make our homes more energy efficient. I know of no other book that takes the reader on such a thoroughly entertaining but equally fact-filled tour of all the options and challenges in making an older home equal to, or better than, new. For anyone who is serious about making their existing home a better custodian of our planet's resources, *The Greened House Effect* is a must read. If I could add an addendum to my own book, *Not So Big Remodeling*, I'd tell my readers, 'To really understand how to do a Deep Energy Retrofit right, read *The Greened House Effect*.'"

> **SARAH SUSANKA**, architect and author
> of *The Not So Big House* series

"*The Greened House Effect* is inspiring, empowering, informative, and entertaining. Jeff Wilson puts a human face on a technical undertaking by relating his family's Deep Energy Retrofit (DER) story as an adventure drama—with defining moments, 'learning experiences,' and palpable joys—interspersed with solid advice about how to carry out one's own DER.

At the same time, Wilson views a single DER in the context of a growing movement that can positively impact our economy, environmental pollution, and national security. *The Greened House Effect* means a better life, for one family and for the world."

CAROL VENOLIA, architect, Come Home to Nature, and coauthor of *Natural Remodeling for the Not-So-Green House*

THE GREENED HOUSE EFFECT

THE GREENED HOUSE EFFECT

JEFF WILSON

RENOVATING YOUR HOME WITH
A DEEP ENERGY RETROFIT

Chelsea Green Publishing
White River Junction, Vermont

Unless otherwise noted, all photographs are by Sherri James.
Unless otherwise noted, all illustrations are by Matthew Baker.

Developmental Editor: Fern Bradley
Project Manager: Patricia Stone
Copy Editor: Kim M. Smithgall
Proofreader: Eileen M. Clawson
Indexer: Lee Lawton
Designer: Melissa Jacobson

Printed in the United States of America
First printing May, 2013.
10 9 8 7 6 5 4 3 2 1   13 14 15 16 17

Our Commitment to Green Publishing
Chelsea Green sees publishing as a tool for cultural change and ecological stewardship. We strive to align our book manufacturing practices with our editorial mission and to reduce the impact of our business enterprise in the environment. We print our books and catalogs on chlorine-free recycled paper, using vegetable-based inks whenever possible. This book may cost slightly more because it was printed on paper that contains recycled fiber, and we hope you'll agree that it's worth it. Chelsea Green is a member of the Green Press Initiative (www.greenpressinitiative.org), a nonprofit coalition of publishers, manufacturers, and authors working to protect the world's endangered forests and conserve natural resources. *The Greened House Effect* was printed on FSC®-certified paper supplied by QuadGraphics that contains at least 10 percent postconsumer recycled fiber.

Library of Congress Cataloging-in-Publication Data
Wilson, Jeff, 1967–
  The greened house effect : renovating your home with a deep energy
retrofit / Jeff Wilson.
    pages cm
  Includes bibliographical references and index.
  ISBN 978-1-60358-450-0 (pbk.) — ISBN 978-1-60358-451-7 (ebook)
1. Ecological houses. 2. Dwellings—Remodeling. I. Title.

TH4860.W543 2013
690.028'6—dc23

                    2013004054

Chelsea Green Publishing
85 North Main Street, Suite 120
White River Junction, VT 05001
(802) 295-6300
www.chelseagreen.com

To Sherri, Winter, and Sylvie

CONTENTS

INTRODUCTION

WHAT IF YOU COULD SLASH THE AMOUNT OF ENERGY IT TAKES TO heat, cool, and power your home by 50 to 90 percent? And what if, by fixing the problems of your energy-inefficient old home, you could help solve some of our country's most pressing problems: the triple threat of a lousy economy, polluted environment, and lack of national security?

When I decided to renovate my 70-year-old house, I was motivated by my own needs and the needs of my family—at first. But the more I learned about the potential of the deep energy retrofit process—renovation methods and materials that have the potential to cut energy usage in half or better—the more I began to dream about the far-reaching changes that might take place in our country if deep energy retrofits became a widespread phenomenon. I'm not talking about band-aid fixes or minor tweaks. I'm not talking about weatherization. I'm talking about a full-scale updating of older buildings to bring them up to 21st century green building standards for energy efficiency, comfort, and health.

Like weatherization on steroids, a deep energy retrofit (DER) takes your older home into the 21st century, by using superinsulation, air sealing, and energy miser appliances to knock your energy use to the ground. Then, in a "one-two punch" with renewable energy generation like solar or wind power, a DER pokes a stick in the eye of petro-terrorism, environmental degradation, and economic recession. Combined with the coming smart grid and green transportation technological advances, the DER process is the keystone of real solutions to our energy problems across the spectrum.

The dramatic, all encompassing approach of a DER will demolish your high energy bills, now and into the future. A DER combines a potent set of building materials including spray foam insulation, radiant barrier sheathing, triple pane gas-filled windows, and insulated fiberglass doors, with superior-quality appliances, energy recovery ventilators, and renewable energy. These aren't futuristic, high tech gadgets, but real "off the shelf" technologies available right now. While serious efficiency sounds like it might cost serious cash, there are loads of incentives, rebates, tax credits, renewable energy credits, feed in tariffs, and low interest energy efficiency mortgages to minimize up-front costs while maximizing energy savings. The bottom line? Pay for your deep energy retrofit improvements with the money you'll save on energy bills and *get paid* to generate your own energy right at home.

During the onset of the worst economic downturn in 60 years, I realized that it was time for my family and me to get to work solving our own problems at home in order to have an effect on the problems of the wider world. We had come to a place in our lives where we had decided to stay put, which meant that the old home where we lived either needed to be torn down and rebuilt or fixed once and for all. Reluctantly, I set aside my dream of building a brand-new, net zero energy home in the country and set to the task of fixing what we had.

This is that story. Over the next three years we designed, financed, and retrofitted our 1940s Cape Cod–style kit home in a small, southeastern Ohio college town. We took some risks and suffered hammer-smashed purple thumbs, clouds of endless dust, a deluge of rain pouring in through the unfinished roof, sore muscles, sunburn, and a host of other setbacks. But we persevered and, as a family, learned a bit about what it means to be a part of the solution. What you'll read here is not only our personal story, but also a roadmap of how you can begin to design your own solution, no matter where you live or what climate you live in. My hope is that you'll find this story compelling enough to get to work on your home, and then share it with your friends, neighbors, and neighborhood contractors.

Is it easy? No, but real solutions rarely are. It ain't easy, but it's worth it. I won't ask you to "believe" or "have faith" in some rosy, green future. I will, however, ask you to *do something*—a little math, a little science, and a little hard labor. This is not about turning down your thermostat, donning a thick sweater, and "freezing in the dark." As a matter of fact, I'll show you how I *turned up* my thermostat and still *cut my heating bills by more than 75 percent*. This grassroots, people-powered solution captures the energy we "drop on the ground" every day to ensure and improve our comfort, health, prosperity, environment, and security in the new energy economy. This is true energy patriotism for all political bents and all walks of life, calling on the best of American values, work ethic, and innovation to lead the world toward a safer, more economically stable, more sustainable future.

Chapter One

WHY A DEEP ENERGY RETROFIT?

THE DAY MY OLDER DAUGHTER TURNED THREE, MY FAMILY AND I moved into a 1940s Cape Cod–style kit home in a small college town in southeastern Ohio. We were new to the area, and our move into town was a precursor to a long-term plan to eventually build our dream home in the countryside nearby. The plan was to fix up a house in town and sell it a couple of years later. Then we'd buy acreage a few miles out in the country, build a brand-new, "green" house, and live an eco-friendly lifestyle in the rolling hills of Appalachia. As plans go, it seemed like a good one to us.

The paint color scheme in the 70-year-old house was, inexplicably, dull pale gray walls with dingy blue-gray trim. We lovingly called it the "Das Boot" color scheme, after the heartbreaking movie about a doomed German U-Boat in World War II. Previous owners had tried to spruce it up by painting the trim in the kids' bedroom bright pink. "Das Boot" meets "Hello Kitty." Some prior renovations had been done poorly, compromising the structural integrity of floors and walls. The attached garage was starting to fall down, but I was hopeful that it would hang on for a few more years. With my construction skills and our joint do-it-yourself experience, I assured my wife, Sherri, we'd have no problem making this house a home. It was all stuff we could handle.

We set about making our fixer-upper beautiful. We tore out interior walls to open up the floor plan, completely renovated the kitchen and bathroom, and fixed damaged plaster. We caused a bit of a stir in the neighborhood when we gave the Midwestern-white exterior a basic facelift with a coat of periwinkle blue paint. We built an outdoor living space with a deck, screened porch, pergola, and outdoor kitchen, complete with a brick bread oven we built ourselves. And that was the key: with our skills and our sweat equity we were making our little house an appealing place to live with little monetary investment. We embodied the "flip this house" ethic of the times. Charge in, make it look great, turn a profit, and move on to greener pastures. We knew the house had deeper problems like a leaky shell and high energy bills, but that's what you get when you buy an old house, right?

⋙ Beauty Yes, Comfort No ⋘

It wasn't long, though, before we realized that the aesthetic improvements we had made weren't really enough. During our first winter, we discovered that the house was cold and drafty, despite $250+ per month gas bills to heat a measly 1,000 square feet. A new kitchen was nice, but it wasn't keeping us warm on frosty winter nights. In gutting the kitchen before we rebuilt it, I learned that the house had no insulation in the walls. That's when we decided to spend a couple of thousand bucks to have a contractor blow cellulose insulation into the empty wall cavities and attic. While cellulose is a great insulator, it has no air sealing ability on its own. We caulked gaps where we could find them and weatherized whatever else we could find. Over the course of winter number two, our energy costs dropped—about 10 percent.

Even with the new insulation, the house was still uncomfortable to live in most of the time. The air conditioner struggled to keep the house passably cool in the summer, and the furnace couldn't quite make up for all the cold spots in the house during the winter. I sweated my way through the long summer days, and Sherri shivered her way through the short winter ones. The upstairs was generally hot and the downstairs cold. The windows were so loose in their frames that outdoor air leaked in, along with plenty of dust, pollen, and neighborhood noise. The basic wood structure of the house was sound, but the shell was leaky as a sieve.

The basement was another significant problem. A musty smell permeated the house from late spring through early fall. On returning from a summer vacation, we would find things we'd stored in the basement, and even the masonry block walls, sporting a fine coating of mold. Since the floor drains and sump pit were open to the air, an occasional swampy smell would accompany the moldy smell. A veritable potpourri of decay.

There was radon in the basement, too (a home inspection before we bought the house had revealed this). The levels were just below the threshold where radon mitigation is suggested by the

Environmental Protection Agency (EPA), but that was cold comfort. Moldy, swampy, *and* radioactive—we would definitely limit the amount of time any of us spent down there. The basement was okay for storage, but useless as a living area.

Still, I figured that old houses are just "like that." If you want quality, 21st century construction and indoor air quality, build a new home for cryin' out loud! We continued concentrating on curb appeal, making this little house look great for a potential buyer. Soon, we'd found 60 acres just 15 minutes from town, with a view of three counties, in verdant, rolling Appalachia. It had creeks and woods and an old barn. It had birds and deer and buzzing bees and all of the other elements of pastoral poetic stanzas. We began actively designing our new country life and home. Things were going along as we had planned.

After buying that land in the country, we began to meet the folks who would become our new neighbors. Some were farmers or college professors or artists, but all had made the move from town to country to live a better and more peaceful life. When we would visit friends in the country, it always seemed that they had the "good life." Their kids frolicked in the tall grass, swam in lazy circles in the mill pond, and fished in the creek—all while the golden sun sank low and the murmuring sounds of the woods crept into the fading dusk (cue the inspirational soundtrack music). The grass was, indeed, greener out there beyond the city limits. The story was a bit different, though, when we met up with those same friends in town.

Most of them had jobs in town, so they commuted morning and evening, all week long. Those with kids made additional trips to ferry their children to lessons and activities. Many complained that having the serenity of country life required spending a lot of time in the car. That was the first time that the reality of a daily country-to-town commute had occurred to me. I'd certainly have to work, whether in construction or at a desk, and that would mean driving to town each day. With our school-aged kids, we'd be making that trip often for school, piano lessons, basketball practice, play rehearsals, or grocery shopping. What if the kids wanted to see a friend or if we wanted a dinner out? That would mean more trips to town in the car. The simple, green country life suddenly didn't sound so simple or so green.

By this time, our older daughter, Winter, had started kindergarten. The elementary school is just three blocks from our house. Families with school-aged kids trickle out of front doors every morning just before nine. Parents holding steaming mugs of coffee kiss their children and usher them in to school, waving at neighbors and commenting on the weather. Those same parents congregate outside the school again at 3:30 p.m. The principal and many of the teachers live within a few blocks of the school, too. It's a real community school, in a real community.

That wasn't the only nice thing we had discovered about the convenience of our little town. The brick streets of "uptown" are about a 10-minute walk from our front door. Uptown features some great restaurants and is adjacent to the university, where all kinds of arts, cultural, and sporting events happen. Our house is also just a quarter mile from the river, alongside which a 20-mile paved bike path snakes upstream through the countryside, all the way to the next town. Going downstream, the bike path will also lead you the mile or so to the grocery store or the farmers' market. We developed a pleasant routine of walking and riding our bikes for many of our errands and family outings.

As the years passed, our younger daughter, Sylvie—who'd been an infant when we first moved in—also started attending that neighborhood school. The number of child-related extracurricular activities doubled, and living in town became even more convenient, especially when compared with how life in a "dream home" in the country might be. It was a tough thing to admit, but little by little we came to realize that the country dream might not be the best choice for our family after all. When I was first confronted by the realities of living in the country, we'd make self-serving justifications and try to keep our eyes on the old dream. As time wore on, though, it was harder and harder to reconcile our quest to live in the country with the realities of commuting. Finally, as the economy took a nosedive and gasoline prices shot through the roof in 2008, we had to face the facts: living in the country, while a nice dream, was full of realities that we would have a hard time justifying. Town life was just too convenient, too simple, and yes, too "green" to think otherwise.

﹥ Finding a New Dream ﹤

Having admitted that, we had to wrestle with another inconvenient truth: if we weren't going to fulfill our lifelong dream of building the perfect, energy efficient home in the country, what would replace that dream? My first instinct was to sell the house we were in and build fresh somewhere else in town. A quick scan of available building lots close to town showed that those parcels were scarce, and expensive enough to be out of reach. My next thought was that we would need to tear down our old, leaky, inefficient home and start over. Really? Send an entire building's worth of materials, time, and energy to the landfill? Not exactly something a green building advocate would promote. I could imagine a happy existence here in town, in this great neighborhood, and yet I couldn't imagine continuing to live in this old, dilapidated house, especially considering its comfort issues, health issues, and high energy bills. We needed solutions for this old house, solutions that were beyond the band-aid of traditional weatherization.

Knocking around in the back of my mind was a renovation method I'd learned about while reading up on various cold-climate solutions for remodel projects years ago. I knew that the method relied on superinsulation to keep a house warm in the winter, and that it had been considered very experimental when it was first developed as a way to drastically reduce heating oil use after the oil crises of the 1970s. I hadn't thought about it in some time, but I wondered if superinsulation would work to keep our house cool in the summer, too. We live in a climate with cold winters, but hot summers, so we needed help in both heating and cooling seasons. I was also well aware of the advances in air sealing techniques used in new home building, and wondered if air sealing and superinsulation could be combined to make an old home work like a new home.

As I delved deeper, I found the old superinsulation method alive and well. It had changed somewhat since the last time I'd read about it, but it had been in the process of development by building science professionals for the last 30 years. The process was now called a deep energy retrofit (DER). What had started as simply adding extra insulation to homes in cold climates had become a range of renovation approaches for buildings in various regions and climates, all aimed at significant reductions in energy use. With a little bit of research, I found that there were many groups, some sponsored and encouraged by the US Department of Energy (DOE), that had been working on DER solutions throughout the country. To superinsulation was added careful air sealing and moisture management, better appliance technology, and advanced building practices. In a DER, every aspect of a home that either uses energy or affects how energy is used is scrutinized to squeeze out every possible bit of energy savings. That includes not only the building shell and insulation, but also heating and cooling systems, water heating, lighting, appliances, and electronics. When the savings from each of those improvements are added together, the results are staggering. By definition, a deep energy retrofit is a building renovation process that cuts energy use by 50 to 90 percent. That's the kind of whole-house solution we needed if we were going to get serious about energy efficiency in our home and the comfort and health of our family.

That rediscovery set us on the course of our own deep energy retrofit. Over the next three years, not only did my family experience the daily trials and tribulations of living through a major remodeling process, but we also discovered the intricacies of planning and financing a DER and talked with building science pros, contractors, manufacturers, and mortgage brokers. We spent countless hours researching every aspect of the process, learning even as we wielded our saws and swung our hammers.

At some point during the research process it hit me: *I'm not the only one*. I'm not the only one who loves his old house but wants something better. I'm not the only one looking for solutions to the problems that older buildings present to their occupants every day. Like others, I've tried lots of small weatherization techniques, but my home still functions poorly. Since the 1970s, builders have learned how to build *new* houses that are much more efficient and comfortable. But too little public attention has been paid to the plight of older homes. I realized that, as a carpenter and home-improvement TV host, I was uniquely situated to help teach a larger audience about how this powerful process could work in their homes, and the potential effect this could have on the larger problems of our economy, environment, and energy security in America.

I felt sure that a TV show based on this idea would be popular—fixing problems in old homes while helping to fix problems in America—but my ideas of telling America about deep energy retrofits fell on deaf ears at the networks where I worked. Television executives told me that energy efficiency wasn't "sexy enough" for viewers. One executive even admitted that they'd been complicit in helping to fill the disastrous housing bubble that had so recently burst in America. Non-stop programming dedicated to "flipping" houses had helped fuel the exorbitant and unsustainable housing prices of the era. "Great," I said, "here's your chance to offer a positive solution to part of that problem." I offered as many sexy show titles as I could—how about *Weatherization on Steroids* or *Green Remodeling Gone Wild*? Still, they declined. If I was interested in spreading the benefits of DERs, I'd have to do it myself.

That would be no small task. I knew that many small, independent neighborhood contractors would be resistant to change. I knew that homeowners would be frightened by the seemingly daunting process. I knew that a lot of the DER ideas would sound outlandish at first blush. Demystified, however, those solutions aren't as wacky as they sound. Sherri and I decided that this would become our work—teaching people about the powerful DER process. Using our two-person video production company, her photographic skills, and my hosting and public relations know-how, we would document our own DER journey. We hoped not only to transform our home, but to help others do the same with their homes. If we could encourage enough people to undertake DERs, our collective efforts could actually make a difference in the world.

➤ What's in It for You? ◀

In theory, you can accomplish a drastic reduction in home energy use by simply not heating or cooling your house or turning on the lights; not unlike living in a tent. Of course, your pipes might freeze and burst in the wintertime, you might have to spend some money on long underwear, and your entertainment options would be limited to something like whittling or knitting, but you'd definitely save some energy. By contrast, a deep energy retrofit provides a dramatic, wholesale reduction in energy use but at the same time maintains or increases your comfort level. There are various approaches to undertaking a DER, none of which are simple, and all of which require some hard work and sacrifice on the part of the homeowner. Yet the benefits far outweigh those sacrifices not only for individuals, but for their families, communities, country, and the world.

You don't have to be a rocket scientist to see that by reducing energy consumption, a DER will save you money. Energy efficiency means lower energy bills immediately, plus a cushion against energy price spikes in the worst case scenario of an energy crisis in the future. Each month that your energy bills are lower, you have that extra money to spend somewhere else, enriching your family instead of helping the executives at the big energy companies make their boat payments. Maybe you'll use the extra money to take more time off work or give junior piano lessons or start a new business. However you decide to use it, you're better off financially after a DER.

Cold, hard cash is nice, but a DER provides other benefits, too. Since the process involves sealing up and insulating the outer shell (also called the *building envelope*) of a house, your home becomes more comfortable, too. Older homes frequently have very leaky building envelopes. Those leaks are sometimes built right in and sometimes develop as a house ages and settles. My home was built in the early 1940s, when energy was inexpensive, and all you had to do was throw another shovelful of cheap, dirty coal on the fire to keep the house warm. As a result, homebuilders of that era didn't bother sealing a home's exterior, and most didn't add insulation of any kind, they simply relied on the air in the empty cavities in the walls for insulation (despite what you might think, air does serve as an insulator). It's that lack of a proper "air seal" and insulation that results in a home being cold and drafty in the winter and hot and sticky in the summer. Sealing up an older home and adding insulation reduces drafts and makes a house more comfortable in all seasons.

That air seal also affects how humidity influences your home and your comfort. Closing off all of those tiny gaps and cracks means that the house will allow less humidity inside during sticky summer months, making your air conditioner work less to keep you cool, and discouraging the growth of mold and mildew. Proper air sealing also keeps humidity from escaping your home during the wintertime. If you live in a dry climate, air sealing helps to keep indoor humidity at optimal levels—not too dry, not too moist. It's humidity loss that makes a home uncomfortably arid in cold seasons, ruining wood furniture and drying out your skin and sinuses. The dry air will also make you feel colder, so a home with even humidity levels will use less energy for heating. The combination of proper air seal and insulation means optimal building performance and better comfort.

Indoor air quality is another factor that a deep energy retrofit can improve. Since air movement through the walls is minimized in a well-retrofitted house, a DER usually includes installation of a mechanical ventilation system that brings fresh air into the home and exhausts stale air. Often, the ventilation system also includes some form of filtration and energy recovery. This controlled ventilation, along with optimal humidity levels discouraging mold and mildew growth, makes the indoor air quality in a home much healthier than it was originally. In the short term, this can mean fewer respiratory problems like asthma. In the long term, it might mean fewer instances of cancer. In any event, it means fewer sick days and a better quality of life.

So the benefits of a DER to your family are tangible: you save money and protect your family from the potential economic stress of an energy crisis while making them more comfortable and healthier. But that's just *your* family. Wait until your neighbors find out how great your old house is performing once it has undergone a DER. As legions of neighbors launch their own DERs, something amazing happens across the broad expanse of our country's communities. Something bigger than the sum of its parts. Something revolutionary. This is what I call **the Greened House Effect**.

➤ The Greened House Effect ◄

Once you retrofit your home and start extolling the virtues of a DER, others will soon follow. Whether they're motivated by the extra dollars in their pockets or the comfort and health of their families, they'll follow. Or maybe they'll follow because they begin to understand how cumulative energy savings from hundred and thousands of retrofitted homes can have an impact on some of the pressing problems we face at the national level. DERs have the potential to save vast amounts of energy—actual British thermal units (Btus) and electrons that can be put to better use. A DER *movement* has the potential to positively change the world in measurable ways.

For our nation, the numbers speak loudly in favor of DERs. As our population grows and as we need more energy for residential, commercial, industrial, and transportation needs, we need to build more capacity. More capacity means more generation. That means more coal-fired or nuclear plants, right? Not so fast. If we avoid that new generation of energy through energy efficiency, we have the same effect as building new plants: freeing up what would have been wasted electrons for other, newer uses. The question isn't which form of new generation is the cheapest, but whether it might be cheaper to avoid that new generation in the first place.

Using Energy Information Administration (EIA) statistics, *Architecture 2030*, a group of architects concerned with reducing energy use and carbon dioxide (CO_2) from the building sector, assembled an interesting bar graph. The graph shows the cost of generating new energy from different sources. The unit of measure is a QBtu, or Quadrillion British thermal units, which is basically an enormous "chunk" of energy. To put this into perspective, the United States uses between 80 and 100 QBtus of energy from all sources annually. The graph shows the cost, in billions of dollars, of generating one new QBtu of energy capacity from a variety of sources.

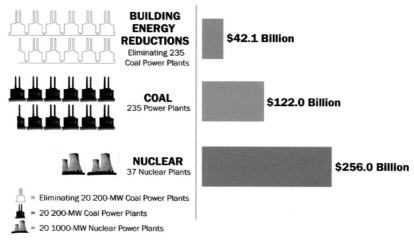

Cost of 1QBtu Delivered Energy

FIGURE 1.1 The least expensive way to solve our energy problems is through energy efficiency in older buildings. Source: © 2010 by 2030, Inc./Architecture 2030. All rights reserved. Data Source: Architecture 2030 Blue Print.

Building 37 nuclear plants to generate our new QBtu needs would cost roughly $256 billion, *if* you can live with the potential drawbacks of a nuclear disaster, of course. Building 235 new coal-fired plants to accomplish the same thing would cost $122 billion. That sounds like a bargain, except that it doesn't tally up all of the environmental and health-related costs associated with coal. Now check out that last number on the graph. There's our old pal, energy efficiency—at a meager $42.1 billion per QBtu. Suddenly, energy efficiency is looking pretty darned sexy, don't you think?

Another statistic shows that we might want to stop looking at our energy problems as problems, and see them instead as opportunities. Start with this idea: there are costs involved in everything, even if we continue with the status quo. You and I are going to foot the bill for that new power plant through our electric bills and taxes, or we're going to pay for energy efficiency in our homes. One way or another, we're going to pay. The question is: Which of the several alternative futures will deliver the biggest bang for the buck? On sheer statistics, the answer is energy efficiency. So the next question is: just how big is the opportunity that energy efficiency represents? From the standpoint of what will put our economy on the soundest footing for decades to come, investment in energy efficiency stands out as an extremely compelling solution.

Figures on American housing stocks from the most recent American Housing Survey of the Census Bureau show that there are nearly 130 million residential housing units that are "heated for year-round use." Of those homes, nearly 82 million are more than 30 years old. Why is "30 years" important? Because in the 1970s, America suffered through debilitating energy crises that taught some people that they couldn't rely on cheap energy to last forever. A few builders and homeowners got smart, at least for a while, and began to build homes that were tighter and better insulated. That means that few homes built more than 30 years ago are air sealed and insulated to higher, late 20th century standards. Oh, and don't think that you're completely out of the woods if your home is newer. Not all builders and homeowners in all parts of the country learned from the 1970s, so many newer homes are still poorly designed and built. More on that later—for now, let's stick to those homes built before the 1980s.

I only use the "30-year" measuring stick to make an easily provable point—remember those 82 million homes? They're the homes most likely in need of retrofitting for energy efficiency. At the height of the building boom, the American construction industry built fewer than 2 million homes per year. Hey, even a math-challenged guy like me can do this calculation: conservatively, if we committed to retrofitting those older homes at the boom rate of 2 million per year, we could be looking at 40 years or more of good retrofitting jobs. That means putting hundreds of thousands of architects, engineers, designers, carpenters, plumbers, electricians, and other tradespeople back to work for decades to come. That's an economic opportunity if there ever was one.

But how do those effects bubble up to the surface to help solve our larger problems? Let's look at possible positive effects on our economy to start with. When you undertake a DER, you'll have to buy building materials and hire some help. This will stimulate the badly damaged construction industry and put folks to work in your own neighborhood. That money will be circulated as contractors hire more carpenters and those carpenters buy new tools. Their families will finally have some extra cash on hand, maybe the first since the recession started, which will be spent on school clothes, a new charcoal grill, a couple of pizzas on a Friday night. Money will be circulating back through the economy like the good old days, driven by your DER.

The money we spend on electricity and heating oil or natural gas goes directly into the pockets of big energy companies and their big profits. Once your DER efforts start generating energy savings, you'll be carrying around some extra pocket change instead of writing such big checks to the energy companies. It's money you can spend at your local hardware store, your favorite Cuban restaurant, or on that computer you need for your new small business. Now your money is stimulating the broader economy. Then there are the even longer term economic benefits. As more and more people demand DERs for their homes, new, innovative products aimed at energy efficiency are invented for the American market. As other countries see the benefits of serious energy efficiency start to accrue here in the States, that innovation can be exported to a world hungry for energy efficiency, bolstering American exports.

Your DER also has obvious benefits for the environment. About half of the electricity produced in America comes from coal. While coal has helped to bring us to our current high standard of living, coal also damages the environment and human health. Smokestack emissions from coal-fired power plants are a source of a cocktail of dangerous pollutants. CO_2 (carbon dioxide) is acting to warm the planet, and SO_2 (sulfur dioxide) is a major contributor to acid rain. Mercury, another hazard from coal, ends up in our rivers and streams, contaminating fish so severely that they're rendered inedible. Fine particulate matter from coal plants is a major contributor to a host of respiratory problems. Even the mining of coal is environmentally devastating. Mountaintop removal mining requires the bulldozing of entire mountaintops, filling the hollows and streambeds below. Having visited mountaintop removal mine sites, I've seen firsthand these permanently ruined landscapes.

As the deep energy retrofit revolution picks up speed, our thirst for energy slows, even while our comfort level, health, economy, and environment improve. The energy we've freed up from our homes is in the form of real electrons that could be put to better use. Most of that savings can be left "in the bank" of a less energy-dependent lifestyle. Some of those electrons could be invested in a safer world. By fixing our homes in a dramatic way, we have the opportunity to transform our transportation sector to use more domestically produced electricity and other non-foreign energy sources.

The opportunity is enormous. Buildings consume nearly 49 percent of the energy we use in America, while cars consume 28

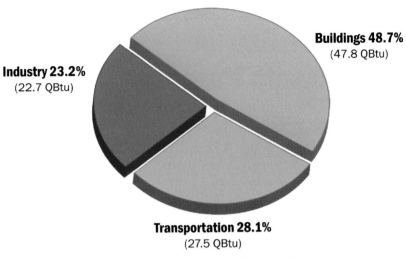

Buildings 48.7%
(47.8 QBtu)

Industry 23.2%
(22.7 QBtu)

Transportation 28.1%
(27.5 QBtu)

U.S. Energy Consumption by Sector

Source: ©2011 2030, Inc. / Architecture 2030. All Rights Reserved.
Data Source: U.S. Energy Information Administration (2011).

FIGURE 1.2 Buildings account for the largest portion of our energy use in the United States and represent the biggest opportunity to help solve our energy problems. Source: © 2011 by 2030, Inc./Architecture 2030. All rights reserved. Data source: US Energy Information Administration (2011).

percent. Plug-in hybrid cars would be partially powered by some of our deep energy retrofit–saved electrons, displacing oil as a major source of energy for our daily commutes. Plug-in hybrids pair an electric motor with a small gasoline engine. With a full charge from an outlet in your garage, a plug-in hybrid car can travel nearly 40 miles on electricity alone. That's far enough to get the average American to and from work without burning a drop of gasoline. Should you need to travel farther, the gasoline engine kicks in, allowing the full-range of a standard, gasoline-powered car. Plug-in technology produces a car that gets more than 100 miles per gallon of gas, which means far less pollution (yes, even if your plug-in hybrid runs on the dirtiest coal-generated electricity, it's still less polluting than gasoline) and a remarkable drop in our dependence on foreign oil imports.

America spends an inordinate amount of its resources, both in terms of lives and money, in oil-rich regions simply to keep the oil flowing. Without a need to protect oil tanker shipping lanes in far-off lands, more of our troops could be brought home. Instead of asking brave Americans to sacrifice themselves on a battlefield to ensure our access to cheap energy, we sacrifice a bit of our own treasure to DER our homes in order to keep our soldiers safe.

The Solar Patriot— A Home with Purpose

FIGURE 1.3 The Hathaway Solar Patriot Home. Image courtesy of Alden Hathaway.

Even before the 9/11 terrorist attacks, many people understood how our energy use affects US national security interests. In the summer of 2001, months before the World Trade Center came crashing down, the Hathaway family of northern Virginia completed construction of their net zero energy solar home. Through advanced building design, the home uses little energy in its daily operation—a solar panel array creates all of the energy they need. They've dubbed the house "The Solar Patriot." Why the name? Carol Hathaway put it best when she said, "We can raise our flags and put our hands over our hearts, but the best way we Americans can fight terrorism and the Middle Eastern leaders supporting terrorism is to eliminate our need for their major export [oil]."

Her husband, Alden, continued, "If just 10 percent of American families were to do what our family has done, we could wipe out our dependence on Iraqi oil and surpass the original Kyoto goals for reducing greenhouse gas emissions. We're offering a simple, grassroots solution to the biggest challenge of our time."

These days, after one of the worst global financial meltdowns in more than half a century, many Americans aren't considering the purchase or construction of a *new* home, solar powered or not. DER homes are the new *Patriots*, offering a positive, actionable solution to major problems of our time.

But What Will It *Cost?*

I won't try to tell you that a DER is an inexpensive undertaking. It's a major home renovation, and that costs real money. Yet when you look at the whole picture—not just the sticker price but life cycle and payback times—a DER costs a lot less than you'd think. Look at it this way; the money you invest in a DER of your home has calculable benefits like energy savings, of course, but it also has many hard-to-calculate benefits. Benefits like better comfort, health, and a sense of purpose that comes from doing something good for your country and your neighbors. Benefits like peace of mind knowing that your family will stay warm through the next energy crisis. Can you think of another place to put your money that would have a more easily justified cost-benefit analysis? Can your new sofa stand that kind of scrutiny? When was the last time somebody calculated the payback time on granite countertops or a new big-screen TV? At least your DER will start paying for itself the minute you start working on it. Try asking a new car to do that. Besides, there are loads of incentives, rebates, tax credits, renewable energy credits, feed-in-tariffs, and low-interest energy efficiency mortgages to minimize up front costs while maximizing energy savings. By piecing together all of the savings, both tangible and intangible, and adding up the incentives, DERs make sense.

So, let's recap: a society-wide investment in deep energy retrofits could be the cheapest way out of our energy woes, while also re-employing the most people from the industry hardest hit in the recession. Can building new power plants make that claim? And what if we include the opportunity for helping to fix our important environmental and national security problems? The DER wins, hands down. If, while we're at it, we become a little richer, happier, more comfortable, and healthier, that's all for the better. I'm ready, are you? Roll up your sleeves, grab a hammer, and let's get to it.

Chapter Two

HOW MUCH CAN YOU SAVE?

ONCE WE'D MADE THE DECISION TO STAY IN OUR HOME FOR THE long term, I quickly realized we were facing more than a run-of-the-mill renovation. Serious problems that I had thought the *next* owner would take care of were now *mine* to fix. The roof was nearly worn out. The windows were cracked and the frames leaky and rotted in places. Old aluminum siding covered up the original redwood siding which, after a quick inspection, I realized was too badly damaged to save. The old attached garage was close to falling down. Even though we'd insulated the walls, there were still full-fledged breezes blowing through the house. The basement was like any other basement in an old house: need I say more? Overhauling our leaky, deteriorating house would demand careful, measured planning before we started hurling our hard-earned greenbacks into the widening maw of the money pit. We wanted to aim for "net zero" on this house, meaning that the home might produce at least as much energy as it would use. Whether we actually would achieve this goal wasn't the point: we simply wanted to get as close as possible within a reasonable budget.

But to do that, we had to know all of the house's weaknesses, large and small. The large ones were easy to see: single pane windows in damaged frames, mold in the basement. The small stuff is much harder because it comes in the form of microscopic, hidden gaps and cracks in the home's protective layer. Most of those millions of tiny cracks and gaps aren't visible to the naked eye, so it would take a professional with experience and sensitive equipment to help me determine their locations and severity. A detailed home energy audit, performed by a pro, was what I needed before I even picked up a pencil to make a plan.

❧ Testing for Leaks and Heat Loss ❦

I turned to Andrew Frowine, a HERS rater in our area, for help. HERS stands for Home Energy Rating System. HERS raters are trained to administer tests and gather hundreds of data points about building components, such as windows, insulation, heating and cooling systems, siding material, and a lot more. They treat your home like a doctor would treat a sick hospital patient, diagnosing diseases and prescribing therapies. The result is a road map that can be used to navigate through the ins and outs of retrofitting your home. The information that a qualified home energy auditor provides will keep you from wasting money on things you might think are important, but really aren't. For example, a home's windows are typically fingered as a major source of energy loss, but replacing them is a big expense. It might be that the existing windows in your home are working just fine, but you really need to invest in a new furnace. A home energy auditor's report will allow you to target the worst perpetrators of energy wasting crimes in your home so that you can concentrate on fixing the big problems first.

FIGURE 2.1 A blower door test will help to pinpoint air leaks, both visible and invisible, in a home. Photograph by Sherri James.

Andrew arrived one morning just after we'd dropped the kids at school, and for the first hour we sat around the kitchen table talking and drinking coffee. He asked to see our current energy bills and asked about the renovations we'd done over the years. We talked about our goals for the house and why we'd hired a HERS rater. Andrew completely understood where we were coming from. He'd seen many homes just like ours and some that were in far worse shape. He feverishly started checking off items and filling in blanks on the myriad data sheets he carried with him. After the interview he walked around both the inside and outside of the house measuring windows, doors, and walls, filling in more of the data points. He checked the air conditioner and furnace, the water heater, lighting, and appliances.

Satisfied that he'd collected every bit of data that he could through interview, observation, and measuring, he set up the physical tests he needed to perform in order to ferret out those problems he couldn't either see or infer. As Andrew was setting up the first pressure test, he commented on the door that led from the master bedroom into the little storage space above the rotting attached garage. My wife and I used that space as a makeshift office, but it could have served as walk-in freezer space in the wintertime. "Are you planning on keeping the garage in this renovation?" he asked. I explained that we were planning to demolish it, because a previous homeowner had removed a load bearing wall, allowing the roof to sag and the structure to become water damaged over the years. The old garage was more like a barn than livable space. "Good," he said. "Then we're going to tape it off and not even consider it in our testing." With so many leaks, the garage would have skewed the results of the pressure test for the rest of the home.

He started by propping open the front door and installing in its place a big red nylon "tent" and fan. The contraption, called a blower door (see figure 2.1), fit snugly and completely covered the opening. The variable-speed fan sucks air out of the house which, in turn, draws air in through gaps in window frames or cracks in the home's protective layer. The fan hooks up to a pressure gauge and a laptop and allows a HERS rater to run a series of pressure tests to measure air leakage in the house as a whole. Then, with the fan still running, Andrew went room-to-room, closing doors and isolating the leaks in each room. Eventually, he was able to pinpoint the specific leaks and tell us just how bad each one was.

❯❯ Leaky Old House: 1; Energy Efficiency: 0 ❮❮

The whole-house tests tallied up the thousands of tiny gaps and cracks in the building envelope. Andrew's laptop calculated the damage: all together they added up to one large, gaping hole 16 inches across. That's like leaving a small window open year-round while trying to heat and cool the place. There's prime suspect number one in the perpetration of energy crimes at our house. As Andrew continued shutting doors and testing individual rooms, he was able to track precisely where the majority of those leaks were coming from. In the girls' bedroom, he stopped dead in his tracks at the new built-in bookcase I'd installed in the knee wall. "Wow! This is a major leak," he remarked, "Right here around the trim." To install the bookcase, I'd cut through the lath and plaster of the interior wall into the small dead space behind it. Now, it dawned on me that I'd created a big hole in the only impediment to air movement from the unsealed outer shell of the house into the bedroom—the interior plaster finish. I should have installed those built-in bookshelves the same way I would have installed a window: by completely sealing around the frame to keep the air infiltration to a minimum.

The same story of my crimes against building envelope integrity was repeated with several of the other built-ins I'd installed to make more effective use of space in our small home. Another modern detail, recessed lighting, proved just as culpable. Just about anywhere I had cut through the old plaster, there was a new avenue to the great outdoors through which air, humidity, and even bugs could gain access to the interior living space. But I wasn't the only one to blame. As with many older homes, the attic was vented to the outside. This was common practice to prevent heat and humidity from building up in the summertime, because exposure to high heat and humidity can shorten the lifespan of a roof and tax air conditioners. In the winter, vented attics keep the attic air cool so that heat doesn't radiate through the roof to cause ice-damming.

The floors in those vented attics are also the ceilings of the upper story, and they usually aren't properly sealed to stop summertime heated attic air from moving into the house or wintertime heated indoor air from escaping. The result is drafts and energy loss not only at electrical outlets on *outer* walls, where you might expect them, but even on *inner* walls. This is because air flows back and forth between the conditioned space inside the home and the attic space (and thus the great outdoors) through holes cut into the attic floor to allow for things like wiring, recessed lighting cans, and plumbing pipe that runs into the wall cavities. Those holes continue down and through to the outlet boxes and fixtures mounted in both inner and outer walls. A surprising number of our inner wall switch and outlet boxes leaked like crazy.

You name it, it leaked. Doors, windows, outlets, recessed lighting, the sill plate where the wood framing meets the basement foundation. It all leaked. I couldn't imagine how I'd ever locate and seal each and every one of those microscopic energy-wasting highways. Figuring that out would have to wait, however, since Andrew had already moved on to thermal imaging. Thermal imaging uses an infrared (IR) camera that shows where surfaces are hot or cold, relative to one another. A good thermal image shows exactly where heat is escaping or entering the house (see "Heat 101" sidebar in this chapter), depending on the season. And it not only shows loss of heat through convection and air movement, which the blower door test had measured, but also where heat itself is being conducted through building materials like plaster, wood, and metal. An IR image shows how heat is being wicked away from where it's supposed to be to keep us comfortable—indoors in the winter and outdoors in the summer.

The differences show up as a rainbow spectrum of colors on the camera's small display screen, red indicating heat and blue indicating cold. For example, if you stand on the inside of a cozy house in the middle of winter and take an infrared picture of an old, single pane window, the image will show red and yellow walls, which would be retaining heat and radiating it back into the room. You'd also see green-blue window frames, indicating that heat is escaping to the outside. If you stand on the outside on that same winter day your IR image would show the blue of the walls, where heat was being kept inside the home, and the yellow of the window frames, where heat was being conducted to the outside of the house.

Our thermal images were telling. Old windows and doors were easy offenders to spot, of course, but the IR camera was also able to see a few small places within the walls that the contractor who had blown in the cellulose insulation several years earlier had missed. The corners of a house, where older construction methods make it difficult to insulate at all, are common places to see heat loss. Interestingly enough, every stud will show up on a good IR image, since the wood stud itself acts as a "thermal bridge," conducting heat. Relative to materials like metal, wood is an insulator, but relative to

Heat 101: How Does It Get from Here to There?

Heat is being transferred throughout our environment all the time. It always moves from warm to cold through these three avenues:

Conduction happens when solid objects touching each other transfer heat between them. Metals are very good conductors, plaster and wood less so, and materials we use for insulation are designed to be very poor conductors. Plaster and wood are good conductors when compared with insulation materials, so heat is even conducted through those materials, affecting our comfort.

Convection is the movement of heat in gases or liquids. As the air in your home is heated, it becomes less dense and, therefore, lighter, so it rises. As the air cools, it falls. This creates a convective current of rising and falling air of different temperatures. Convection is a main reason homes tend to be warmer upstairs than downstairs.

Radiation is the transfer of heat via electromagnetic waves. Those waves travel through empty space, without relying on gas, liquid, or solid objects for transfer. The sun's energy is a good example—you can feel warmth as your skin is heated via radiation when you're outside on a sunny day.

Your home is often experiencing all three of these avenues of heat transfer simultaneously. For example, on a sunny summer day, heat radiated from the sun will warm the shingles on your roof. That heat is conducted through the shingles and rafters until it heats the air inside the attic. That warm air then travels via convection loops, warming other parts of your home, eventually transferring heat to the interior.

a well-insulated wall cavity, wood is a conductor, and wooden studs channel heat in or out of a house. The IR images also revealed the lack of insulation around the window frames. The space between the window frames and the studs of the wall structure wasn't typically insulated back when our home was built in the 1940s. Some of the IR images reinforced what the blower door test showed and some of the images showed flaws that the blower door test alone couldn't measure. The two tests together were a powerful tool.

Most HERS ratings will also include a test of a home's ductwork. This test works similarly to the blower door test, pressurizing heating and cooling ducts to show how well the joints of the ductwork are sealed or if there are any restrictions reducing air flow through the ducts. This is especially important if any ducts pass through an unconditioned area, like an outside wall or attic. Since all of my home's ducts were within the heated and cooled conditioned space,

FIGURE 2.2 The same wall in a standard photo and a thermal image. This thermal image shows heat loss through air leaks, but also through the thermal bridging (conduction) of building materials. Notice how each stud inside the wall is conducting heat from inside to outside. The studs show up as brighter, vertical lines. The darker spaces between the studs are the insulated wall cavities. Images courtesy of FLIR Commercial Systems, Inc.

duct leakage wasn't much of an issue—any conditioned air would simply escape into the space I heat and cool anyway. However, duct leaks that allow heated or cooled air to escape to the outside of a building can be a major source of wasted energy, and many older homes will benefit from having the ducts thoroughly sealed.

Soon, Andrew was wrapping up the testing. Before he left, he explained how he would analyze all of the information he had gathered that day. At his office, he would put all of the numbers through software that calculates where the worst energy-sapping culprits were in our home. Then the same software would indicate the best places to attack first with our deep energy retrofit. A couple of weeks after the testing, a very detailed report landed in our mailbox.

A lot of the report was Greek to me since it consisted

FIGURE 2.3 A Minneapolis Duct Blaster is used to determine air leakage in heating and cooling ducts. Once leaks are sealed, the duct system will perform much more efficiently. Photograph courtesy of The Energy Conservatory, Minneapolis, MN.

of raw data from the testing. But it also included easy-to-read graphs and charts that showed where the energy dollars were going in our house. The report wasn't a page-turner, but it did shed a lot of light on the major failings of our old house. The graphs showed that heating was the worst of our worries, and that we weren't doing too badly on lighting, since we'd already replaced many old incandescent bulbs with energy efficient bulbs. Our cooling bills rated above normal on the graphs for a house the size of ours, but the energy consumed by our efficient appliances and water heating rated below normal. The report went on to explain what part of our energy bills were likely a result of a leaky house and what part could be attributed to its various working systems. The specific leaks Andrew had found during testing were detailed in the report, so I could tackle those first.

Our Home Energy Audit Report included a final HERS Energy Rating Certificate score. These scores compare the tested home with a standard newly built home. The standard home is given a score of 100, and a good score will be lower than that. The best score would be zero, which would indicate a net zero energy home that produced all of the energy it needed through renewables like solar or wind power. Our home, like the home rated on the certificate shown in figure 2.4, scored surprisingly well at 84. That took into account the fact that we had gone to the trouble to insulate the empty wall cavities and that we had replaced the old furnace and

HOME PERFORMANCE WITH ENERGY STAR
ENERGY RATING CERTIFICATE

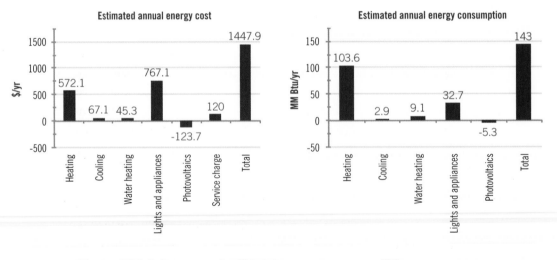

Address:	2342 Maybee Ave.	Annual Estimates*:		**TITLE**
	Denver, CO 80333	Electric (kWh): 9762		**Company**
		Natural gas (Therms): 1096		Address
House Type:	Single-family detached	CO_2 emissions (Tons): 16		
Cond. Area:	3000 sq. ft.	Annual Savings**: $669		Certified Rater: H.I. Scorer
Rating No.:	XYZ-22233			Rater ID: 303 333 2222
Issue Date:	October 02, 2012	* Based on standard operating conditions		Registry ID:
Certification:	Verified	** Based on a HERS 130 Index Home		Rating Date: 4/12/95

FIGURE 2.4 The HERS certificate distills all of the data gathered during a home energy audit into a single score, comparing the tested house with a standard, baseline home. A lower score indicates a more energy efficient home than a higher score. This certificate shows the energy use and costs for each component of a 3,000-square-foot Colorado home. Image courtesy of Architectural Energy Corporation.

air conditioner when they failed a year or two before with a high-efficiency model. I realized, though, that the score had excluded the worst part of the house by cordoning off the dilapidated old garage and office. Had we included those, the score would have been well above 100. Since our goal was to aim for zero, I could see some big savings on heating and cooling costs over the long term coming our way once the deep energy retrofit was complete.

Although we wanted to make a smart investment in energy efficiency with our remodeling dollars, we also had major issues of comfort and poor indoor air quality to address. What was I willing to pay each year to have a comfortable house? I was already paying unwillingly and through the nose to have an *uncomfortable* house. What would my monthly energy bills be if I simply turned the thermostat way up in the winter and way down in the summer so that we could be more comfortable? And what was it costing us in health-care bills and lost time at work from the unhealthy quality of the air in our house? More importantly, what would those costs be later if we continued to breathe the poor air in our house over decades? By fixing the problems with a DER, I was saving money beyond the obviously lower energy bills.

But is saving money the only reason to undertake a DER? Solving health issues in a home saves real money on health-care costs but has less tangible benefits as well. Like most people, once you become aware of a problem like poor indoor air quality, you experience a nagging anxiety until the problem is solved. Will my children get sick from the air in this house? Will one of us end up with cancer because we haven't dealt with the problem? Being constantly uncomfortable negatively affects quality of life as well. Why can't my own home be a place where I can relax without feeling too hot or too cold? The piano goes out of tune and my skin dries out because the air gets so dry inside my home during the winter—even those seemingly unrelated issues are caused by the poor function of my home. Fixing problems of comfort and health provides the illusive benefits of peace of mind and quality of life.

Looking at the HERS rating, it was clear to me that our better-than-average score was attributable more to the fact that we're cheap misers than the efficiency of our home. Or, as my Czech friend, Libor, would say, "Cold and dark is cheap!" His wife, Helen, even had a T-shirt emblazoned with that saying made for him because of his distaste for turning on the furnace in the fall. Libor would good-naturedly poke fun at us Wilsons because our house

Energy Awareness = Energy Savings

Most of us are blithely unaware of exactly how much we depend on energy in every facet of our lives. When an energy bill comes in the mail, we only see one number: the dollar amount we have to pay. But we don't really understand exactly where we're using the most energy in our homes, or just how our habits might affect our energy use. That ignorance costs us: without knowing where we're really wasting energy, we don't know precisely how to best change our habits to save energy.

Oberlin College's stone buildings and leafy green lawns evoke a quintessential college campus. Located in northeast Ohio, Oberlin often shows up on "10 Greenest Colleges" lists for its highly efficient new buildings, its use of renewable energy, and its commitment to reducing energy use in its older facilities. Recognizing that human behavior is a factor in energy usage, researchers in the Environmental Studies Department developed a program to engage students living in the residence halls on campus.

It started as a competition between dormitories to see which buildings could use the least energy over a set period. In order to show residents their progress, students and professors in the Environmental Studies Department created an "energy orb" display. The display, placed in the common area of each dorm, was little more than a light that glowed green when the building was using less energy and red when it was using more, relative to what would normally be used at that time of day. This made students aware of the effect of their energy use

Figure 2.5 Oberlin College Energy Orb. Photograph courtesy of Oberlin College.

habits and allowed them to make a change of habit to affect the status of the glowing display light. After a month of monitoring, the initial results were startling.

Some dorms reduced their energy use by more than 20 percent. This, simply from being made aware of energy use patterns and changing deeply ingrained habits. That original competition has now morphed into the "Ecolympics," which is run every April at Oberlin, pitting dormitories against each other for the top prizes, which include bragging rights and an ice-cream party during finals week. The old green light has been replaced by a high-tech, online Building Dashboard that can be used to monitor energy and water use across campus. Surprising what a little "green-lightenment" can do for energy efficiency.

was so "balmy" at 68°F (20°C). "Wow," he would say as he walked through the door on a cold November night, "I should have worn shorts to your house!"

While not as hard-core as Libor, we had been turning the thermostat down in the winter and up in the summer, sacrificing comfort for slightly cheaper energy bills. We thought we had to make the choice: comfort and healthy indoor air quality, or lower energy bills. But now I was realizing that I wanted—and could have—both. By retrofitting my home, I could minimize spending on energy bills while still enjoying a comfortable and healthy home environment.

⚡ Multiple Benefits from an Energy Audit ⚡

Our HERS report showed that the bulk of our energy use and waste came from heating our leaky old home. It was clear that the improvements that would have the most dramatic effect on our bills would be air sealing and insulating the building envelope. That's easier said than done on an older home, since leaks can be difficult to reach without first removing finish materials to expose the bare exterior sheathing. On the one hand, this can mean removing and replacing roofs, siding, doors, and windows—not a solution for the meek. On the other hand, you may find that previous homeowners had already mitigated air sealing and insulation problems and your score might indicate that it's only an outdated furnace or water heater that is pushing your bills into the stratosphere. Either way, you're a smarter consumer when you get the details only a professional home energy audit can offer.

Whether you're simply planning a few renovation projects right now, or you're ready to go whole-hog into a complete deep energy retrofit, a home energy audit performed by a certified professional is a valuable tool that's well worth the cost and the time it takes to analyze the results. You'll see the good, the bad, and the really ugly, which will help you prioritize. While there is a cost to a home energy audit (typically $250 to $450), many states and utility companies offer either free or heavily discounted home energy audits to citizens or customers. My natural gas utility offers professional audits for $50 ($20 for income-eligible customers) and then will help consumers find incentives to help pay for the upgrades. Consider the money you spend on a home energy audit well spent. It's an investment that will pay itself back many times over, helping you make educated decisions about your home improvement plans over the long term. Check out the Resources appendix at the end of this book for links to help you find a certified home energy rater in your area.

A home energy audit will come in handy even if you're only con-templating renovating a single room in your home. It would work like this: say you're going to update your old kitchen. That might include new cabinets, countertops, flooring, and appliances—a big investment and, in the short term, a big mess. If your home energy audit has indicated that your home lacks a good air seal and insula-tion and that the windows need to be replaced, you might decide to take the opportunity to fix those problems in the kitchen at the same time you deal with the aesthetics. While that will add to the overall cost of the renovation project, it's much cheaper to add retrofitting into an already planned renovation than to remove finish materials after the fact just to get at the wall cavities for deep energy retrofit purposes. If the opportunity to expose wall cavities arises during an unrelated renovation, whether from the interior or the exterior, grab the chance to make deep energy efficiency upgrades.

Over time, you can continue to consult your home energy audit whenever you take on a new project, such as replacing the siding or roofing on your home, and include energy efficiency measures in the project. I call this a "rolling DER." When considered as an add-on to a home improvement project, deep energy retrofit may only add 20 to 25 percent to the cost of that particular project. By contrast, if you attempt a DER on a home that already has solid, modern, updated finishes, the costs of retrofitting may have to in-clude new finish materials, and the cost-benefit ratio of a full DER may not make sense.

Having a home energy audit in your pocket is handy in case of an emergency, too. Furnaces and air conditioners usually fail when they're being taxed the most. That typically occurs on the hottest or coldest days of the year. Left with the choice of freezing or swelter-ing in your own home, you might make a hasty decision about a large ticket item without having all of the information you need. A heating and cooling contractor can use the data from a home energy audit to help carefully size the new HVAC system so that it's not too big or too small for your house. This, in turn, can save you money now on the installation of the new unit and even more over its lifetime of operation. Without the home energy audit many heating and cooling contractors simply make "rule of thumb" calculations, which may or may not result in your getting the properly sized system for your home.

Professional home energy audits may also be required in order to participate in some mortgage or incentive programs linked to energy efficient home improvements. This is a way for a lender or incentive program official to quantify the potential energy savings in a given home. One of the reasons technology like solar and wind power are so widely subsidized is the extremely predictable flow of power that can be calculated to forecast the exact amount of clean energy that will be produced by a solar array or wind turbine over its lifetime. Gains resulting from energy efficiency improvements are harder to quantify. Different buildings require different approaches to fix their energy efficiency problems, and each solution will have a different effect depending on factors like the climate where a building is located and the occupants' habits. That makes estimating energy efficiency gains more complex, which has led to a push to improve energy audits and associated computer modeling. Those improvements will help in the quantification effort so that energy efficiency can stand on the same ground, worthy of incentives, as renewables like solar and wind.

A home energy audit can also benefit you if and when you decide to sell your home. Homebuyers are able to be pickier in a tight sales market. If you've skimped on air sealing and insulation but your neighbor does it right, his house might sell before yours does. Being able to document the quality of your home renovations and prove that quality to a prospective buyer can make a big difference in whether or not your home sells. Home energy audits before and after major renovations can establish baselines and then document and demonstrate efficiency improvements.

Any way you look at it, when you're trying to reduce your energy use, a good home energy audit is one of the best tools in your toolkit. I know it's trite, but I'll say it anyway: knowledge is power.

Chapter Three

DESIGNING A
DEEP ENERGY RETROFIT

THE DETAILED HOME ENERGY RATINGS SYSTEM REPORT THAT OUR HERS rater generated for us showed just where the problems were in our old house: everywhere. It was going to take a major makeover to bring our home into the 21st century.

Apart from the problems that the HERS report revealed, we also had plenty of maintenance issues to confront. Roof replacement, window and door replacement, basement condensation and odors, the dilapidated garage, and a band-aid patched exterior were on the must-fix list if we expected to live happily in the house long-term. These were issues outside of our energy efficiency goals but included decades of neglected maintenance we could no longer avoid. Planning would have to start at the triage level for this particularly wounded patient.

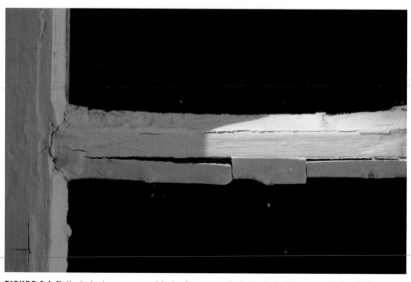

FIGURE 3.1 Failed glazing on our old single pane windows is just one example of the many delayed-maintenance problems we factored into our retrofit design plan. Photograph by Sherri James.

✕ Analyzing Our Problem List ✕

It was easy to see that we would have to replace the roofing and the siding, both of which had outlived their useful lives. It was also time to replace the 70-year-old, single pane, wood-framed windows, many of which were cracked and rotting. Even the better windows didn't open, having been anchored to the frames under layers of paint over the years. While we were at it, we might as well replace the old exterior wooden doors, since they had long ago split at the joints and sagged at their hinges, making it necessary to give them a good hard slam to get them fully shut. The old attached garage was a complete loss; it would have to be torn down, the concrete slab floor removed, and a new structure built in its place. The basement would require some kind of interior insulating layer to keep humid air from condensing on the cold masonry surface, and we'd need to somehow deal with the radon problem once and for all. In retrospect, it might have been easier to list the few things that would remain the same, rather than the things that would be changing.

The key was to design our deep energy retrofit elements around those maintenance-related renovations. Since we were replacing the roofing, we would have the opportunity to add insulation and air sealing. The same went for the siding. But did that mean we'd have to remove all of the roofing and siding and start over? I didn't like the idea of sending so much debris to the landfill if it wasn't completely necessary. Then again, how would you get to the leaky sheathing underneath if you didn't remove the siding? Accessing the problem areas could mean major destruction, and major destruction could mean major money.

⊸ A New Protective Shell ⊸

As we began looking at our options, one kept popping out at us as a good, all-around solution that balanced material costs and labor costs, but still gave us all the benefits of an air sealed, superinsulated wall and roof structure. I call it a "curtain wall" (shown in figure 3.2). The term is used in commercial construction to describe a framework or structure that hangs on a building's surface without bearing any of the weight of the building. Our curtain wall would consist of a ribbed frame, securely attached to the outside of the house, with 3-inch deep cavities between ribs spaced 16 inches apart. We would fill those cavities with expanding closed cell polyurethane spray

FIGURE 3.2 Our curtain wall adds an exterior shell of wood framing and spray foam insulation. Later in the retrofit process, it gets covered by new sheathing panels, house wrap, and siding. It works well for both walls and roofs. Photograph by Sherri James.

foam insulation, which is applied wet and then expands into all of the little gaps and cracks as it cures to a rigid state. Not only is spray foam great at air sealing, it's also a very effective insulator. With the curtain wall in place, our finished, retrofitted walls and roof would have more than double the insulation value of a standard home.

Over the new curtain wall would be layers of sheathing, housewrap or roof membrane, and finish materials like siding and roofing. This would have the effect of thickening the old walls and roof on the house by about 4 inches. It's like adding a winter coat with a windbreaker shell over a sweater. The blown-in cellulose

Spray Polyurethane Foam Insulation

Spray polyurethane foam (SPF) is a highly effective insulator and air sealing product and is getting more and more use these days as a superior replacement for fiberglass and cellulose insulation in either batt or loose form. Why? Because fiberglass and cellulose don't offer air sealing themselves, so they must be painstakingly air sealed using other methods so that they perform up to their rated R-values. The two main types of SPF are open cell and closed cell. Both are sprayed on wet, mixing two chemicals that react with one another to foam up and expand as they cure. Initial curing happens quickly, usually over a minute or two, but a full cure can take up to 72 hours. Open cell SPF expands aggressively, is soft to the touch after it cures, results in an insulation value of about R-3.5 per inch, and is less expensive than closed cell SPF. The cells, or bubbles within the foam, are open to each other, permitting some limited degree of moisture and air flow. Closed cell SPF expands less aggressively, is denser and harder to the touch, and results in an insulation value of about R-6.5 per inch. The closed cells act as an air, moisture, and vapor retarder or barrier, depending on the thickness applied.

Both versions can either be professionally applied or purchased as do-it-yourself kits, but beware: in its liquid form and as it cures installers must take careful safety precautions not to breathe the fumes or get the wet foam on their skin. A proper ventilator mask, goggles, and protective clothing should be worn.

insulation in the existing wall cavities (the sweater) was a good start, but alone it allowed the winter winds to blow right through. A curtain wall of spray foam insulation (the windbreaker) would block the air movement, making the cellulose insulation much more efficient. Since reliable, do-it-yourself spray foam kits had recently come on the market, this was a job that I felt I could do myself. I would save a little money on labor and would also be in control of the process. That way I could make sure every little gap and crack was filled properly.

Next, we would replace all of the old windows and doors. The windows would be super-efficient, triple pane, krypton gas filled. The new doors would be fiberglass with closed cell foam insulation, and any glass in the doors would be the same triple pane glass as the windows. With thicker walls we decided to install "new construction" windows, as opposed to "replacement" windows, flush with the exterior plane of the new siding. The extra 4 inches of wall thickness on the exterior meant that indoors we would have 10-inch deep window sills that would need to be finished out once the

FIGURE 3.3 Retrofitting with highly energy efficient building materials can produce a very handsome finished appearance, like the fiberglass doors and triple pane windows we installed. Photograph by Sherri James.

exterior retrofit was completed (see figure 3.4). Making a change over *here* meant a corresponding change over *there*, whether you liked it or not.

That was especially true on the exterior. It would take careful planning to ensure that the bump-outs of exterior roof and wall surfaces came together in an aesthetically pleasing way and that architectural elements stayed proportionate to one another. While we were at it we would upgrade the trim and siding and add a few pleasing visual elements to give the house better curb appeal. A faux slate, recycled-rubber roof would give the house a cottage look while allowing us to incorporate recycled materials at the same time. We also opted to include art glass in several of the doors and windows to provide beauty and privacy. Cedar-relief engineered wood trim and siding, half-round gutters, and small copper roofs on the bay windows would also give the house a charming but updated look.

FIGURE 3.4 Installing new windows on the outer plane of the new exterior wall retrofit materials gave us deeper window sills once they were finished out. Photograph by Sherri James.

FIGURE 3.5 The inadequate size and inconvenient positioning of the doorway from our house into our pre-retrofit office is painfully apparent. Photograph by Sherri James.

Making things fit on the interior was complicated as well. The worthless office space over the garage was accessed via a small, 4-foot-tall, "Alice in Wonderland" door in the master bedroom (see figure 3.5). The door height was constrained by the old roofline. Whacking your forehead on the way into the office wasn't uncommon, so we hoped to reframe the entrance into what would be our new replacement garage and office addition to accommodate a full-height door. To make the roofline on the addition integrate with the retrofitted house, we'd have to make changes to the original house's roof as well. See what I mean? Things get complicated quickly.

⊷ Simple Addition ⊶

Changing the structure of the house in this way would be a major undertaking, but I was committed to having a full-sized door into the new office space—and no more head-whacking woes. Besides, raising that roof pitch would provide us with some other benefits. First, the nearly flat surface would give us an ideal place to mount a 4kW solar array. Second, by matching up the roof pitch with that of the replacement garage addition we would end up with spacious, 14-foot ceilings in the room over the garage. This allowed us to design a loft apartment–style interior, build more up than out, and minimize the expansion of the home's footprint on the property. The additional space wouldn't be visible from the front of the house, keeping the curb appeal of our quaint, Cape Cod–style cottage intact. Raising the rear dormer roof on the house wouldn't be easy or cheap, but it turned out to be an elegant solution to several problems at once.

The garage replacement addition wasn't technically part of our DER, but it was a necessary part of our family's comfort and the expansion of our home businesses. The 1,000-square-foot two-bedroom house worked fine when the kids were little, but now things were getting cramped. We were shoehorning two adults, two kids, and two businesses into the same space, which seemed smaller and smaller as the girls grew older and needed room to work on science fair projects or English papers. Sherri's work, reclaiming wine bottles to make artful housewares and furniture, was also growing. She needed not only more workshop space, but also a desk in an office to handle the business part of her business. With my work, I desperately needed a workshop and office to write and produce how-to videos and books. The key was to design a replacement addition that wouldn't overpower the small house.

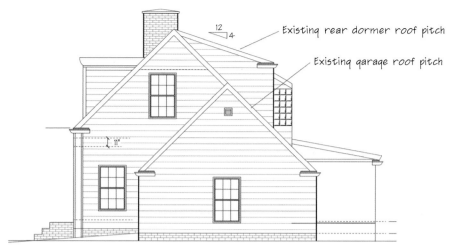

EXISTING NORTH ELEVATION

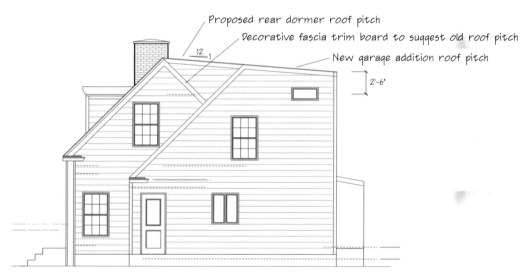

PROPOSED NORTH ELEVATION

FIGURE 3.6 Before and after views show how the existing north side of the house would change to meet our design goals. The taller, flatter roofline maximizes space in the addition, allowing us to install a full-height interior door for access from the original house. Illustrations courtesy of Tommy DeLoach, LP Building Products.

We settled on enlarging the footprint of the new garage by 6 feet toward the property line on the north side. On the front, we matched the original, steep roof pitch of the main house. By treating the rear of the roof like a dormer, raised to the pitch of the main house's rear dormer roof, we would gain extra space without changing the house's overall look. That left the details: the new replacement garage addition would have to be the polar opposite of the one we were tearing out in terms of energy efficiency. The new slab foundation would be insulated against heat loss into the soil. The walls would be thicker and superinsulated. The windows and doors would have the same energy efficient properties as the retrofit on the main house. The garage door would be the best insulated door on the market, with an effective weather seal. The interior materials would be as local and sustainably made as possible.

⬦ The Working Systems ⬦

But how would we heat and cool the additional space? I had paid good money to replace the old central heating, ventilation, and air-conditioning (HVAC) unit less than three years before, and it had been specifically sized for our older, inefficient house. Would I now need to replace it? I sought the advice of our HERS rater, Andrew Frowine. He thought that, with the major building envelope improvements we had planned, we wouldn't need extra HVAC capacity. He counseled us to wait and see. If the new space was too hot in the summer and too cold in the winter then we could add on a ductless mini-split system that would service just that end of the

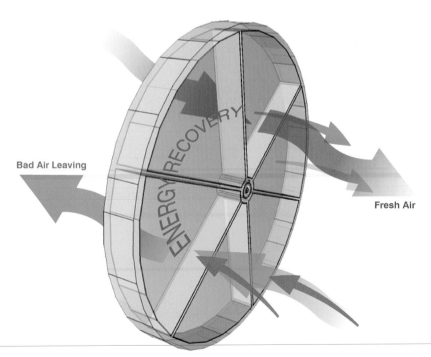

FIGURE 3.7 An energy recovery ventilator brings in fresh air and exhausts stale air, recovering the heating or cooling energy from the exhaust stream into the fresh air stream. Illustration courtesy of UltimateAir®, Inc., drawn by Matthew Baker.

house. On the other hand, if his calculations were correct, our current HVAC should be more than enough to do the job. Didn't I mention that a HERS test might come in handy later?

Once the main house was retrofitted and the addition was in place, the house would be nearly airtight. This meant that very little fresh air would be leaking *into* the building and very little stale indoor air would be leaking *out*. Our indoor air quality would steadily deteriorate, with contaminants and humidity buildup, if we didn't open a window for fresh air. Of course, an open window not only lets fresh air in, but it also lets the energy we use to heat and cool that air out. The best answer to this problem is an Energy Recovery Ventilator (ERV). This appliance works with your heating and air-conditioning to provide the "Ventilation" part of the HVAC acronym. Basically, an ERV constantly circulates fresh air and exhausts stale air from the house. As it does this, it collects the energy (heating or cooling) from the exhaust air and "recovers" it into the fresh air using a special energy exchange medium. As an extra bonus, one of the best ERVs on the market, the UltimateAir RecoupAerator, was made right in my little town. So I could support a local business while tackling my indoor air quality and energy efficiency problems.

Our relatively new, high-efficiency HVAC system was a start, but there were other systems to consider. Over the few years prior to our major DER work, as each system had worn out, we'd carefully researched replacements. When our old water heater tank failed, we replaced it with a high-efficiency tankless model. Like a lot of people, we had already replaced nearly all of our lightbulbs with either compact fluorescent (CF) or light emitting diode (LED) bulbs. Over time, as appliances failed, we replaced them with high-efficiency models. We had finally retired our family's last energy-sapping desktop computer, relying instead on energy-sipping laptops. The old television and several of the smaller appliances used sizable "vampire" power to keep them in standby mode. I used a plug in meter (called a "Kill-A-Watt" meter) to check power consumption of these devices when both on and off. Grouping devices with high vampire power usage on power strips makes them easy to turn off when they're not in use.

⊶ Automation, Monitoring, and Solar Panels ⊷

Our approach to automation had been piecemeal, and other than the use of the Kill-A-Watt meter, our energy monitoring relied on intuition. We used simple automation in the form of a program-mable thermostat, motion and light sensing switches for outdoor lighting, and timers on bathroom exhaust fans to keep from leaving them on too long. I was on the fence about installing anything more high-tech in the automation and energy monitoring department. Once we had deep energy retrofitted our home, our energy use would be so small that expensive whole-home automation and energy monitoring wouldn't likely make a big difference in our bot-tom line. While studies have shown 5 to 15 percent savings from simply monitoring energy use and adjusting habits, some high-end systems can cost thousands of dollars—not easy to justify if your home barely uses any energy to begin with.

What we could justify was installing a 4kW solar panel array on the new dormer roof on the back of the house. I originally didn't think our home would work for solar, but my local installer, who also happens to be a friend, offered to come by the house and do a quick assessment. We were pleased to find that a photovoltaic sys-tem would do well on our site, and the system now provides about 90 percent of our electricity. Financially it made sense, too—panel prices were falling, and several grant and tax incentives brought the price of the installed system down to a reasonable level.

⊸ Putting Pen to Paper ⊸

With all of this in mind, I drew up some plans. Nothing fancy—I started with 1/4-inch grid graph paper, drawing the footprint of the original house and the proposed addition so that 1/4 inch equaled 1 foot. Then I took measurements of the roof height at the peak and the eaves, as well as the size and placement for each window and door. I transferred those measurements to my graph paper, count-ing each grid square as a foot. Keeping everything proportional along the way, I was able to turn simple overhead drawings into very rough elevation drawings (views of all four sides of a building) that would give us an idea of how the finished structure would look from the outside. Those simple, handmade drawings worked fine to help us make decisions about how different changes, like window placement or the roofline, would affect the final exterior aesthetic.

Once my wife and I had settled on a basic plan I turned to an engineer friend, Tommy DeLoach, of LP Building Products, to help clean up those drawings and specify the structural elements. Tommy is a whiz at computer-aided drafting (CAD) software, so he was able to translate the sketches I sent to him into his computer in

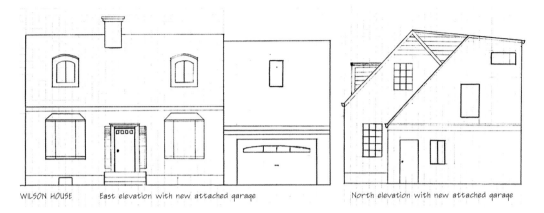

WILSON HOUSE   East elevation with new attached garage   North elevation with new attached garage

FIGURE 3.8 This handmade, graph paper sketch shows some of our original design ideas, including a skylight in the garage roof, which we ultimately decided not to install. Illustration by Jeff Wilson.

no time. What he sent back to me were clean, digital drawings of elevations (those are his drawings in figure 3.6). He also created drawings of various components of the house with each structural element—beams, rafters, studs, and headers—carefully mapped out. The more technical drawings included a materials list that I could use to order lumber. With those in hand, I felt confident that our DER could become a reality.

⤜ Designing Your DER ⤛

So that's how Sherri and I eventually worked out the DER plan for our house, but what will *your* DER plan look like? It could be very different from ours, depending on where in the country you live, what style of house you have, how old it is, and what condition it's in. Every DER plan is the result of a unique decision-making process, and this book can serve as your guide throughout the process. To start with, let's look at the main elements of a deep energy retrofit. This is just an overview; each one of these components is covered individually and in depth in the coming chapters.

Deep energy retrofit design starts with the building envelope, which constitutes your home's outer skin and protection from the elements. Other DER elements include your home's systems: HVAC, water heating, lighting, appliances, electronics, automation, and energy monitoring. Bump-outs or additions are also often a part of a DER plan. Finally, renewable energy generation, such as solar or wind power, is considered after a home's efficiency has been maximized.

← A Hole in the Bucket: Sealing the Envelope →

The building envelope is just what it sounds like: everything that goes into keeping the outdoors *out* and the indoors *in*. Starting from the exterior surface of a house, a building envelope consists of siding and roofing, housewrap or roof underlayment, a sheathing material (usually plywood or oriented strand board, which is not particleboard, but an engineered wood panel made by layering strands or flakes of wood in specific directions, which are then bonded with resins under heat and pressure), the structural members (studs and rafters, for example), insulation material, and even interior finish surfaces (such as drywall and paint). Fixing the building envelope is the most critical part of a DER because it affects everything inside the envelope—heating and cooling efficiency, humidity levels, indoor air quality, and comfort all depend on a well-designed building

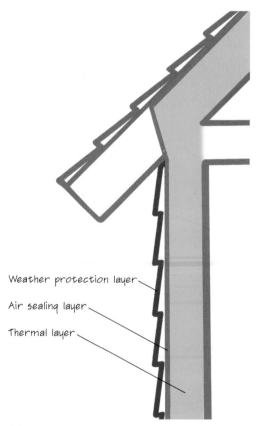

Weather protection layer

Air sealing layer

Thermal layer

FIGURE 3.9 The building envelope is made up of a weather and water barrier layer, an air barrier layer, and a thermal or insulation layer. The insulation layer is sometimes referred to separately from the building envelope as the "thermal envelope." Illustration by Jeff Wilson.

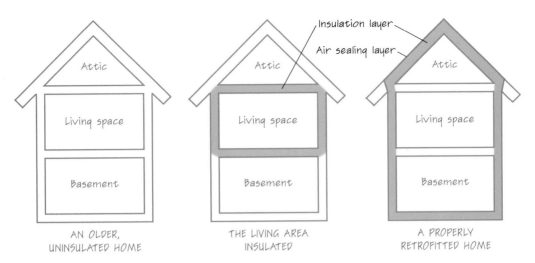

Insulation layer

Air sealing layer

Attic

Living space

Basement

AN OLDER,
UNINSULATED HOME

Attic

Living space

Basement

THE LIVING AREA
INSULATED

Attic

Living space

Basement

A PROPERLY
RETROFITTED HOME

FIGURE 3.10 Often, older homes are not insulated. When insulation is added later to walls and ceilings, the attic and basement aren't usually included and air sealing is rarely addressed. The ideal deep energy retrofit brings the building envelope, thermal envelope, and air seal layers into alignment to act as one continuous protective barrier from the elements. Illustration by Jeff Wilson.

envelope. A leaky building envelope is the basic stumbling block in trying to make older buildings more energy efficient.

To put it simply, the building envelope consists of three elements: an outer layer to protect from weather and water, an air-sealing layer to keep air from moving through the wall and roof cavities, and a thermal layer of insulation to slow the movement of heat. If any one of the three elements is missing or defective, the building envelope won't function optimally. Many older buildings have a good weather barrier but lack air sealing and thermal layers. That lets air and heat move freely through the weather barrier layer, compromising energy efficiency, comfort, and air quality.

The thermal envelope is the insulating part of the building envelope. Some homes have no insulation whatsoever, while some have had insulation added later, but only to certain parts of the home. That results in a home where the thermal envelope and building envelope are not aligned. A house may contain spaces that are inside the building envelope but outside the thermal envelope. In builder-speak, we say that these spaces are not "conditioned," meaning that they're not heated or cooled. Crawl spaces and attics are often outside the thermal envelope but within the building envelope. In the best of all worlds, the thermal envelope and the building envelope will be one and the same, avoiding some problems that can crop up in spaces that are not conditioned. This must be done carefully, however, because there are some hazards that can develop if the retrofitting of these spaces is done incorrectly. I explain this in more detail in chapters 5, 6, and 7.

For now let's just say that air sealing and insulation, which improve your building and thermal envelope, are the first things you'll want to concentrate on in your DER design. Like I said before, insulation is like a sweater that your home wears and air sealing is the windbreaker. And just as a windbreaker alone won't keep you comfortable in frigid temperatures without an insulating layer, a sweater alone won't keep you comfortable in a biting wind. You need both, and these layers are the foundations upon which your DER rests. Depending on where you live, different levels of insulation may be recommended, but homes in all heating and cooling climates can benefit from air sealing. As a matter of fact, if your house has oodles of insulation but no air seal, your insulation is not living up to its potential, so getting a handle on air sealing your home is vital.

The quality of your building envelope also plays a role in determining what size HVAC system you'll need. A leaky envelope requires more HVAC capacity while a tight envelope requires less. With a tight building envelope, you'll save thousands of dollars now on buying a smaller system and thousands more into the future as that smaller system uses less energy. Properly sized heating and cooling systems will also last longer and work more effectively than systems that are too large or too small. That will mean savings in maintenance and premature replacement costs, and your house will be much more comfortable in terms of both temperature and humidity year-round.

Air sealing and insulation can be done from the interior, exterior, or both, depending on your preference and your particular circumstance. For example, if you're doing a major "gut" renovation, where all interior finishes will be removed anyway, retrofitting from the interior makes sense. If completely gutting your home is not in your renovating future and your significant other will throw you out on your ear if you make another mess, then an exterior retrofit will help keep the indoor chaos to a minimum and your relationship intact. Sometimes, like in our retrofit, a little of both is in order. On our home, we worked from both the exterior and the interior to accomplish all of our DER goals. A year after we moved into our house, for example, we had a contractor blow loose cellulose into the empty wall cavities. Now we would add air sealing and extra insulation to the building envelope with spray foam

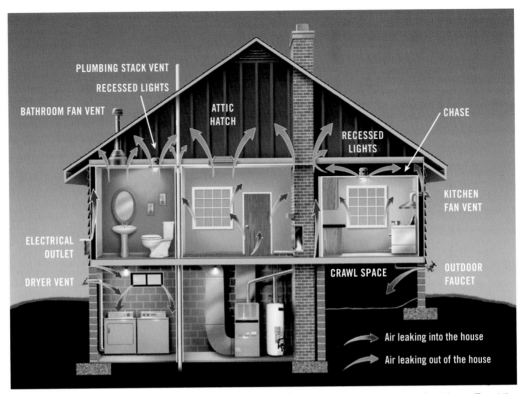

FIGURE 3-11 There are many avenues for air to travel back and forth between the indoors and outdoors. To get the most out of a DER, the building envelope must be carefully air sealed. Illustration by US Department of Energy.

(see chapters 5 and 6). All of that was done from the exterior of the house. In our basement, however, where accessing the exterior of the old block walls would have required major disruption and earth moving around the foundation, we opted to work from the interior, installing the spray foam on the interior of the walls (see chapter 7). Whether you choose an interior or exterior strategy, that tight air seal is paramount.

Interior strategies usually include removing some or all finish materials from walls, exposing the studs and the back side of the exterior sheathing inside the wall cavity. Then spray foam is applied into the cavity for insulation and air sealing. This approach can be costly, since spray foam insulation commands a premium. In order to get the air sealing benefit of spray foam without breaking the bank, it's possible, under certain circumstances, to partially fill the cavity with spray foam and then fill the remaining space with batt or loose fill insulation. In either case, a home retrofitted from the interior is usually not habitable during the retrofit process due to the amount of demolition required.

Exterior strategies typically require little interior demolition, so occupants can remain in the home during the retrofit process. The typical approach includes expanding the exterior wall or roof surface outward with spray foam or rigid foam insulating panels. While spray foam naturally air seals as it expands and cures during application, rigid panel materials require careful manual sealing at the joints with tape, caulk, or foam. It's also possible to perform an exterior "gut" retrofit by removing all siding and sheathing before filling the cavities with spray foam from the exterior. Once the insulation and air sealing is complete, new exterior finish materials are installed.

Many people overlook basements and crawl spaces in energy efficiency improvements, but studies show that bringing the foundation into the thermal envelope can potentially save 30 percent on heating costs. Exterior approaches, which require removing landscaping and copious amounts of dirt from around the foundation, can be very expensive and disruptive. Once the foundation is exposed, the exterior surface is waterproofed and layers of foam board are attached. Often, new foundation drains are installed and then dirt is backfilled against the foam and landscaping is replanted.

Assuming that a basement doesn't have serious water infiltration and only suffers from condensation problems, interior retrofitting can be a cost-effective, viable choice. Spray foam or rigid foam is installed against the masonry surfaces of the walls and floor, and then finish materials are installed over the foam. In the case of crawl spaces, the preferred method is to cover the floor of the crawl space with thick plastic sheeting and then spray foam the foundation walls all the way up to the underside of the floor above. In some cases, however, a foundation has water and structural problems that need to be addressed before any retrofitting for energy efficiency take place. Insulating and air sealing the foundation of your home is just as important as walls and roofs, so make sure to include it in your DER plan.

Doors and windows are part of your building envelope, too, and require the same qualities of weather, water, air, and thermal resistance as the rest of the building envelope. This is a place where research will pay off. For better weather resistance and efficiency, long-lasting operation, and beauty, you'll want to look past the standard, off-the-shelf grades of windows and doors available at consumer big box home centers and concentrate on higher quality contractor grade models. It's also important to have your new windows and doors installed by properly trained professionals. This is especially true in retrofitting applications: air sealing, insulation, and water management techniques that may be straightforward when installing windows in new homes can become tricky when incorporating new windows into an older home. The energy efficiency and operation of many high-end windows have been compromised by a second-rate installation. This makes it doubly important to hire a well-trained, competent installer.

– The Working Parts: DER Systems –

Once the building envelope strategy has been designed, from the roof and walls to the basement or crawl space, then you can move on to the systems. Your HVAC system is likely the biggest energy consuming system in your home. If there were such people as "average Americans," their biggest single point of energy use would be heating, which accounts for nearly 30 percent of all energy consumed at home. Cooling costs come in second in the energy hog race. Those elusive average Americans spend about 17 percent of their energy budgets on cooling. If you live in the south, your heating and cooling percentages might be swapped, with cooling costs eating up the lion's share of your energy bill.

Water heating comes in next at 14 percent of the average American's energy use. Whether or not you're replacing your water heater, there are a few things you can do to make your water heater perform up to its potential. To start with, make sure that the tank is well insulated. Inexpensive water heater "blankets" are available that can help slow heat loss from the water sitting in your tank. Use pipe insulation on hot water supply pipes to minimize heat loss between your water heater and the fixture. Shutting off your water heater when you go on vacation is a good idea, too. Still, with a DER, where we're gleaning energy savings from all of the disparate parts of a home, water heater replacement might be in your future, so making a DER water heating plan will help.

Next up are appliances. Refrigerators, stoves and ovens, dishwashers, clothes washers and dryers, microwaves, coffeemakers, toasters, and other modern conveniences eat up about 13 percent of our energy pie. Part of the point of a DER is that you won't have to "freeze in the dark," and I, for one, know the importance of cold beer *and* being able to toast your pastries, no matter the cost of energy. That's why, on top of building envelope and major systems solutions, scrutinizing the energy use of your appliances is also an important aspect of a full DER. Following Energy Star recommendations is a great start. Bright yellow Energy Star labels ensure that you're buying an appliance that is at least 20 to 30 percent more efficient than others in its class. But you can go further by comparing those labels and choosing the most efficient appliances within the Energy Star class. That label will also help you make a better decision when an appliance fails and has to be replaced quickly—Energy Star has done most of the research for you and made it easily accessible right at the point of purchase.

⚊ Automation and Monitoring ⚊

Last, consider energy monitoring and automation as part of a well-rounded DER plan. Energy monitoring can show you where most of the energy is being used in your home and, therefore, where your money is going. Once aware of those facts, you might opt to change your habits in order to save energy. According to a University of Oxford study, people made aware of their energy use through energy monitoring save between 5 and 15 percent. There's that expression again: knowledge is power. I used a Kill-A-Watt meter to sample the individual energy uses of all of my appliances. The Kill-A-Watt meter is plugged into the wall and then a single appliance is plugged into the meter. The Kill-A-Watt's display then shows how much energy that appliance uses, either instantaneously or over time. Whole house energy monitoring systems are also available that mount to your existing electric meter and show your home's energy use in real time while keeping a running tab over time. By inputting your utility rates, that data can be expressed in dollars, so you can actually see the effect of using an appliance on your pocketbook. This will give you a good picture of your overall energy use and motivate a change of habit. Still more elaborate energy monitoring is possible that will incorporate automation as well.

Home automation is just what it sounds like—the ability to monitor and control anything in your house automatically. While in the past home automation has mostly been used for high-end home theaters and home security, it's now targeting energy efficiency to control HVAC, lighting, outlets, appliances, and even motorized window shades. This allows a homeowner to monitor energy use in different systems and then automate them to perform in the most efficient manner. Like a programmable thermostat, a whole-home automation system will allow you to control and program your HVAC system from a touch screen display. Lighting can be automated to turn off when rooms are empty, appliances automated to operate when electricity rates drop to off-peak pricing, and outlets automated to turn off when not in use, avoiding the "vampire loads" of electronic devices in standby mode. Even window shades can be automated to let sunlight in or shade it out, depending on the season.

Does all of this sound a little bit "Star Trek" to you? Not these days. We live in a land of touch screens and smart phones—it's about time our homes caught up. Using tablet technology, many home automation systems provide easy user interface apps to control any system in the home. These systems can cost from a few hundred dollars for an off-the-shelf model to many thousands of dollars for a custom system. Once these automation controls are installed, you can enjoy both energy monitoring and automation for the most energy efficient operation of your home, so beam me up, Scotty! While a lot of home automation is wireless these days, it pays to make a plan before your DER starts, so that any wired elements can be installed with the least amount of disruption to finish materials. For more about home automation and other home systems, see chapter 8.

⊷ Renewable Energy ⊶

After all of your home's various parts and systems have been carefully examined and redesigned for maximum energy efficiency, you should give serious consideration to renewable energy generation like solar, wind, or biomass. Like many people, I never thought that renewables could produce enough energy for my home's operation. With a DER, though, our electricity use would drop dramatically, making a roof-sized photovoltaic solar array big enough to power most of our home.

Once you've defined the changes that you'll make to improve your home's energy efficiency you can begin designing your renewable energy system to fit in with your plan. Maybe you'll need to raise a roofline like I did, or maybe you only need to make minor structural changes. Maybe you just need to trim back a couple of tall trees to take advantage of more sunlight on your roof. Even if you don't think your home is well situated for renewables, it's worth asking an installer to give you professional advice, since he or she will usually do this free of charge. If renewables will work at your house, these professionals will design, install, and help you find incentives for your system.

What Happened In Vegas

FIGURE 3.12 A rags-to-riches retrofit in Las Vegas—the ReVision House. Illustration copyright © 2009 J. David Thorpe used with permission

What happens in Vegas stays in Vegas—unfortunately, that even applies to the housing bust of the Great Recession. When the Department of Energy's Building America Consortium for Advanced Residential Buildings (CARB) research team went looking for a pilot deep energy retrofit project in a hot, arid climate, they had a lot of foreclosed homes to choose from in Las Vegas. One in particular stood out: a classic 1960s, midcentury modern-style house that had been abandoned and had become an eyesore in the neighborhood. CARB set out to breathe new life into the home, calling it the "ReVision House."

The project was ambitious: take a run-down, poorly insulated home and make it net zero for energy use, so that it produced all of the energy it needed. At the same time, the home would be restored aesthetically to its hip, 1960s roots. Since the interior was in good shape, the retrofit was attacked from the exterior, removing the old stucco, siding, roofing, sheathing, and fiberglass batt insulation to fill cavities with high-performing spray foam insulation. Once superinsulated and air sealed, the home's HVAC system could be downsized by 50 percent from the old unit to a new, energy miser model. Leaving no stone unturned, the home's appliances, lighting, water heater, and pool pump were replaced with models using a fraction of the energy of the originals.

After vastly improving the building and systems, a solar thermal water heating system was installed and photovoltaic array was added to generate electricity. The results were shocking—while the original home tested in with a HERS rating of 123 (23 percent worse than the average new home), it hit a final, post-retrofit score of -2. This means that the new home creates 2 percent more energy than it uses over the course of a year. Another example of the power of a deep energy retrofit.

❯ Dream of Big Energy Savings ❮

That's the grand overview of a DER. Are you overwhelmed yet? Don't worry, it's natural to feel that way when considering a project as involved as a full deep energy retrofit of your house. Take your time—don't rush the critical design stage and give yourself the leeway to dream big at the outset. Remember that a DER doesn't have to be done all at once, but can be phased in over time, making the individual phases more manageable.

By the time you're ready to start designing your deep energy retrofit, you'll have a professional energy audit in your hands, and your auditor's report will be a guide that you'll refer to over and over again during the design process. Depending on your comfort level you may want to hire an architect or you may feel confident creating your design yourself. Either way, it helps to start by sketching out your ideas. I'm not much of an artist, but I can usually use helpful guides like graph paper and a ruler to get fairly decent results. Working with a pencil allows you to erase and redraw portions of your sketch as your ideas evolve. You'll inevitably run into design problems that need to be solved, but that's a natural part of the process. As you engage with professionals like architects, engineers, building science pros, and salespeople along the way, they'll be able to help make all of the puzzle pieces fit.

Start by dreaming big—not in terms of size, but in terms of your energy efficiency and comfort goals. Dreaming is the one part of this process that won't cost you a red cent. By using your HERS test as a roadmap, carefully research and plan each element. There are some kinds of jobs you only want to do once, so make sure not to skimp on them just because they aren't the most visible after the retrofit is finished. Specify the best windows and doors, the best insulation, and the best high-efficiency appliances and equipment. Even if you'll have to scale back your plans later to stay within your budget, it helps to know how different products stack up. Is the premium you'll pay for high-end windows, compared with the next step down, worth it? Can you get the same quality of air sealing and insulation from a lower cost solution as you would from spray foam?

You may be able to spread out the project and the costs over time instead of doing everything at once. With a good, overall plan, you could choose to retrofit the roof one year, for example, and move on to the walls the next. With HVAC and appliances it rarely makes sense to replace everything at once, so a rolling DER of your home's systems will work better, replacing items as they fail. Our DER took three years of physical work because we opted to do parts of the project ourselves.

While an entire deep energy retrofit is, by nature, not a do-it-yourself project, you might have the skills to attack some parts of your DER yourself. Sherri and I hired a contractor to handle the very heavy lifting and steep roofing jobs—things that would have taken me months to accomplish alone. Once the house and new addition were under roof, she and I did the rest of the project ourselves, including the exterior curtain wall retrofit and all of the exterior and interior finish work. This took time but allowed us to minimize the expense of our DER while still stimulating our economy by hiring a local crew. Whether you're a hands-on or hands-off kind of person, researching and planning carefully will save you money and result in a higher quality finished product.

⨞ Other DER Design Considerations ⨞

Among other factors that will affect the design of your DER, your regional climate is probably the most important. In some parts of the country, water conservation is as important as energy conservation as a design consideration. Aesthetics, especially when retrofitting historic homes or complying with neighborhood association rules, are also potentially significant. Local building codes may limit what you can do, either by the codes on the books or by ignorance of DER materials and techniques on the part of codes officers. Structural integrity, materials selection, working with a contractor, designing for indoor air quality, dealing with construction waste, and the possibility of certifying the actual energy efficiency of your home will all come into play as you map out your DER. And if you're retrofitting for the long haul, you may even want to consider Universal Design or aging-in-place elements that will accommodate people with disabilities or the elderly.

⁃ Climate and DERs ⁃

Consideration of climate is very important—there is no cookie cutter way to deep energy retrofit a home. In the frigid, dry northeast your approach will differ from someone who lives in the sultry, humid south. While things like the amount of insulation you need and the type of windows you choose can be debated for a particular climate, proper air sealing and ventilation are universal. While basic HVAC equipment will need to help control humidity and indoor air quality, it will also need to have the right attributes to perform optimally in your climate: heating in cold climates and cooling in hot climates.

Your home's "micro-climate," the climate of the area immediately surrounding a house, may be somewhat different than your regional climate, and that can affect your design. For example, even though your region may be considered "hot-humid," if you live in a deep hollow where a dense tree canopy and hills shade and cool your home, you may not need the kind of high-capacity air-conditioning that a home in direct sunlight in that region might require. Also, think about your home's particular orientation to the sun. While you may not be able to reorient the house by picking it up off its foundation, a major remodel may allow you to add on or shift space uses on the interior to help your home function better within its environment. Called passive solar design, it's a way of allowing sunlight in to help heat during cold months and shading sunlight out during hot months to aid in cooling. This is most commonly done in modern renovations by removing interior walls to create an open floor plan or by carefully placing or removing windows to allow sunlight in or keep it out. A similar effect can be achieved by designing extended roof overhangs to shade windows in the summer but allow sunlight in during the winter as passive solar heating.

Outside, you may be able to plant or remove trees strategically to provide shade or allow sunlight in. Trees can also help regulate breezes, shielding your home from frigid northern gusts in the winter. Evergreens will provide shade and wind blocking year round, while deciduous trees will provide shade in the summer and then lose their leaves and allow sunlight through in the winter. Just because you're starting with a home already situated in a particular place in a particular way doesn't mean that you can't creatively and wisely adapt the building to work more harmoniously with its surroundings. A major renovation like a DER is an opportunity to transform your home.

⚫ Water Conservation and DERs ⚫

Depending on where you live, your water bill might be nearly as high as your energy bill. Even if water use isn't a major concern, clean drinking water takes a tremendous amount of energy to produce. Should energy prices spike, residential water rates would necessarily rise as well. Considering water conservation as part of your deep energy retrofit plans makes good sense.

Aesthetics and DERs

The only people I've met who don't care for the process of deep energy retrofitting are historic preservationists. At first I was surprised that someone would deny the benefits of a DER in favor of mere aesthetics, but after a bit of thought I've concluded that a DER might not be the best solution for some truly historic buildings and historic districts. *Green Restorations,* an excellent book written by Aaron Lubeck, helped me understand this point of view. Some historic buildings are, by nature and design, inefficient. Their inefficiency helps tell a story of the time in which they were built, so these buildings should be treated as works of art or historic documents. You wouldn't spray foam a Monet, would you?

That said, I believe that the number of historic buildings kept in their original condition for the purposes of art and history should be limited; at least those buildings intended as residences for 21st century people. Insisting that every old building has some inherent aesthetic and historic value that shouldn't be altered for posterity's sake is unrealistic. Those buildings that we still wish to use as homes, for the most part, need to be altered to conform to a high standard of energy efficiency. These retrofitted homes will someday be held up as historic homes themselves; examples of the significant changes we humans were willing to make at the beginning of the 21st century in light of energy issues of the times. These examples will eventually tell *our* story of conservation and efficiency.

If you're an owner of a historic home and you're considering a deep energy retrofit, be sure to plan carefully and work with preservation experts to ensure your home retains its historic aesthetics and significance while you improve its performance.

Think about installing low-flow, aerated fixtures at sinks and showers. The aerator in a fixture mixes air with the water stream, forming bubbles that help keep the pressure high while using less water. Newer toilets with dual-flush capability allow the user to use less water for liquid waste and more water for solid waste. Dishwashers and clothes washers vary widely in their water use, too. Energy Star–labeled dishwashers and clothes washers are rated not only for their lower energy use, but for their lower water use as well, so the bright yellow label is a good rule of thumb for choosing a new appliance for water conservation as well as energy conservation.

Outdoors, plan landscaping and gardens for low water use by planting native, drought-tolerant species. When irrigation is necessary, use soaker hoses over sprinklers, and automate the watering schedule with a timer so that water isn't accidentally left on. The latest technology in irrigation includes a rain sensor that won't water plants if it's rained recently, and some whole-home automation systems will even use weather forecasts to delay watering if rain is imminent.

Simple changes of habit can yield big results, too. Turn off the water in the shower while soaping up or at the tap while brushing your teeth. Only run the dishwasher and clothes washer when they're full. Scrape dishes instead of pre-rinsing. Like investments in energy efficiency, water conservation pays off.

⬩ Complying with Rules and Codes ⬩

As you would for any major renovation, you will need to retrofit within certain guidelines. To start with, many homeowners' associations and planned neighborhoods enforce rules about simple aesthetics that will need to be followed as a DER plan is developed. These rules, called "covenants," may legally restrict you from making certain changes to your home or property even though you own it. It's best to know ahead of time what aesthetic restrictions you may be under before you get too far in the planning process.

Zoning rules and building codes will need to be examined as well. These rules will cover everything from property line setbacks and lot coverage to precisely how systems need to be installed and by whom. If deep energy retrofitting is a new concept in your area, you'll want to become friendly with your local building codes officers. Some may be initially reticent to accept newer,

Planning for the Future

A deep energy retrofit will add many years to the lifespan of your home, so while you're at it, consider including Universal Design (UD) or aging-in-place elements in your plan. Universal Design means that your home will be usable to all occupants, regardless of their age or possible impairments. Aging-in-place is a similar concept, preparing the home so that it is still useful as the occupants become elderly. Adding aging-in-place elements into your design ensures that you'll be able to stay in your deep energy retrofitted home as the natural process of aging makes navigating your home more difficult. These elements can include ramps instead of stairs, wider door openings, and functional access to things like appliances and light switches. Whether you're impaired or not, UD will make your home more useful for everyone.

somewhat radical-sounding DER methods, but many will welcome the education and challenge DERs represent. You might also need the okay from a local planning or zoning board, depending on the extent of additions or renovations. Start talking with officials early in the planning process to ferret out any potential zoning or planning conflicts so that they can be resolved before groundbreaking day. You might suggest this book to officials who are unfamiliar with DERs as an overall picture of the process, but you'll also find more in-depth and technical information, books, and links in the Resources appendix.

Happily, my experience with local officials was smooth and without conflict. I took my basic pencil drawings showing property line setbacks, lot coverage, and the differences between the old building footprint and the new building footprint to our building codes office. I sat down to several brief, informal meetings with the codes director and the city planner to discuss what I had in mind. They brought up several salient points and were able to indicate where minor changes would keep my design within the building code and zoning rules. I found both guys to be amiable and interested in our project, and I think we all learned something from the process of talking it through. I still can't go to a basketball game without having a conversation about "the project" with our codes director, since his daughter plays basketball in the same league as mine. Through this process we addressed all of the potential problems to the satisfaction of everyone involved by the time I needed my building permit.

⬧ Hiring Building Professionals ⬧

Like I said, a DER is not a DIY project. You'll need the advice of experienced, qualified people who are either familiar with DER methods or willing to consult with other professionals along the way. During your planning process, you may need to hire an architect, engineer, building science pro, and contractor.

An architect can be a great ally throughout the process of either building or renovating, performing tasks as common as producing a set of plans and as complex as consulting during the whole project. An architect can be especially helpful on more difficult projects like major additions or historic restorations. Depending on your budget, your project, and your willingness to take on an active role in the day-to-day construction activities, an architect can either be a big help or just an added expense.

Whether or not you opt to hire an architect, you'll most certainly want to vet your design plans with an engineer. An engineer will be able to tell you if your plan is viable from a structural standpoint. Most likely, you're making some other serious changes to your home at the same time that you're deep energy retrofitting. Those changes, which may include removing walls or raising roof pitches, might add stresses to parts of your home that are not built to properly support them. In a worst-case scenario, part of your home can collapse. Less drastic, you can end up with cracking and buckling of finish materials, or windows and doors that don't work as the building settles under the new weight of the remodel. Having a structural engineer do an assessment of your plan will help ensure that your retrofit is structurally sound and will stand the test of time. An engineer might also be able to save you some money by properly sizing and placing structural members like studs and joists and suggesting techniques like advanced framing (a way of framing with less lumber to achieve the same strength but better insulation in walls). Where a contractor without engineering training might overbuild to cover any eventuality, an engineer can help optimize your plan so that you're not spending more on materials and labor than is necessary. An engineer also usually has the skills and software needed to transform your pencil drawings into professional-style blueprints. This might allow you to skip the expense of an architect for simply drafting your plans.

Deep energy retrofit plans demand careful vetting by building science professionals, as well. A deep energy retrofit changes a building so radically that unintended consequences can arise after the fact if good building science isn't followed. For example, moisture movement through the empty wall cavity of an older home isn't seen as problematic because the cavity is able to become damp and then dry through the cracks and gaps in the building envelope. Many historic buildings have stood for hundreds of years, going through cycles of wetting and drying with little structural effect. Add fiberglass or cellulose insulation to that cavity, and suddenly moisture can be trapped within the insulation, posing the risk of damage from mold and rot. Seal up the building envelope incorrectly, hindering its ability to dry out, and moisture damage can occur. Building science has been developing over the last 30 years, ferreting out confounding issues that arise from dramatic changes to a building. That's why you won't want to design your DER alone—be sure to consult with a well-trained building science pro to ensure you avoid serious long-term damage to your home. This can be a properly trained architect, contractor, or energy auditor. If you choose a contractor without building science training, be sure to hire a separate building science pro to ensure that all of your plans and your contractor's building practices pass building science standards.

On top of that, a building science pro can also help design your retrofit holistically, considering how each individual element affects others and optimizing how they work together as a whole. This can save you money on the project during both the construction phase and in the long-term operation of your home. The Building Performance Institute helps to set standards and best practices in energy efficient building. The organization also certifies professional building workers at many levels. Check out the Resources appendix for links to finding a building science pro in your area.

With a viable plan in hand, you now have the choice of whether to work with a contractor or manage the construction yourself. If you know enough about construction, or have time to educate yourself on the process, acting as your own contractor can save you some money. Many smaller remodeling contractors will manage a crew of jack-of-all-trades carpenters of various skill levels and then hire out work like electrical, plumbing, tile, or concrete to subcontractors. These subcontractors are paid by the contractor for their work, but the contractor will charge you the subcontractor's fee plus a contractor's premium. If you can handle hiring subcontractors, you'll write the checks to pay them directly and avoid the contractor's premium.

Not all contractors are willing to work this way, but many will understand. When my contractor and I first met to discuss the project, we very specifically laid out what he would be responsible for, leaving the rest up to me. I explained that I would hire the few subcontractors we needed but would mostly be working on things myself, alongside the contractor's crew. Though he was a bit skeptical at first, he told me that he was willing to try it as long as I didn't hold up his work schedule. If I could keep up with his crew of 20-plus-year-old carpenters, he would work with me. As a 40-plus-year-old, semi-retired construction guy, it made me tired just thinking about it. My ability to swing a hammer was still strong, but could I really keep up with an entire crew half my age and double my bicep size? Besides, over the last 10 years I'd spent more time in an office writing about construction than on a job site doing it.

We made sure that my tasks were wholly separate from the contractor's tasks, and as things turned out, I kept up pretty well, usually working into the evening to make sure that my part was done by the time the crew started again the next morning. Once or twice I had to leave town on business, so I paid them extra to finish a task that I wouldn't be able to complete on schedule. While this method of working stretched the project out a bit, I was able to save some money (and a gym membership) while still putting some local guys to work, balancing my goals on the house. I paid my contractor and his crew to do the framing, roofing, and window installation. I hired the HERS rater, concrete guys, and solar installer myself. Later in the project I paid one crew to install the gutters on the outside and another to hang and finish the drywall on the interior. The rest—demolition, exterior curtain wall installation, spray foam insulation, trim, and siding, and the rest of the interior finish work—Sherri and I did ourselves.

How to Find the Right Contractor

Hiring the right contractor isn't a simple matter, especially if you're serious about finding a contractor with building science training or a familiarity with deep energy retrofitting techniques. Give yourself plenty of time; one or two months isn't sufficient. Not only will you need to find a reliable and competent contractor, you'll also need to be slotted into that contractor's schedule, which can sometimes be backed up quite a few months. The better the contractor's reputation, the longer the waiting list. To find a contractor, start by asking friends and neighbors, or knocking on the doors of homes that have recently been remodeled. By talking with people who have just been through the process, you'll get a version of a remodeling story that isn't softened by the fog of time. Ask them about whether the contractor is open to new ideas and whether the project stayed on schedule. Even simple things, like end-of-day site cleanup or a willingness to show up on a weekend to reposition a tarp that's blown off, can tell you a lot about the character of a contractor. Don't be afraid to ask how disputes were handled, and whether the contractor's prices are reasonable.

You'll also be spending a lot of quality time with your contractor and crew, and you're investing lots of your time and money to make this project work, so interview at least three contractors to find someone who fits your budget and personality. You might pay a little more for someone who is willing to try some newer

DER techniques, like advanced framing or spray foam insulation, and that contractor might jump at the chance to learn some new skills related to deep energy retrofits. DERs could potentially be a big part of new business for a contractor, so being among the first contractors in a given locality to acquire those skills and training could give him or her a leg up on the competition.

Even when working with an excellent contractor, unforeseen problems will undoubtedly arise. Unexpected structural problems may come to light in the midst of the retrofit, or changes may need to be made to the original plan. Both you and your contractor will need to be flexible in working through such problems. In most cases, the cost will lie with the homeowner and deadlines will have to change. Being reasonable and calm is the best thing you can do to keep the process moving forward in the most positive way possible. Keep all of this in mind, and select a contractor who scores highly in enough categories to make sure your project is a success.

If you're hiring an HVAC contractor yourself, it's also important to learn about certification and licensing of HVAC contractors in your state, and call only contractors who qualify; HVAC trade groups can help you educate yourself. You should expect prospective contractors to do a thorough analysis of your home to ensure proper HVAC and duct sizing and to provide a detailed, written estimate. And as with any contractor, check references carefully. See the Resources appendix for more details.

⇉ DER Materials ⇇

Generally speaking, materials for DER projects are no different from materials for standard renovation projects. Still, you may want to consider "green" materials when making design and purchasing decisions. These materials may be labeled as sustainably produced or harvested, made with non-toxic and low-energy techniques, manufactured or harvested locally, no- or low-maintenance, or super energy efficient. Whether you're a true green-believer or not, it's fair to consider the benefits of green materials. By choosing products that fit into as many of these categories as possible, you're likely to rack up savings on many levels.

For example, "sustainably harvested" is a fancy name, but what it means is harvesting practices that will ensure more of the product will be readily available to you when you need a replacement in the coming years. If a product is made using non-toxic techniques, your family isn't going to get sick down the line from exposure to that product in your home. If a product is made using low-energy techniques, that means production costs are lower and that savings is passed on to you. The same goes for the locally produced products. Since my local sawmill doesn't have to send its lumber halfway across the country, they can offer beautiful cherry flooring for a lot less than I'd pay at a national chain home improvement center. If you're working with low-maintenance materials, this means that you won't be back up on a ladder in five years fixing or replacing what you've just paid to fix or replace. And we know that the stuff that uses less energy during its lifetime is good. On all counts, installing green materials makes sense.

"But green is too expensive!" I hear this comment all the time. Most likely, the cheap product that you would use in place of a green product won't last as long and will off-gas volatile organic compounds (VOCs), which could make your kids sick. Or it won't perform as indicated by the manufacturer, wasting lots of energy over time. This is what they mean by being "penny wise and pound foolish." It's important to calculate the lifetime cost of a product, not just look at the sticker price. Many times, the more expensive item will cost less to operate and maintain than the cheaper one. For example, when I had to replace my 25-year-old HVAC system, I ended up going with the more expensive unit (by about 25 percent) because it was better made, properly sized to my home, and much more energy efficient. By the time I started calculating the difference in operating costs alone, it was easy to see that buying the more expensive unit now would save me money over the medium- to long-term. Plus, my family would be more comfortable. I say this to make a point: green products aren't just a fad. They can be a sensible alternative to overmarketed, mass-produced, lower-quality materials.

If you're buying new materials, you're likely going to be getting rid of old materials in the form of construction debris. Instead of pitching it into a dumpster, consider donation and recycling programs instead. In our neck of the woods, semi-clean, used building materials can be donated and will be picked up by a local company, ReUse Industries, which then makes them available at deep discounts through its warehouse. As a matter of fact, many communities across the country have similar programs. Habitat for Humanity runs ReStore outlets nationwide that sell gently used furniture, home accessories, and building materials. The proceeds from selling donated materials are used to help fund Habitat projects (search by zip code for your nearest ReStore at www.habitat.org). While our municipality doesn't support construction debris recycling, there's a chance that yours does. In Seattle, Washington, for example, a recycling dumpster costs the same as a garbage dumpster. Where landfill space is limited, recycling may save you money on tipping fees at the dump. In still other areas, a local ethic of recycling means that it's subsidized by local taxpayers. This not only generates less garbage but is often connected to a low-income works project that provides jobs for those who can't find work elsewhere. Just remember that planning for recycling of job site waste is something to do long before groundbreaking day and will require the full cooperation of your contractor and subcontractors to be effective.

If you're deep energy retrofitting your home and you're serious about green materials, then you may be interested in certification programs. Certification means that you open your project to inspectors who will ensure that your project meets certain green standards. Once completed, you're issued a certificate that can be shown to prospective buyers, which may mean a nice premium on closing day if you someday decide to sell your deep energy retrofitted home. On the minus side, it's another hurdle in getting your DER done. Waiting for inspectors and the cost of attaining the certification can divert your attention from the real DER goal.

Keeping your eye on the DER ball through a long process can be trying, but as a DER survivor and beneficiary, I can tell you that the results are worth it. Take your time, make a lot of lists, and break the big chunks of work down into manageable goals. After that, the trick is to just stay at it. An old Chinese proverb puts it well: "To get through the hardest journey we need take only one step at a time, but we must keep on stepping."

⇝ Retaining Your Sense of Home ⇜

Home: it's one powerful word. Once, when Sylvie was about two, we were traveling far from our home to visit family. It was late in the day, and she was hot, tired, and hungry. Sherri was holding her as she began to weep quietly. Heavy tears welled up and spilled down her chubby red cheeks. "What's wrong, honey?" Sherri asked. She buried her head in my wife's shoulder and cried, "I just want to go back to my little blue house!" Even there, visiting Grandma and

Credit where Credit Is Due: Green Remodeling Certification Programs

You'll be shelling out some greenbacks to deep energy retrofit your house, so why not get credit for it through a green remodeling certification program? Most programs require pre- and post-retrofit energy audits to assess performance, as well as inspections by credentialed experts. Costs range from $300 to $1,000 for inspections and certification.

- The National Association of Home Builders (NAHB) offers the National Green Building Standard "Green Remodel Path" for renovations: http://www.nahbgreen.org.
- LEED (Leadership in Energy and Environmental Design) for Homes Program is part of the US Green Building Council. LEED will certify a renovation only if it is a gut-remodel that exposes the wall cavities and replaces most systems: www.usgbc.org.
- EarthCraft is based in the southeastern United States and offers EarthCraft Renovation certification in the region: www.earthcraft.org/renovation.
- Energy Star Certification is handled by different entities by region. For example, Energy Star Northwest offers certification of homes in Washington, Oregon, Idaho, and Montana: www.northwestenergystar .com. Search your region for your Energy Star partners.

Grandpa and all of her aunts and uncles and cousins, Sylvie was homesick. Even there, on a trip she had looked forward to so much, the comfort and familiarity of her own home beckoned. Why not? That's what home is.

In the midst of planning your DER, don't forget to hang on to those sentimental details that make your house uniquely, lovably yours. One night when Sherri and I were sitting at the kitchen table in a pile of paint chips, trying to decide what color we might paint the new version of the "little blue house," Sylvie came into the room. She figured out what we were doing as we held up the chips in the light, comparing them. Hoping she'd share our excitement about all of the changes, I cheerfully told her how we would have new siding when the project was over, and that we could paint it *any color we wanted*. Would she like to help pick the color? She turned quiet. "Papa," she asked tentatively, "what color *are* you going to paint the house after you redo it?" I looked across the table at my wife and down at the multi-colored pile of chips. I thought a bit about all of the big changes we were about to go through, which were good on so many levels. I thought back on that day, long ago, and the tired, homesick, two-year-old Sylvie in her mama's arms. I thought about home. "Blue," I told her. "*Exactly* the same color blue, honey."

Chapter Four

FIGURING COSTS AND FINDING FINANCING

SHERRI AND I WORKED HARD DURING THE DESIGN PROCESS FOR OUR DER, and we felt confident that we had created a good plan. But when it came to financing a project like ours—especially in the middle of a recession—I was really at sea. Still, being frugal people at heart made the process easier.

Frugality is a part of our DNA; a strand that, if you follow it back to when Sherri and I met, started with both of us rereading Henry David Thoreau's *Walden*. We'd both read it in high school but had missed the point. We read it again in our twenties, together, but this time the ideas really hit home: if we kept our wants down to a minimum and we were honest about our needs, we would naturally consume less. Less consumption meant working less at jobs, giving us more freedom.

While many of our peers were working overtime to pay for their lifestyles, we opted to pay cash for used cars, live in a smaller home, and maintain a generally frugal, creative, and unique life. Our shorter workweek left us time to brew our own beer, read a lot, play music, hike, shop in thrift stores, and cook dinner for friends. We lived within our means in order to have more time for what was truly important to us: family, friends, and enjoying a stimulating daily life.

On top of our frugal ethic, we both work as freelancers. That means our income doesn't arrive in equal, biweekly paychecks, but sporadically. If you charted my income as a television host, actor, voiceover talent, and writer over the years, it would look like an elevation view of the Himalayas (with the early, deep troughs filled in with construction work). That experience led us to maintain our frugal behavior even when times were good, stashing away a little when we could to carry us through the next low.

Sure, we had strayed from Thoreau's simplicity a bit by the time we hit our forties. We had added two kids and two businesses to the mix. But when the recession hit, we were in an enviable position: no car or credit card debts, a smaller house with a manageable mortgage payment, and a solid roster of regular clients for both of our businesses. We felt the sting, but we were surviving, and we felt lucky. As we thought about it, we realized that our luck had something to do with our deep distaste for debt. Avoiding debt took some creativity and hard work while our income was falling. Thomas Jefferson would have been proud. "I am a great believer in luck," he said, "and I find the harder I work, the more I have of it."

Our little blue house was a big part of that luck. We had bought this small fixer-upper and *fixed it up*. Our house was inexpensive, and we had refinanced when rates were low. As we pondered the big DER project, things looked positive. Our home had appraised well, we owed little on the mortgage, and it would be paid off by the time I hit 52. We could afford to take on some debt for our DER—it was an investment that would pay us back in many ways over the coming years.

⇒ How Much Will It Cost? ⇐

The question of cost swirled through our DER dreaming, sometimes raising our anxiety levels. No matter how frugal we might be, major renovations cost real money. Getting a handle on exactly how *much* money proved to be tricky, because we had decided to do a lot of the work ourselves.

Most homeowners hire an architect to help design a renovation or retrofit project and draw up the plans. Those plans are passed to general contractors who bid the entire project, soup to nuts, and come up with a single figure. The homeowner never has to do any number crunching. But for our DER, I planned to be the general contractor for many aspects of the project. We would hire a professional contractor only for certain big jobs that we couldn't manage ourselves, like installing windows. So, as general contractor, I had to shoulder the responsibility for figuring the total cost of the project. I'd done a fair amount of this kind of figuring earlier in my life when I worked as a remodeler, but I lacked the skills and resources of modern contractors. I was out of practice at creating an estimate for a construction job.

I began to do some rough figuring of materials and labor costs. I compared costs of materials in catalogs and online and used actual labor bids from contractors and subcontractors to figure the rest.

How We Used Incentives

I had hoped that incentives like tax credits and grants would be available for big retrofit projects like mine. After all, it was clear from the data that energy efficiency is the cheapest way to "generate new energy." The truth was disappointing. There was a modest $1,500 tax credit for materials related to energy efficiency upgrades, but it applied only to the cost of materials (up to 30 percent of the total cost), not to installation costs. I wasn't completely surprised that energy efficiency wasn't better supported at a societal level. The networks where I hosted TV shows rarely paid much attention to energy efficiency—they were more concerned with how a home looked than how it worked. I'd been told by network executives that energy efficiency wasn't "sexy enough" for viewers. "With energy efficiency," one programming executive told me, "there's nothing to see. At least with solar panels and wind generators we can see something." I guess solar power *is* sexy, huh?

Solar panels and wind power are even sexier when you consider that renewable energy installations qualify for a 30 percent federal tax credit on the cost of both materials and installation. On top of that I found a State of Ohio grant for $3 per watt of installed renewable energy. What's more, I discovered that individuals who generate their own power from solar panels can sell Solar Renewable Energy Credits, or SRECs. SRECs are valuable due to the fact that the clean power they generate displaces power on the grid, which would otherwise be generated from dirty sources like coal. An electric utility would claim my solar panels as part of their generating system portfolio to satisfy renewable portfolio rules, and in return they would pay me for the privilege. The going rate for every 1000kWh (or 1MWh) that I could generate was $250. All of those incentives didn't even count the "free" power that my solar panels would generate, saving me money on my electric bill.

In the end, I was able to take the $1,500 Federal Energy Efficiency Tax Credit for the retrofit, but the big savings came on the 4kW solar array. Since the system had a sticker price of $32,000, the State of Ohio grant would knock about $11,000 right off the top. That left me with an initial solar bill of $21,000. The Federal Renewable Energy Tax Credit is 30 percent, so I'd get another $7,000 in tax savings. Then my SRECs would net about $5,000 over the five-year contract, which would bring the total cost of the system to $9,000, even before I'd saved a dime on electricity. At that rate, my system would pay for itself in fewer than 10 years.

After a lot of research and sessions with the calculator, I was able to come up with a rough total out-of-pocket cost—and the number wasn't pretty. Over time, we could recoup some of the cost through tax credits and Solar Renewable Energy Credit incentives, but we would have to make this big investment first.

Sherri has always been the voice of reason when I advocate for financial risk-taking, and I knew that the figure I'd come up with wouldn't meet her approval. But what was the alternative? Assuming we put off the deep energy retrofit, we still had maintenance work to do. The roof, windows, doors, and siding were at the end of their useful lives. Within the next five years we would have to bite the bullet and pay for replacing them. So I ran a new set of calculations, figuring the cost of renovating the items that were the most pressing but leaving out the costs related to an energy-efficiency retrofit. I tallied up the cost of replacing the roof, siding, windows, and doors using standard construction techniques and materials rather than a deep energy retrofit approach. The results were surprising. The new total cost estimate was only 20 percent less than my original.

I was very surprised that the cost of the deep energy retrofit materials and installation represented only 20 percent of the cost of the total project, and became even more committed to figuring out a way to make things work. After all, if we were going to have to spend a big chunk of money to renovate our home anyway, wouldn't it be well worth an extra 20 percent to also implement a deep energy retrofit, so we could live in a super-efficient, more comfortable, healthier home?

But before I could present all this to Sherri, I had to come up with ways to offset some of the costs of the project and reduce the total amount of financing we would need. I started with our HERS report. Based on that data, we could expect to save as much as $150 each month on energy costs after our DER.

As I cast about for other ways to offset costs, I remembered what many of our friends and neighbors in this college town had done to make ends meet: they had become landlords. What would stop us from doing the same? If we designed the upstairs of the new garage-replacement addition as a fully contained loft apartment with its own entrance, we could easily rent it for $400 a month—probably much more. This could be our emergency, fallback plan. If things continued to improve and the Wilson family's economic engine chugged along at the current rate, we could keep the extra space to ourselves. If the economy took a second nosedive, we could move back into the main house and rent out the addition until conditions improved. That idea also worked long-term. Once the kids left home, Sherri and I would be left in a house with more space than we needed. At that point the addition could become an income source for us as we entered semi-retirement. As an investment, the addition looked better and better.

Getting even more creative, I realized that Sherri and I could use our media skills as a way to offset some costs. We had previous experience creating video for the websites and training programs of many construction-related companies—me on-camera and Sherri working on production. If we could trade our skills for materials, it would be like taking out a loan from our "time bank"—promising future work in exchange for materials. I spent six months pitching the idea to companies and successfully landed several work-for-materials agreements. Now it was time to look for a loan, and little did I know what was in store for us in the search.

⤜ How We Found Financing ⤛

As frugal people with little debt, our credit scores were sky high. We were sure that we'd have no problem either getting a second mortgage or refinancing our first mortgage to fix up the house. With our proposed groundbreaking date eight months away, there was plenty of time to have financing approved in time to write the first check. Talking with lenders, we had a rude awakening. Every bank or broker commended us on our credit scores and lack of debt. Compared with average Americans, we were model citizens on the economic front. Our assets were nothing to write home about with a Mont Blanc pen, but we were virtually debt-free. What concerned them was my income.

Like many people in the recession, I'd seen my income fall over a couple of years. Those two years just happened to be the exact span of time that lenders were examining as a qualifier for the loan. Don't get me wrong, we weren't destitute; we just experienced less income during the recession years. Not uncommon. Combine that with a belt-tightening banking system that was less than willing to lend, and our little world-saving journey looked like it was going to be a very short trip. Bank after bank simply said, "No." No matter how much I cajoled, or how much I waxed poetic about our lofty DER mission, they said, "No."

I even tried to explain to one bewildered loan officer how being a self-employed freelancer was *better* than being an employee in a poor economic climate. Because we relied on dozens of different income streams each year, we could never lose our jobs entirely, the way a regular employee could. We might see a drop in work activity, but never a sudden end to it. But the answer, time and time

A Community DER

FIGURE 4.1 Castle Square Apartments, after the retrofit. Photograph by Damianos Photography.

Residents of Boston's Castle Square Apartments were ready for a change. The seven-story building, with its 192 units of affordable housing, looked the part of a low-income housing block and worked about as well as any 1960s structure might be expected to function—poorly at best. Residents reported sleeping with their heavy winter coats on during cold, northeast winter nights and enduring the constant smell of cooking odors drifting between apartments. Many children in the complex suffered from asthma.

When it was time for Castle Square's scheduled rehabilitation, the Castle Square Tenants Association expressed its desire to do something better: something "green." Since members weren't completely sure what that would entail,

again, was "No." No to a refinance, a home equity line of credit, or a personal loan. We were sunk before the ship set sail.

That's about the time that my neighbor showed up with a brand-spanking-new pickup truck. Not just any pickup truck, but a shiny, black, tricked-out, high-end model, with some kind of aftermarket muffler that made it purr enticingly. When I commented on it, he said, "It was hard to pass up. We were down at the credit union and they were offering home equity lines of credit at prime they looked for direction from Heather Clark, principal at Biome Studios and consultant to Winn Development, which co-owns the building with the Tenants Association. Heather had helped Winn Development, one of the largest affordable housing developers in the United States, target 1,500 properties nationwide for energy reduction measures and oversaw the installation of 1 megawatt of solar panels on the company's buildings. "What I saw, even with the best energy efficiency measures in an older building, was a sort of 'invisible ceiling' at about 30 percent energy savings," Heather said. "We recognized that, if we were really going to make a difference, we would need much deeper energy savings at Castle Square, so we recommended a deep energy retrofit."

Once educated on the process and what it would entail, residents were eager to get started. The original rehabilitation project called for new boilers, windows, exterior masonry repairs, and new kitchens anyway, so it was the perfect time to perform a DER on the old structure. An air sealing spray was applied to the exterior first, after which a metal insulated panel "skin" was installed. New, high-efficiency windows and a reflective, well-insulated roof completed the building envelope renovations, after which a solar thermal water heating system was installed. LED and CFL lightbulbs and high-efficiency appliances rounded out the project.

Those improvements would help to decrease the building's energy use by a whopping 72 percent with a savings of around $430 per unit per month. It also allowed the tenants to live comfortably despite Boston's severe winter weather.

Individual apartments were air sealed from one another, and then carefully controlled ventilation was installed to keep the indoor air fresh. The number of asthma attacks among children at the complex dropped almost immediately. This prompted the Centers for Disease Control to study the effect of such air sealing and ventilation techniques on childhood asthma rates. Residents report much higher levels of comfort from the completed DER, but also a sense of pride in how their newly retrofitted building enhances the general aesthetic of the neighborhood. Once finished, a Green Resident Community Organizer was hired to help tenants learn how to live with their newly retrofitted building in the greenest manner possible.

Through a combination of community involvement and education, the Castle Square Apartment deep energy retrofit represents a way forward in fixing the energy efficiency problems of the nation's older multi-unit housing complexes. This way forward offers not only energy savings, but better comfort and health for residents, as well as neighborhood pride from being a part of the solution to America's energy problems.

minus a half percent. My loan is 2.75 percent! The rates might go up, but with the way things are, it'll be a long time before they raise 'em." I nabbed the loan officer's name and beat a hasty path back to the house to tell Sherri. It turned out to be just the tip that would help to turn our DER dream into a DER reality.

The loan from the credit union was better on all accounts than any of the bank refinance options I'd been looking at. Where a standard refinance would have cost many thousands of dollars in fees and closing costs, the credit union home equity line would cost a total of $400 to close. Interest would only start to accrue when I actually spent the money. It was just the solution for our financing needs, so I started the application process right then and there.

⇥ Financing Your DER ⇤

Once you're satisfied with the design of your DER, you'll need to figure out the costs and how to find financing, just as Sherri and I did. But as I mentioned above, if you plan to work with an architect for your DER, he or she will do the cost estimating for you. In that scenario, a lot of the risk in calculating the final costs of a project lies with the general contractor. Many homeowners seek bids from more than one contractor. If a contractor bids too high, the home-owner will go with a lower bid, and the contractor loses the work. If the bid is too low, though, a contractor can easily lose money when the costs of labor and materials go beyond the original estimate.

If all the bids you receive seem too high, you may have to go back to the drawing board and make some changes in your choices of materials. Or, like I did, you may be able to figure out a creative way to offset some of the financing needed. Are there parts of the project, even small ones, that you could accomplish yourself? Is there any potential for renting space in your home?

Once you have a bid you're satisfied with, you will have to figure out where the money for your DER is going to come from. Everybody's economic situation is different, but there are plenty of options. Whether or not you'll need a loan, you'll be able to take advantage of some great incentives. In the end, doing your homework on incentives, as with everything else, can really pay off.

Nothing is more stressful for me than dealing with money. As a debt-averse kind of guy, a loan is like a big, hairy monster that follows me around. Or maybe a small, dark cloud overhead. I'd sooner celebrate the final payment on a loan than my own birthday. Whether this kind of emotion is healthy or a little obsessive, debt is serious business and shouldn't be taken lightly. That's why it's important to minimize your debt at the outset of a deep energy retrofit project by using incentives.

⇤ Finding Incentives ⇥

Incentives can come in all shapes and sizes. These days, entities from the federal government to state governments to local municipalities are offering tax credits and grants. Even utility companies, pressed by the governments and people they serve, are offering rebates for energy efficiency measures and recycling programs for older appliances. Private markets are getting into the act as well, using brokers who buy and sell solar and wind power Renewable Energy Credits (RECS). Incentives can also come in the form of loan guarantees or special mortgage rates for energy efficiency upgrades. Everywhere you look, you'll unearth some kind of incentive for energy efficiency and renewable energy.

Grants for energy efficiency and renewable energy are usually either a set amount for a project accomplishing certain efficiency goals or, in the case of renewables, a rate per watt of installed generating capacity. Renewable projects are rated against an ideal system, and the grant is reduced by the percentage your system deviates from the ideal. For example, my system was 4kW (4,000W) installed, and my grant was $3 per watt, so the baseline for the grant was $12,000. Since my system was angled slightly to the west it was 89 percent of ideal, so my grant was reduced by 11 percent, to $10,680. My installer assured me that most systems fall into the 85 to 95 percent of ideal range, like ours. Usually a homeowner must pay the total cost of the system and then receive a check for the grant after the system has been installed and inspected. My system's total cost was $32,000, but my installer offered to accept the approved grant application as a credit on my account, which meant that I only had to pay the balance, or $21,320, when the installation was complete. Then the installer received the check for the grant once the system was approved.

The grant application can usually be done through your installer and must be done as much as a year prior to installation to ensure the application is approved before work starts. I told the installer that I would only sign the contract to have the system installed if the grant application was approved. In most places, the pool of money for grants is limited and given on a first-come-first-served basis, so it pays to get grant applications in early.

Tax credits are dollar-for-dollar reductions of your income tax bill. The renewable energy federal tax credit is 30 percent of the total cost of the system installed, less any grants received. That amount is then deducted from your income tax bill at the end of the year. If your tax bill is not large enough to use the entire tax credit the first year, the credit can be carried over into future years, as long as the credit remains in effect. Tax credits are a way of directing your tax dollars directly into renewable energy and efficiency—it's money you would pay to the government anyway, so it's nice to be able to have a say in where it goes. This tax credit can not only be used for solar and wind electric power, but also for solar water heating, geothermal heat pumps, and even hydrogen fuel cells (there are some limits on fuel cell credits).

Utility companies offer rebates and recycling programs, too. Whether you have an all-electric home or you use natural gas as well, utilities offer a wide range of rebates for heating and cooling equipment, duct sealing, insulation, air sealing, appliances, lighting, and more. They also offer free or reduced-rate energy audits. Many will also offer recycling incentives. Old appliances are picked up for recycling, free of charge, and the homeowner gets a rebate check. Any time you consider energy efficiency improvements or replacing any of your home's working systems, make sure to look at rebates offered by your utility companies.

Renewable Energy Credits (RECs) are sold through brokers or directly to utilities. Once a renewable system is installed, you contract with a broker or utility so that, over a period of time the broker will issue you a set payment each time your system generates 1,000 kWh of power. My initial Solar Renewable Energy Credit (SREC) contract is with the broker, SolSystems, Inc., for five years. Each month I log on to my SolSystems account and input the total kWh generated by my system. Each time my system rolls over another 1,000 kWh, SolSystems sends me a check for $250. SolSystems then sells that SREC to a utility company, which uses it to satisfy state regulations that require them to generate a percentage of their total power portfolio from renewables. RECs work as an acknowledgement that your renewable system is creating clean power on the grid, displacing power generated from coal, natural gas, or nuclear.

If you're considering using solar or wind energy in your DER, incentives can really take a bite out of the initial sticker price. Once you take out the money that's available up front, though, you still may be faced with a fairly high out-of-pocket expense before you can cash in on the tax credits, rebates, and SRECs. The same can be said for the actual money saved on your energy bill—it takes time to add up. That's why many of the larger solar installation companies around the country now offer solar leasing. With little or no out-of-pocket expense, your home is evaluated and a solar photovoltaic system is installed on your home's roof. The company installing the system guarantees a savings on your electric bill and uses the incentives to help pay for the initial installation. The company recoups its costs over the life of the system as it generates power by taking a slice of the savings that you would normally get if you purchased the system outright. You get solar panels and up to a 20 percent savings on your electric bill and the company gets a long-term income stream. At the end of the lease period, you have the option to extend it with new equipment, purchase a new system at a reduced rate, or have the solar panels removed for free.

The best place to start looking for incentives is the Database for State Incentives for Renewables and Efficiency (www.dsireusa .org). This website is a regularly updated database of incentives at the federal, state, local, and utility level. The listing is presented as an interactive map, allowing you to click on your state and then dig down from the state level into local municipalities and utilities serving different regions. Most of those listings are fairly detailed, showing whether a particular tax break, grant, or rebate is available to commercial or residential consumers, how much the maximum incentive can be, and the basic rules for claiming the incentive. You can usually "click through" a link to get to the official rules for each incentive. Make note of any limits, including actual amounts of incentives, which are often a percentage of a total amount spent on materials and/or labor. Also be sure to note the end dates on incentives. You may find that you need to speed up your retrofit to take advantage of a certain incentive, or that you need to apply early to get into next year's pool of accepted applicants. Time spent on the DSIREUSA website will definitely pay dividends.

The federal government's Energy Star website also offers a page that will help you look for incentives on everything from lighting to electronics to insulation. A coalition of public non-profit groups, called the Tax Incentives Assistance Project, helps to list many of the incentives available and links to regional and local groups working on incentives for energy efficiency and renewables. The American Council for an Energy Efficient Economy keeps abreast of news on current and proposed incentives and is actively involved in encouraging incentives at all levels. Another organization that spends a lot of time lobbying for energy efficiency is the Alliance to Save Energy (ASE). ASE is a great place to get wind of up and coming legislation so that you can contact members of government to encourage them to support those bills and find out if new legislation on the books will affect your DER timing. Check the Resources appendix at the end of this book for links.

Local Incentives

When it comes to incentives, don't limit your research to the federal level; check with your city government and utility company, too. Some locally based programs offer better incentives than the bigger entities. The incentives available for retrofitting and renewable energy projects vary depending on what state, or even what city, you live in. While federal tax credits can be enjoyed by all Americans, there are definite advantages to living in places where energy efficiency is a priority. Here are just a few of the many state and local programs available:

Mass Save is a Massachusetts-based program that, among other incentives, offers a $25,000, 0 percent interest loan for up to seven years for homeowners completing approved energy efficiency measures. You can also get $50 for recycling your old refrigerator, or get a free home energy assessment to see if you qualify for more savings.

The city of **Gainesville, Florida**, offers a Feed-In Tariff for qualified photovoltaic installations, including those on homes. Gainesville's city-owned utility will pay homeowners a premium for photovoltaic-generated electricity over a 20-year period.

The **Pittsburgh Home Rehabilitation Program Plus** offers a 20-year, 0 percent loan up to $25,000 for renovating older homes. The "plus" part of the program offers a $2,500 grant for energy efficiency measures, as well.

Duluth, Minnesota, may not be a large town, but it offers a local rebate of up to $2,500 for approved deep energy efficiency measures and low-interest loans for up to $15,000 and 10 years.

⇥ Finding a Loan ⇤

Once you've lined up as many incentives as you can, you'll need to find the money to pay for the rest. With the home energy audit in your hands, you may consider retrofitting at the "pay as you go" pace, expending money to retrofit one portion of your home at a time as you can afford it. More often, though, deep energy retrofitting will be accomplished as part of a general renovation or addition, and you'll need to come up with a chunk of money at one time to pay for it.

If you have equity in your home, it's a great place to look to finance improvements. When mortgage rates are low, this will make your DER even less expensive. Assuming your credit scores and income levels allow, you can tap into that equity by refinancing your original mortgage, taking out a second mortgage, or opening up a home equity line of credit. Any bank or credit union can typically help, and there are mortgage brokers galore out there, even in post–housing market bust America. After your credit eligibility is confirmed, a professional appraisal is performed on your home to establish its current value. Then a new loan can typically be written for up to about 80 percent of that value. Or, in the case of a home equity line of credit, a credit line is established in the amount of the 80 percent loan to value, less any principal you still owe on your first mortgage. Pretty standard stuff and the way most homeowners will find the financing for their DERs.

Other financing options exist in the renovation loan department. The Federal Housing Administration (FHA) offers a 203k renovation loan that will allow you to either purchase or refinance a home and include renovation costs in the loan. The loan amount is based on the home's projected value at the end of the renovation process. The Fannie Mae "HomeStyle" renovation mortgage is similar, but with some different provisions. In both cases, down payments are low and requirements for income and credit scores are

Advice from a Mortgage Professional

David A. Krebs, a licensed mortgage broker in Florida, is one of several professionals I interviewed while researching my DER and writing this book. David has helped clients secure mortgages of all kinds, and he's an expert on loans for renovations and energy efficiency improvements. He had great answers to my questions about how to deal with the various types of mortgages available for construction and energy-improvement projects and how such mortgages related to either purchasing and remodeling or refinancing and remodeling a home. Financing is one of my weakest spots, and I found his reassuring words very helpful.

Here's what David has to say about the benefits of a renovation loan:

"A great advantage of a renovation loan is its lower rate as compared to a 'cash out' refinance. If you go the traditional refinance route in order to get cash for renovations, you're likely to pay a premium of up to .25 percent.

Lending institutions classify renovation loans as 'rate and term,' the same as when you purchase the property, so there's no penalty for an increased mortgage amount. A renovation loan can help make up to $35,000 available for home renovation. When combined with an Energy Improvement Mortgage, an additional $10,000 can be borrowed, for a total of $45,000 to be put toward renovations and upgrades. Another plus of this type of loan is that the bank has strict guidelines to follow to protect the homeowner and other parties involved. The bank is not going to allow a check to be cut if the work is not up to code or not done correctly. If work isn't being done satisfactorily, the homeowner won't have to find out after the fact and chase down the contractor later. In my opinion, this is the best insurance policy around. It's fair to the contractor, too, as there's no doubt he'll get paid for his properly completed work since the bank is overseeing the project."

THE GREENED HOUSE EFFECT

a bit lower than conventional loans because they're backed by the US government. These types of loans have rules about establishing the projected value of the home after renovations are completed, and all renovations are inspected to be sure they're built to current building codes. Otherwise they're just like standard mortgage and refinance options.

Then there are loans directed specifically at energy efficiency: the Energy Efficiency Mortgage (EEM) or Energy Improvement Mortgage (EIM). The first is aimed at building a new energy efficient home, while the second is aimed at renovating an older, inefficient home. Both allow the homeowner to pay for energy efficiency improvements using the money that he or she will save on utility bills. With a new home and an EEM, the energy savings are projected by considering how the new energy efficient home compares with a home built using standard construction measures. Those savings then become available to the homeowner to spend on energy efficiency measures and become part of a monthly mortgage payment, since that money isn't being spent on energy bills. An EIM is similar. Projected energy savings of the renovated home are compared with current energy usage in the home, and the savings are calculated. This is done with the help of a HERS rating and software that can closely estimate how certain energy efficiency improvements will change how the home performs. The homeowner is then able to borrow a bit more up front than would be normally allowed and pay for the excess with the money saved on energy.

⟫ The Real Bottom Line ⟪

While you're figuring out something as complicated and expensive as a major home renovation, it's important not to fall into what I call the "payback trap." Payback is a term used to project if and when an improvement will recoup its original investment cost through its contribution to energy savings. That seems straightforward, but it's not just a simple calculation of money spent versus money saved. Unless you're a trained economist, calculating payback times is a complicated, convoluted process. Simply calculating how long it will take for the energy savings from a given upgrade to pay for its sticker price results in an oversimplified, incorrect answer to the payback question.

Start with the prices of energy and inflation. There is no guarantee that energy prices will stay the same over time. While it is possible that they will fall in the short term, it's more likely that they will rise in the long term. For example, according to a report from the Edison Electric Institute, since the year 2000, electricity prices have increased at a rate of 2.5 percent per year. Inflation over that time averaged 1.99 percent. Both of those numbers should be included in any attempt to calculate payback time. As energy prices rise, the savings from deep energy efficiency measures become larger. As inflation makes building materials and labor more expensive, deferring maintenance and retrofit projects becomes more expensive.

Next, I would argue that there are few home improvements that actually *earn* anything for the homeowner over the long run, let alone pay back the original investment. Most improvements begin to depreciate the moment they're installed and begin to age. Granite countertops, swimming pools, media rooms, and many of the other home improvements we consider will never pay for themselves. Deep energy efficiency improvements, while not always able to immediately pay back an original investment in the short term, actually do have a payback period in the long run. That's an important thing to remember as you think about the concept of payback.

In your calculations, you'll also need to consider the fact that a portion of most renovations is for regular replacement and maintenance of the building. In order to see the true cost of deep energy efficiency, make sure that you compare it as an upgrade to the cost of a basic, standard renovation, not as the entire cost of the renovation. For example, we needed new windows because the old ones were failing. The cost of replacing them would normally include basic, double pane replacements. The cost of the deep energy efficiency upgrade to triple pane windows was about 25 percent more than the double pane windows. The 25 percent extra is part of the DER cost, not the cost of the standard replacement window. Think the same way about upgrades in insulation, HVAC, appliances, and other DER elements.

It's also important to consider the baseline at which you start the payback calculation. This is the idea that comfort, while not a concept that lends itself to perfect mathematical measurement, has a real cost in terms of energy. Most people are uncomfortable in their pre-DER homes because they keep the house colder in the winter and warmer in the summer than they would really like, in order to avoid high energy bills. Once a home is deep energy retrofitted, they'll be able to set the thermostat for optimum comfort and *still* save energy and money. It's important to compare the original, uncomfortable baseline with the same temperature range in the retrofitted home to make a fair payback comparison. Or, conversely, you could set the thermostat in your pre-retrofitted home to a more comfortable level, record the resulting, higher energy cost level, and compare that with the more comfortable, deep energy retrofitted home. This solves the problem of computing payback time from different comfort baselines.

If you've ever sat through an economics course, you're familiar with including the costs and benefits of externalities (things that are affected by, but not directly connected to, your economic choice) when making decisions about money. From a strictly monetary standpoint, consider the effect that better air quality would have on your family's health. With cleaner indoor air, you'll miss less work, your kids will miss less school, and your health-care bills will be lower.

Last, there are the non-monetary benefits that accrue from paying a DER premium, such as these outlined by Martin Holladay, a senior editor at Green Building Advisor (GBA), in an article on the GBA website: "A house with triple-glazed windows will ride out a wintertime power outage better than a house with double-glazed windows because it won't cool off as quickly [and they] provide comfort advantages that can't be quantified. When it's below zero outdoors, you can sit in a chair beside a triple-glazed window and not feel cold. That's worth something." I agree. There are also non-monetary benefits to good health, including simple well-being and the avoidance of the stress and anxiety associated with sickness in a family. Finally, if you had asked my wife what she would pay to get rid of the swampy basement smell in our house before the retrofit, I'm almost afraid of her reply. Fixing that, for her, was priceless.

❯ Be Prepared ❮

In the end, be sure to include a little "wiggle room" in your budget calculations for unforeseen problems that might crop up. On our project, once we got up onto the roof, we found that the mortar joints in our brick chimney needed to be repointed to preserve the structure. This had little to do with deep energy retrofitting the house, but it was a necessary repair nonetheless that set me back several hundred dollars. The job included grinding out some of the old mortar before replacing it, which sent dust and grit in all directions. While I wasn't happy about it, I was glad to have the messy job done before we installed the beautiful new faux slate roof, so I forked over the cash. These types of issues are common in older buildings, so adding 5 to 10 percent to your total estimated costs to plan ahead for them can give you some peace of mind.

Our home equity line came through while we were trying to enjoy a summer vacation during the month before launching into our DER project. I remember the phone call from our credit union loan officer. By this time, we'd spent two years dreaming, designing, and planning the deep energy retrofit of our old home. I'd had dozens of conversations with lenders, all of which had ended without a loan. Each of those conversations took away another of the threads we were trying to hang onto—what if we'd done all of this planning for nothing? When she called, even the loan officer sounded excited when she said, "Your appraisal came back and everything on your home equity line looks good. All you have to do is come in to my office and sign the papers when you get back. Congratulations!" One more hurdle cleared, with a hundred more to go on our DER. But the hardest work was ahead: everything we had dreamed on paper now had to be created in real life. I thanked my loan officer profusely, hung up, and immediately called my contractor. "We're on," I told him. "When can you start?"

Chapter Five

RETROFITTING ROOFS

WITH OUR FINANCING IN PLACE, WE SPENT THE NEXT TWO WEEKS getting ready for the blitzkrieg of major remodeling. The demolition work on the old attached garage was project number one; Sherri and I had decided to do that ourselves to keep costs down. Days came and went as we sledge hammered, pry barred, hauled, and heaved hunks of rotted old wall and sagging roof. I carefully tore off the old aluminum siding and recycled it, reaping enough cash to pay for some dinners out and ice-cold beer at the end of those long work days. Ahh, the benefits of being green. We worked in the oppressive, sticky heat day after day, punishing our muscles and cooking our skin. We drank gallons of ice water, ate ravenously, and slept well.

⇻ Our Roof Retrofit ⇺

Following demolition, the deep energy retrofit could begin, starting with the roof. In places, we would install a new roof right over the existing roof; in other places, we would be reconfiguring the roof, too (as described in chapter 3). The new dormer roof would be built 10 inches thick so that we could maximize the space available for insulation. The space between the joists would be insulated with a combination of spray foam and fiberglass batt, achieving a near R-60 insulation value. The interior gable end walls of the attic would also be insulated with fiberglass batt, awaiting a layer of spray foam on the exterior when we got around to that part of the DER work. On the front roof, which faces the street, we would lay 2×3 studs on edge over each of the old rafters. The studs would be attached through the old shingles and sheathing into the rafters using 4½-inch deck screws. Once the new 2×3 rafter "extensions" were installed, I would apply the spray foam insulation directly onto the old shingles, between the 2×3s. On the existing roof areas, we'd be adding R-17 of spray foam insulation to the R-30 insulation already in place to give us nearly R-50. By leaving the old shingles in place, we avoided the cost and environmental impact of disposal.

Since the spray foam insulation came in kits that I could install myself, I was able to save some money on labor. That spray foam would not only give us the powerful insulation punch we were looking for, but it would also seal up any possible cracks or gaps we would encounter. This was less important on the roof slope itself, which was already well sealed against the elements, but would certainly come into play at the eaves and soffits and on the gable end walls, where cracks and gaps were plentiful.

With the spray foam installed over the entire roof, radiant barrier sheathing would go on next, forming the base for all of the roof finish materials. On the nearly flat rear dormer, we would finish with a white thermoplastic polyolefin (TPO) membrane roof. A membrane is important because gravity is less effective to help drain water away on flat or nearly flat surfaces. With lapped roofing materials, such as shingles, wind-blown water can work its way up the spaces between the lapped layers on a nearly flat surface, resulting in leaks. A membrane has no lapped layers; it's one continuous—and hopefully leakproof—surface. The reflective white color of the TPO would also help to keep that dormer roof surface cool once the solar panels were installed. Solar panels lose some efficiency when ambient temperatures rise too high, so the cooler, white roof would help the panels to operate at the highest summer efficiency possible. Since this portion of the roof wouldn't be visible from the street, there were no aesthetic considerations—the white, featureless roof would never be seen.

R-Value Demystified

Ever wonder what R-value is? It's essentially a measure of insulation's resistance to heat transfer from one place to another. It's a value derived from a standardized test resulting in a number that can be used to compare different types of materials. The higher the R-value, the better the material is at blocking heat transfer, and the better insulator it is. Beware, though, the standard tests for R-value are administered under ideal conditions, resulting in "pure" numbers. Under real world conditions, such factors as improper installation, air leaks, moisture, and settling over time can dramatically reduce the R-value of insulation from the manufacturer's stated rating.

FIGURE 5.1 The Stalwart Construction team sets the rafters for the new, flatter rear dormer roof, on which our solar array would later be installed. Photograph by Sherri James.

However, the steep, 45-degree front roof faced the road, so its aesthetics *would* be important. For this surface we selected a recycled rubber faux slate shingle. These shingles looked remarkably like slate, and we were excited to give the old house such a stylish facelift. The new roof, installed with a special underlayment, would likely last 75 years or more. While the material costs nearly three times as much as standard shingles, I wouldn't have to replace it in my lifetime. Over 75 years I might have to replace a standard shingle roof twice. The initial premium on the faux slate material would save labor costs of installing a standard roof two more times over that period; not to mention the waste associated with those two roofing jobs and the fact that our recycled rubber roof would be recyclable itself at the end of its lifetime. I liked the sound of all of that.

Groundbreaking day burst through in a brilliant dawn, with a sound and fury that made me feel more than a bit sorry for my neighbors. Both Ben Stolzfus' concrete crew and Matt Cooke's Stalwart Construction crew were on the scene by 7:00 a.m., along with Tony from Trace's sanitation, who had come to swap out the dumpster. A backhoe, dump truck, front-end loader, Tony's container delivery truck, and several air compressors were humming away all at once. I slurped down my coffee, kissed the girls as they left for school, and headed off to work. It was a short commute, since my workplace for the foreseeable future would be my own house.

Sherri picked up her cameras and started shooting the mayhem. We planned to document every inch of this journey, from start

Radiant Barrier Sheathing: A Space Blanket for your House

Attic with standard roof sheathing

Attic with LP TechShield radiant barrier sheathing

FIGURE 5.2 Illustration courtesy of LP Building Products.

NASA originally developed the "space blanket" as an emergency heat shield for the space station, Skylab, back in the 1970s. Just by using a simple, thin, reflective parasol, enough radiant heat could be deflected from Skylab to keep it cool. Without the parasol, it would overheat.

Roofing material is primarily heated by the sun's radiant energy. As the materials warm, that heat travels into the attic space via all three avenues of radiation, conduction, and convection (see chapter 2). Traditional insulation materials are effective at slowing the transfer of heat via conduction, and somewhat effective at slowing convection, but aren't as effective at slowing radiant heat transfer.

Using the same principle that NASA used with Skylab's reflective parasol, one simple way to address heat buildup in attics in warmer climates is to use radiant barrier sheathing, which is simply a standard sheet of oriented strand board (OSB) or plywood sheathing that is laminated with a thin layer of aluminum foil. The sheathing cuts and installs just like standard sheathing, but the reflective layer helps to block a large percentage of radiant heat from entering the attic, helping to lower summertime attic temperatures. This simple, inexpensive solution can save up to 17 percent per month on air-conditioning costs and earn points toward green building certification programs.

to finish. Today there was plenty to see. Guys clambered over the roof, shouting down through the noise, "I need more nails!" or "Six more of those at 11-foot-3!" The concrete slab and driveway of the old garage was being demolished and removed to make way for the new, insulated foundation slab and driveway. Diesel exhaust and dust permeated the heavy morning air. The reverberations were bone shaking—there was no turning back now.

The Stalwart Construction crew wasted no time getting to work on the roof. The first order of business was to raise the rear dormer roof to create a new, nearly flat surface. I flinched as the crew from Stalwart, wielding reciprocating saws, ripped into my roof. I would wear out my work boots doing anti-rain dances for the next couple of months as we transformed the house, inevitably opening it to the weather.

Our shared work plan went like this: first, the crew would add on the structure of the new rear dormer roof. While that was happening, I would retrofit the rounded dormers out front. I had to work quickly. Once they were done framing the rear dormer roof, and before they could put on the sheathing, I would need to insulate back there. This setup meant that I'd be on the front while Stalwart was on the back and then we'd swap. While I was insulating the back they'd be adding the exterior rafter "sleepers" to the front roof. Then we'd swap again. They'd install the sheathing on the back roof, and I'd spray foam the front. After that, they'd add the sheathing to the front roof surface. If I could keep up with the younger, stronger Stalwart crew, it would end up being a well-choreographed dance, which would minimize the time the house was open to the elements.

One day, hard at work on the front roof's rounded dormers, I heard something on the breeze. Singing. It started low and soft, building in dramatic intensity until it hit the chorus, "I would do *anything* for *LOVE!* I would do *anything* for *LOVE!* But I *WON'T DO **THAT**!*" Somewhat off key, but with a kind of gusto rarely heard—especially on a construction site—it caught my attention. I gathered my safety rope and clambered up the front roof to the top of the house. There I found Will from Stalwart working away, belting out the hit single by Meat Loaf. His Stalwart colleagues, Rem, Patrick, and Travis, were shaking their heads quietly. When Will ended his construction site aria with a flourish, Rem offered, "So, what exactly is 'that'?"

For a solid minute, the crew kept working, contemplating Rem's dry, pseudo-intellectual, hilarious rebuttal to Will's equally funny choice of repertoire. "Yeah," Patrick concurred, "what *is* 'that'? I mean, Meat Loaf really never says." A few more nails were fired through a bracket into the next rafter to secure it to the ridge beam. Travis, the barest hint of a smile crossing his lips, asked, "Who's the girl who sings the duet with him at the end of the song?" Someone offered Chaka Khan. Somebody else said it was Meat Loaf's wife

FIGURE 5.3 Intent on keeping up with the younger, experienced guys from Stalwart Construction, I set to work retrofitting the arched dormers on the front of our house. Then, for spray foam application, I donned protective gear. No fun on a summer day, but worth the discomfort to protect my skin, eyes, and lungs. Photographs by Sherri James.

(Mrs. Loaf?). Neither was right, Will countered, but he couldn't bring the name to mind right then. This was going to be a long conversation, so I headed back to work. But the seed had been planted. "Hmm," I thought to myself, "what exactly *is* 'that'?" The hits just kept coming, with Will often butchering the lyrics and always a little north or south of the melody line. His Stalwart compatriots suffered this abuse silently and by and large without malice, often using the diversionary tactic of asking probing questions. Once the philosophical conversation began, the singing stopped, and the peaceful activity of building continued. I was beginning to like having these guys around, not just for the way they solved problems

FIGURE 5.4 The Stalwart Construction crew installs exterior sheathing as they integrate the new, raised rear dormer roof with the old house. Photograph by Sherri James.

that arose on our deep energy retrofit project, but also for the camaraderie and company that a do-it-yourself project lacks.

The Stalwart crew wasn't a bunch of stereotypical construction workers. Between them they held degrees in education, biology, and psychology, and a new recording deal (for Rem and his band, Southeast Engine). Sure, like regular construction workers, they were known to eat doughnuts on Fridays. They even drank the beer I would offer on some Friday afternoons, but the construction site banter was a bit different from what you might expect, and there was a noticeable lack of ego involved in everyday working affairs. Whenever a problem arose, it would be solved by the group, not by an individual.

Work progressed quickly. By the end of the first week, the place was looking like a low-budget circus. Big blue plastic tarps covered the portions of the roof that were open to the elements and piles of debris and new materials were scattered about the backyard. Everybody wanted to get the roof on as soon as possible, but the roofing materials hadn't yet been delivered, so the Stalwart crew moved on to framing the addition. That left us Wilsons under the enormous blue tarps that constantly flapped in the slightest breeze, like the massive sails of a landlocked ship. It was during the time between sheathing the roof and installing the roofing that we had our first crisis.

A storm blew in from the west, with the ferocity of the changing season. A shifting, ravenous wind huffed and puffed, and a

FIGURE 5.5 Our "little blue house" wears a wrapper of bright blue tarps to keep out rain in this mid-retrofit view. Photograph by Sherri James.

horizontal rain hammered at our naked home. In a lull, late that evening, I went out to inspect the tarps. All seemed well, though the sound of them rippling and slapping against the house made me wince. We finally went to bed, assuming the worst of the storm had passed, but awoke in the wee hours of dawn to a renewed onslaught from the skies. At some point, a tarp had come loose from its moorings and laid open a swath of the new dormer roof to the weather. That's when I heard Sherri yell, "There's water coming in down here!" Sure enough, water was leaking through the ceilings in the living room and upstairs bathroom. Not a torrent, but a steady drip. It was the tarp on the back of the house that had come loose and was allowing rain to be driven against the old siding, behind some exposed flashing, and into the house. Sherri rushed to set up a line of plastic bowls to catch drips and gathered old towels to soak up the mess. I got on the phone.

"There's water coming in," I told Matt, one of the owners of the construction company. The expletive he led with was followed by a promise that they'd be there in a minute to batten down the hatches. Luckily, even though the crew hadn't planned to come to work that morning in the bad weather, they all lived in my neighborhood and were on the scene in less than five minutes to secure the tarp. Once the water stopped dripping, and the house had a chance to dry out, we found that the casualties were minimal. With the house still open to the air, and so many gaps and cracks anyway, the long string

FIGURE 5.6 Stalwart's Travis and Patrick install EcoStar roof tiles on the front of the main house. These look like slate but are actually made from 80 percent recycled rubber and should last up to 75 years. Photograph by Sherri James.

of good weather that followed soon dried everything out thoroughly. Still, we wouldn't be able to rest soundly until the whole place was under a watertight roof.

The recycled rubber faux slate and white TPO roof would be slowly and carefully applied over the next couple of weeks. Once the rear dormer roof was dry, the TPO went on quickly, with the crew tending to the careful flashing, edging, and seam-sealing. The faux slate was a different matter. First, a thick, adhesive membrane was installed and then a rolled, high-tech underlayment was applied as a backup to the faux slate. Finally, the faux slate itself was installed in a staggered fashion that gave the roof a cottage look when it was completed. To complete the aesthetic appeal of the new roof, I would eventually add half-round, faux copper gutters and real copper bay window roofs on the first floor. With the deep energy retrofitting and the new roof, our little blue house would be able to weather anything Mother Nature could throw at us.

⌇ DER Roof Options ⌇

When you hash out a solution for your deep energy retrofitted roof, you'll have plenty of things to think about. What is best for your home will depend on your climate, the load-bearing capacity of your roof, the complexity of your roof's structure, how your home sits on your lot, and your budget. Are you close to needing a new roof?

Vented and Unvented Attics

Attics and roof assemblies come in two flavors: vented and unvented. Venting of an attic or roof assembly simply means that outside air is allowed to circulate between the floor of the attic (usually the ceiling of the rooms below it) and the underside of the roof sheathing. The space in a vented attic is, therefore, not "conditioned" space, because it's outside the thermal envelope (see "A Hole in the Bucket" in chapter 3 for an explanation of conditioned space). Historically, there were practical reasons for venting an attic. Venting allows hot air to escape during the summer months, helping to cool the space. This lightens the load on the air conditioner and extends the life of the shingles. Allowing cold air to circulate through an attic during the winter helps to prevent ice-damming—and the leaks that may result—on the roof above dams (Ice damming occurs when snow melts on a roof and then cold temperatures refreeze the water into dams. As air temperatures rise again, those dams melt more slowly than the surrounding snow. The snowmelt is held behind ice dams, where it can back up behind the shingles and possibly infiltrate the sheathing). And good ventilation allows moisture and humidity to dry, helping to prevent mold and rotting of the structural roof members. Vented attics are time-tested, and many contractors swear by them.

Unvented attics seal off any potential air leaks from outside and bring the attic space into the conditioned thermal envelope of the rest of the house. They must be designed carefully to avoid any of the problems I noted above but can then avoid some of the drawbacks of vented spaces. First, if HVAC equipment or ductwork is installed in an attic, an unvented roof assembly can prevent loss of heating or cooling energy from the equipment to the outside air. Second, an unvented space will block any air leakage into or out of the home's living space through the attic to the outdoors, saving energy. One caveat, though: the warranty of some roofing materials may be voided without proper ventilation beneath the roof deck. Installing the roof sheathing with a small air space beneath it will allow you to have the best of both worlds: an unvented attic and a full roofing warranty.

Feeling lucky? Don't bet on it. The choice of whether to go with a vented or unvented attic should be left to a building science expert—your properly trained architect, engineer, or contractor. See the Resources appendix at the end of this book for links to find pros in your area.

Are you trying to keep the old look of your home, or is a complete change a possibility? Should you plan for a vented or unvented attic (see sidebar)? Are you planning to add solar? The more questions you ask, and answer, the better.

In your design considerations, for example, you might want to lengthen or change the eave overhangs, especially on the south and west sides of the house, to help your home take advantage of passive solar heating and cooling. Properly designed, these overhangs can allow wintertime sun into the house to help with heating, but shade summertime sun out to ease the cooling load. Perhaps adding a porch with a roof is in your plans. Again, a careful porch roof design might shade a portion of your home's exterior that is prone to catching direct sunlight and overheating the indoor space. The shading helps save you money, and you also get a nifty new porch out of the deal. The point is to consider all of your options carefully, and think creatively along the way.

Maybe, like us, you want to avoid changing the outside appearance to your home too much. We wanted to keep the Cape Cod charm of the front and sides of the home, but weren't quite so worried about the back, since it's not visible from the street. This led us to keep the rounded dormers and 45-degree front roof pitch, and to match that pitch on the front of the new addition. In the back, where the Cape Cod aesthetics were less important to us, we raised the pitch to make our home more solar panel friendly and to allow for a more open floor plan. Maybe you want to change the features of your home to give it more visual appeal and style. Remember, a deep energy retrofit is a major remodeling project, and the roofline is one place you'll have the opportunity to help reinvent your home. Coupling your energy efficiency goals with your aesthetic goals can result in reinvigorating your home's overall visual appeal at the same time you bring it up to a 21st century energy standard.

Those efficiency goals start with serious air sealing and insulation. Depending on your particular circumstance, you might choose to retrofit from the exterior of your home or the interior. While the approach might change, the fundamentals stay the same. A properly retrofitted attic or roof assembly will need to completely air seal the conditioned space from the outdoors. This will include appropriate flashing and sealing of chimney, skylight, waste vent, and similar penetrations through the thermal envelope. Then superinsulation is added for thermal performance. Finally, all roofing finish materials are installed to manufacturer recommended standards. The result is a greatly improved "lid" for your home, and major energy savings in your pocket.

⊁ Exterior Roof Retrofitting ⊰

Retrofitting a roof from the exterior means that the roof is uniformly "bumped out" with a layer of foam insulation, or that all roofing and sheathing materials are removed and the open rafter cavities filled

Skylights and Tubes

DOMED ROOFTOP COLLECTOR

TUBE WITH HIGHLY REFLECTIVE INTERIOR

CEILING LIGHT DIFFUSING FIXTURE

FIGURE 5.7 A Solatube daylighting system. Illustration courtesy of Solatube International, Inc.

Nobody wants to live in a cave. Making sure all spaces in your home benefit from plenty of daylight is a good way to save on energy for lighting, but it's also a way to make your home feel airy and inviting. Skylights, including standard skylights and "tube" types, are great ways to add light to a space. However, since even the best skylights on the market can't compete with a well-insulated and air sealed roof as a good thermal break, it's important to balance the need for, and savings from, skylights within your overall deep energy retrofitting strategy. This calculation can be done easily by your HERS rater; you may find that the loss of heat energy through a skylight vastly outweighs any lighting benefit you might get.

Tube skylights address potential energy loss while still allowing natural light into the home. They consist of a glass dome, which is installed on the roof surface, and a 10- to 14-inch-diameter tube that passes through the attic space and terminates in a ceiling-mounted lens fixture. The tube has a super-reflective interior surface that maximizes the amount of light delivered to the interior of the house. This arrangement neatly balances the need for interior daylight with heating and cooling energy efficiency needs.

Thermal Bridging and Thermal Breaks

FIGURE 5.8 This is a graphic depiction of thermal bridging through a typical home without continuous insulation. The yellow areas illustrate heat loss through uninsulated wood studs. The second image illustrates the same home with exterior continuous insulation. Actual results will vary. Images courtesy of Dow Building Solutions.

It's not common knowledge that the wood commonly used in framing roof and wall systems is a fairly good conductor of heat. Check out your neighbors' roofs on a frosty morning before the sun is fully up. You'll see dark lines where the frost is melting, which indicates warmth. That warmth is being conducted from the living area into the attic air space and through the rafters and roofing materials, melting the frost. In this case, the wood acts as a "thermal bridge," which can work both ways—conducting heat out of the house in the winter and into the house in the summer, straining your HVAC system.

Any place in your home where the materials act to allow heat transfer in or out of the home is considered a thermal bridge. Metal, solid glass, and even wood are good thermal bridges, while insulation materials like fiberglass, cellulose, and foam are not. A thermal break interrupts that flow of heat, slowing its movement in or out of your home, depending on the season. A layer of exterior foam sheathing, for example, will act as a thermal break between the roof or wall structural materials and the finish materials, greatly increasing the efficiency of your roof or wall assemblies.

Overhangs and eaves tend to be good thermal bridges; they are also difficult to retrofit. It's not uncommon for serious retrofitters to remove existing eaves, install a thermal break of foam sheathing, and reinstall new overhangs, whose structures are thermally "divorced" from the original structure. This technique was originally called a "chainsaw retrofit" after a 1982 DER project in Saskatoon. There, some retrofitting pioneers removed the eaves of a home with a chainsaw, wrapped the home in foam, and then built new overhangs outside of the thermal envelope.

with foam. If you're using the bumped out exterior retrofit approach on the walls as well, you'll want to design the roof to integrate with the wall retrofit. This may mean extending roof overhangs to keep the same geometric shape of the house as it expands outward. We were careful to make sure the roof retrofit, which came first, would extend far enough to incorporate the wall retrofit, even though the exterior wall retrofit wouldn't happen until a few weeks later. Since we knew the dimensions of the lumber, sheathing, and finish materials ahead of time, it was easy enough to sketch out details to scale and then plan ahead for the areas where the rooflines and walls would join.

Because the insulation and air sealing is being done at the same plane as the roof sheathing, exterior roof retrofits should result in a fully sealed, unvented attic space. This is because of the principle I talked about in chapter 3 of aligning the thermal envelope and building envelope. Installing insulation on the exterior of a roof and then allowing the cold winds of winter to blow through a vented attic would negate nearly all of the benefit of that exterior insulation layer. Exterior roof retrofits are ideal where cathedral ceilings exist below, since the cathedral ceiling already works similarly to an unvented attic and the thermal properties of the retrofit will enhance the overall effectiveness of the cathedral ceiling assembly's insulation value.

Here are a few possible ways to approach retrofitting a roof from the exterior:

⟢ Curtain Walls ⟣

The retrofit approach we took—the exterior stud and foam "curtain wall" method—has a few advantages. For example, installing the 2×3s on the exterior of the front roof is actually a job that a skilled do-it-yourselfer could tackle alone. And because we encapsulated the old shingles with spray foam, we avoided the expense of shingle removal and disposal. Remember, though, your old roof will need to be able to handle the load of the new material if you add a curtain wall, so a structural engineer should sign off on whatever plan you make. If a curtain wall is designed and applied correctly, though, it can actually add strength to the old structure.

⟢ Exterior Gut ⟣

If your home needs a new roof anyway, and if the existing sheathing is damaged or in need of replacement, consider an exterior gut retrofit. In this scenario, all roofing and roof sheathing is removed from the building. If the home has cathedral ceilings, spray foam is sprayed down into the open rafter cavities, against the back side of

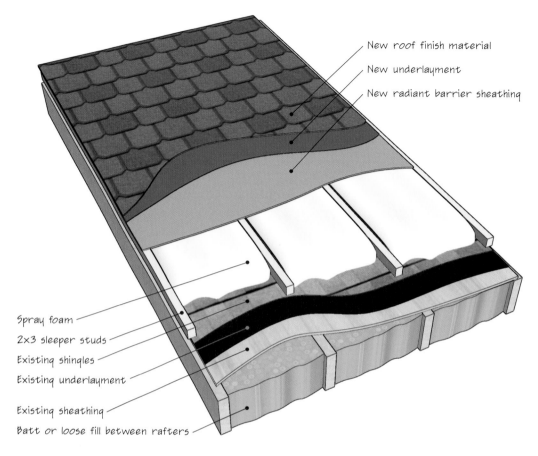

New roof finish material

New underlayment

New radiant barrier sheathing

Spray foam

2x3 sleeper studs

Existing shingles

Existing underlayment

Existing sheathing

Batt or loose fill between rafters

FIGURE 5.9 The Wilson curtain wall spray foam roof retrofit approach adds 2×3s and spray foam to the old roof before sheathing and finish materials. Illustration by Matthew Baker.

the drywall or plaster. If there is an attic below, then a simple barrier, like kraft paper, is attached to the bottom of the rafters from inside the attic. Next, closed cell spray foam insulation is sprayed down into the rafter cavities. Once the cavities are filled with foam, new sheathing is put in place. Finally, the new roofing is installed.

⊷ Structural Insulated Panels ⊷

Another strategy is to add Structural Insulated Panels (SIPs) to your roof. SIPs are made by sandwiching polystyrene foam between pieces of sheathing. This results in a panel that is both superinsulated and structurally strong. SIPs are typically custom manufactured offsite for new homes, but they can be used in retrofits as well. Custom manufacturing means that each piece will fit to your specific project without much modification, so they'll install with less labor and less waste on the job site than standard construction methods. Careful,

FIGURE 5.10 A worker installs new roof sheathing over an exterior gut, spray foam retrofitted roof structure in Las Vegas. Photograph courtesy of Building Media, Inc.

detailed planning is needed to be sure each piece integrates with the existing structure, and a crane may be needed to install SIPs on a roof. Each panel is attached to the house using long screws, and seams between the panels are foamed to complete the air sealing. A properly sealed SIP installation is quick and offers all the benefits of spray foam retrofitting. While SIPs cost a bit more up front, some of that extra expense is recouped in fewer labor costs during installation.

⊷ Nailbase ⊶

Nailbase material consists of a layer of foam laminated to a single sheet of sheathing. Nailbase makes a bit more sense to use in retrofitting applications than true SIPs. The second piece of sheathing on the SIP sandwich allows finish materials to be attached on the interior of a new SIP built home, but that isn't usually necessary in an exterior retrofit. However, nailbase is typically sold in standard panel sizes, which require the extra labor of cutting and shaping on the job. Installation is similar to SIPs, with long screws attaching the nailbase to the old roof sheathing and anchoring it in the rafters. A proper foam seal is required between each panel. Nailbase is available in different thicknesses and configurations, depending on your specific application. Some nailbase materials are manufactured with blocks between the sheathing material and

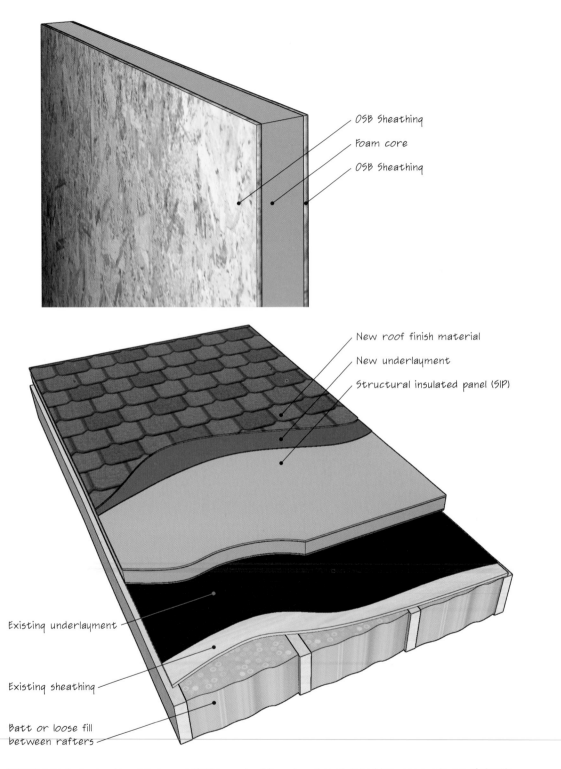

OSB Sheathing

Foam core

OSB Sheathing

New roof finish material

New underlayment

Structural insulated panel (SIP)

Existing underlayment

Existing sheathing

Batt or loose fill
between rafters

FIGURE 5.11 A structural insulated panel (SIP) is made of foam board sandwiched between two layers of sheathing. SIPs are one good way to retrofit a roof. Illustrations by Matthew Baker.

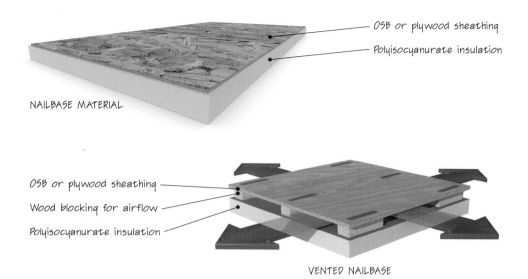

NAILBASE MATERIAL

OSB or plywood sheathing
Polyisocyanurate insulation

OSB or plywood sheathing
Wood blocking for airflow
Polyisocyanurate insulation

VENTED NAILBASE

FIGURE 5.12A The two types of nailbase panel material. Illustration courtesy of Hunter Panels, www.hunterpanels.com.

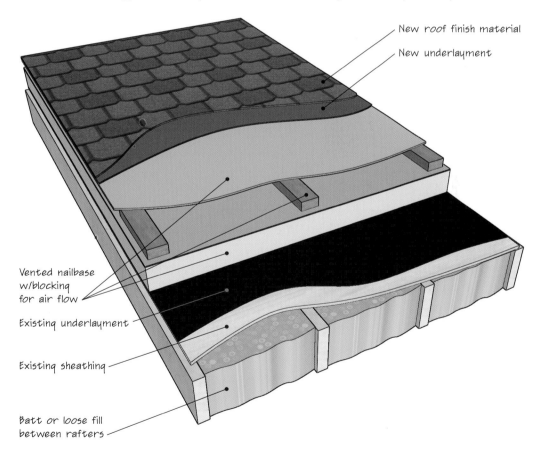

New roof finish material
New underlayment

Vented nailbase
w/blocking
for air flow

Existing underlayment

Existing sheathing

Batt or loose fill
between rafters

FIGURE 5.12B This is one possible configuration of a nailbase roof retrofit. Illustration by Matthew Baker.

the foam insulation to allow air to flow freely, which will fulfill the requirements of many roofing manufacturers' warranties for venting behind the sheathing.

► Rigid Foam Sheathing ◄

It's also possible to simply add layers of foam sheathing to the exterior of the roof. The attraction of using foam sheathing is that it's less expensive and, unlike spray foam, SIPs, or nailbase, is also commonly available at local home centers. It's also easy to handle and cut to shape and size. Since screws would simply drive straight through a foam sheet, furring strips are laid on top of the foam boards and long screws are driven through the furring strips, foam, and old roof sheathing and into the rafters below. Then full sheets of sheathing are installed, followed by underlayment and finally shingles or other roofing material. The key to using rigid foam panels is to install them over an existing roof sheathing deck for structural support, use at least two layers and stagger the seams, and use spray foam and/or tape to seal the edges of the panels. This will ensure you're getting the critical air seal. The thickness of foam you'll need depends on your region and what kind of performance you need. Widely available rigid foam sheathing boards range in thickness from ¼ inch to 2 inches, and can be layered to achieve greater thicknesses. There are three basic types of rigid foam sheathing to choose from for an exterior roof retrofit:

Expanded polystyrene (EPS) delivers about R-4 of insulation value per inch of thickness and is the least expensive of the three types of foam board. This is the type of rigid foam that most people are familiar with—the same stuff as white foam coffee cups or the white foam inserts used for packing materials.

Extruded polystyrene (XPS) delivers R-5 per inch thickness and is stronger and more rigid than EPS. It has low permeability, which means it won't soak up moisture, so it's often used as below-grade foundation and slab insulation. It costs about 50 percent more than EPS. While EPS is white, you can recognize XPS by its green, pink, or blue color. Both EPS and XPS tend to lose a percentage of their insulation value as they age, and many brands contain a flame retardant that is considered a persistent, bioaccumulative toxin. While the flame retardant is used in extremely low levels, some choose not to use EPS or XPS for that reason.

Polyisocyanurate (ISO) is considered the most environmentally friendly of the foam boards available because it doesn't need

FIGURE 5.13A At least two layers of foam board, with staggered, taped seams, are used in foam board roof retrofits. Photograph used by permission of National Grid and David C. Legg.

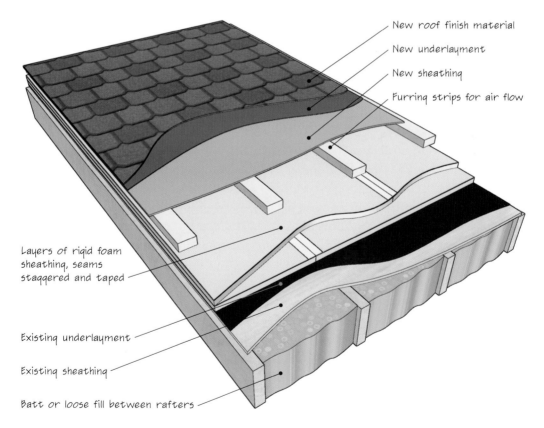

New roof finish material

New underlayment

New sheathing

Furring strips for air flow

Layers of rigid foam sheathing, seams staggered and taped

Existing underlayment

Existing sheathing

Batt or loose fill between rafters

FIGURE 5.13B This is one possible approach to an exterior rigid foam board roof retrofit. Illustration by Matthew Baker.

the flame retardant of EPS and XPS and uses water instead of more environmentally damaging chemicals in the manufacturing process. It also delivers the best insulation value—R-6.5 per inch thickness—of all three foams. The foam itself is cream to yellow in color, and always has a facing, usually foil. ISO is permeable, but the facing is impermeable, so with properly sealed seams it performs as an exterior vapor barrier. Due to the fact that ISO is permeable, it's not used where it will come in contact with the ground, as in below grade foundation or slab insulation. ISO is the most expensive of the three types of foam, costing about twice as much as EPS.

With any of these exterior retrofit approaches, use only the optimal, manufacturer-recommended number of metal fasteners to attach retrofit materials to the house. This is important to limit the amount of thermal bridging that might occur through the fasteners. Thermal bridging can happen as heat absorbed by the old rafters is transferred through the highly conductive metal of the new fasteners, or through the sleeper studs of the spray foam approach, and out of the house. Lots of metal fasteners mean lots of pathways for heat to escape.

⍟ Interior Attic Retrofits ⍟

Roof retrofits can also be achieved by working from the attic interior. Again, air sealing and insulation are paramount, so any interior approach has to cover both of those bases. This is most easily done in a house with an attic but can also be done in homes without an attic, as in the case of cathedral ceilings. An interior attic retrofit is the best choice if you've recently replaced your roofing material. Retrofitting from the interior means that you'll have the option of choosing a vented or unvented attic. There are benefits and drawbacks to both approaches, so consult a competent building science professional. In the end, your decision may depend largely on your climate conditions and local building codes.

In the case of an unvented attic, insulation and air sealing is applied to the underside of the roof sheathing and rafters. Spray foam is more expensive but faster to apply and more effective than other insulation materials. Spray foam is applied to the back side of the roof sheathing, layering as much as is needed, depending on the R-value desired and the performance required of the retrofitted cavity. The foam is applied all the way up to the ridge beam, sealing off vents. Spray foam is also applied to the gable end walls, sealing vents there as well. A minimum of several inches of foam will be necessary to prevent ice damming on the roof in cold climates, as explained earlier in this chapter. The key is to have enough spray foam insulation on the underside of the roof deck to keep heat from inside the house from crossing the thermal bridge to the roof's surface, which could cause snow there to melt. Also, getting a layer of foam over all exposed surfaces of both the back side of the roof sheathing and all sides of the rafters will help to create a reliable

FIGURE 5.14 Spray foam is applied directly to the underside of the roof sheathing in an interior, unvented attic retrofit. Photograph courtesy of Dow Building Solutions.

thermal break. Once a thick layer of spray foam insulation is applied, it's possible to add batt insulation or blown-in insulation over that for added R-value. Unfaced batts or loose blown-in insulation is held in place with nets. The nets are permeable, which lets air circulate and allows any moisture to dry, should condensation ever

FIGURE 5.15 In this vented attic retrofit, the attic floor is sealed with spray foam. Photograph courtesy of Sustainable Structures, Hallowell, ME.

occur. Again, with a thick-enough layer of closed cell spray foam (thicker layers are needed in colder climates), the likelihood of condensation is small. Still, running your plan by a building science pro will let you rest easy that ice damming and condensation problems will be prevented or minimized.

In a vented attic, the insulation and air seal must be installed on the attic floor. In many older homes, you'll usually find a thick layer of blown-in or batt insulation between the attic joists, resting against the back side of the ceiling finish materials. Sometimes there will be two, or even three, layers since it tends to compact over time, losing some of its insulating value, and previous homeowners might have "topped up" the amount of blown-in insulation. While all of that insulation is great, it doesn't address the air leaks into the house via interior wall structures, electrical wire runs, HVAC duct runs, plumbing vents, chimneys, recessed lighting, built-ins, and more. Attempting to seal every leak individually is possible, but very difficult to do correctly. Inevitably, some leaks would be missed, compromising the insulating value of the retrofitted attic system. Here's where spray foam comes in handy again.

In this approach, you first remove the old blown-in and batt insulation completely. If the insulation is in relatively good shape—that is, if it's not damp, moldy, rodent or bug infested, or otherwise contaminated—it's possible to save this insulation for use later. Once the attic is completely free of any insulation, a layer of spray foam can be applied over the entire surface. Since this is a vented attic, any vents, such as soffit vents, are not covered. Penetrations, such as recessed lighting, require special attention, since some of these types of enclosures are not rated to have insulation installed in contact with the housing. (See the "Be Safe with Recessed Lighting Fixtures" sidebar.) Also, if any HVAC ductwork runs through the attic, it will need to be completely sealed and insulated against the unconditioned attic air, as well. Once careful sealing of the attic floor is accomplished, the old batt or blown-in insulation is reused or new batt or blown-in insulation is installed on top of the foam air seal. Again, it's important to be sure that any soffit vents aren't inadvertently covered when the batt or blown-in insulation is replaced.

One drawback to this approach is that the blown-in or batt insulation on top of the layer of foam will allow air to circulate through the insulation, compromising its effectiveness. While it will still offer part of its insulating value, it won't perform at its advertised R-rating per thickness. To avoid this, a very thick layer of spray foam would need to be applied to the attic floor, adding to the costs of the retrofit. That's one of the reasons that I prefer the unvented attic to a vented attic. Unvented attic retrofit strategies, whether interior or exterior or a mixture of the two, maximize insulation performance and make air sealing the attic an easier, less error-prone affair. That said, an unvented attic needs to be designed carefully, with the help of a building science pro, to avoid common pitfalls.

Be Safe with Recessed Lighting Fixtures

Recessed lighting fixtures can be a serious energy drag. That's especially true of fixtures that have been installed so that they're exposed in a vented attic. Those fixtures, particularly older models, allow lots of air to circulate around the big flood lamp bulbs to keep them cool. That hot air flows up and out of the fixture, into your attic. With it, in a "chimney stack effect," that air drags the air you've paid to heat or cool up and out of your house, creating serious energy waste. Because the fixtures can get very hot, many older recessed lighting fixtures are rated as non-insulation contact (non-IC) fixtures. That means exactly what it sounds like: when installing insulation around a non-IC fixture, leave a space a few inches wide between the fixture housing and the insulation material to avoid overheating and the possibility of fire.

These older, non-IC fixtures pose a problem when retrofitting for a vented attic because they do not allow for insulation like spray foam to be sprayed over the leaky housing. While these housings can be carefully sealed with high temperature caulk, the problem of lack of insulation around the housing remains.

When retrofitting, these older recessed light housings should first be replaced with housings rated as "air sealed insulation contact" (Sealed-IC), which means that they're safe for insulation to come in direct contact with the housing. Even with the new housings installed, the safest way to retrofit an attic with exposed recessed light housings is to first cover them with a fire-rated cover (such as commercially available Insullite covers) before insulating around the fixtures.

That advice also extends to choosing how much foam insulation to use in your retrofit. The key to a successful roof retrofits, especially in colder climates, is to add enough thickness of foam—whether in the form of spray foam, SIPs, nailbase, or rigid foam sheathing—to avoid condensation from occurring within the roof or attic floor cavity. That amount varies by climate and region, so make sure to include your building science pro's advice in your plan on foam thickness, as well.

❯ Finish Materials for Retrofitted Roofs ❮

Once the insulation and air sealing have been completed, standard finish materials like asphalt shingles or metal roofing are perfectly acceptable. Still, if you're interested in saving energy at home, you might also be concerned about the environmental impact of your

Florida Home Keeps its Cool

FIGURE 5.16 The Cool Energy House. Photograph by Andy Frame.

Florida's mild climate has made it the fourth most populous state in the nation, as well as one of the most visited by American vacationers, even in the heat of summer. It's likely that much of that popularity would not have been possible without the one technological advance that helped make Florida more habitable: air-conditioning. These days it's the high-energy demand of air-conditioning that drives folks in hot, humid climates to deep energy retrofit their homes.

On a trip to Orlando for the annual International Builders' Show, I was invited to tour the *Cool Energy House*, a deep energy retrofit pilot project spearheaded by the US Department of Energy's Building America Retrofit Alliance (BARA). Building Energy Optimization (BEopt) software, developed by the National Renewable Energy Lab and released for free use by the public, was used to calculate the effectiveness of potential improvements.

The leader of the BARA team, Craig Savage of Building Media, Inc., said, "BEopt essentially allows you to quickly determine which energy efficiency measures to apply to your home to get the best return on investment."

After a thorough energy audit assessment and based on recommendations from the BEopt software, the home's walls were retrofitted from the interior with densely packed blown-in fiberglass insulation and thoroughly air sealed to block hot air and humidity infiltration. Spray foam was applied to the underside of the roof structure, creating an unvented attic space where HVAC equipment and ductwork could be housed without competing with the Florida heat and humidity. New high-efficiency windows and doors, HVAC, lighting, and appliances were installed. The pool pump was replaced with a unit that uses 90 percent less energy than the original. Finally, a 3.5kW photovoltaic array was added. When all of the improvements were added up in BEopt, the home achieved 52 percent savings, and indoor comfort levels improved dramatically. At the same time, the home's interior and exterior were thoroughly renovated to bring the house up to date.

The dramatic savings of the Cool Energy House, which was just over 20 years old when retrofitted, shows how deep energy retrofits can be applied even to newer homes in milder climates to reach serious energy efficiency goals.

material choices. Here are some recommendations for more environmentally benign roof materials.

Roof color can affect roof temperature in all seasons, affecting heating and cooling loads. A lighter colored roof will reflect more radiant heat in hotter climates, reducing the amount of heat that enters the home so that the air conditioner works less to keep the home cool. Darker colored materials will absorb more radiant heat, helping the furnace keep the house warm on a cold-but-sunny day. The amount of sun reflected by a given roofing material is called the Solar Reflectance Index, or SRI. The higher the SRI, the more reflective it is. You can find help choosing the right SRI for your roof from your roofing contractor or through the US Department of Energy's website, which features a good overview of cool roofs.

A roofing material's recycled content and recyclability help determine its effect on landfill space, as well as the amount of energy used in its production. With recycled content roofing, like our 80 percent recycled rubber faux slate roof, material originally headed for the dump is remanufactured into a usable product. Conversely, if a roofing material is easily recyclable the likelihood that the material will enter the waste stream at the end of its life is small. Metal roofing is the most easily recyclable roofing, but asphalt shingles, which have historically not been recycled, are becoming more widely recycled as road materials in various regions.

Choosing extra durable materials can save on future costs, extending the time between new installations, and keep construction debris from future installations out of the dump. Better yet, choose a roof that's not only very durable, but recyclable and includes recycled material as well—a metal roof will last 50 years and a recycled rubber roof like ours can last 75 years.

Finish materials don't have to be the only green part of your roof system. Using engineered wood products in the roof's structure (in rafters, joists, and sheathing) means that you're using a lumber material that is made from sustainably harvested, small diameter, rapidly regenerating trees. The resulting structure will also be straighter and stronger than the same structure built with traditional lumber.

⤜ Mea Culpa ⤛

As you can see, there's no "one size fits all" solution in deep energy retrofitting, but rather a range of approaches for different climates and home types that all aim for the same building performance level. Usually, depending on your climate, a properly retrofitted roof or attic should achieve between an R-30 and R-60 insulation rating, and completely air seal the living space from the exterior air, whether you have a vented or unvented attic or a cathedral ceiling. It's worth repeating that with all retrofits, consulting with a building science pro is paramount. Ditto the structural engineer. In some cases, the extra load on a roof can be considerable, so a structural engineer should do proper load calculations to avoid any unpleasant surprises down the road. That said, it's time for me to tell a cautionary tale about my own roof retrofit, and why I should have heeded my own warnings.

On the structural side, I had sound advice. I ran my pencil drawings by Tommy DeLoach of LP Building Products, who carefully vetted them for strength and stability. Tommy's the guy who turned those rough sketches of our DER plan into neat prints. He also specified all of the load-bearing joists, rafters, beams, and studs, so I knew we were good to go from a structural standpoint.

I was somewhat less diligent with the insulation plan for the new dormer roof on the rear of the house. As I sized up our plan, I realized that by leaving the old dormer roof in place, the space between the top of the old roof and the bottom of the rafters on the new roof would be quite small. It would be a wedge-shaped space about three feet tall at the bottom end where it met the wall, diminishing in size to the point where it met the ridge beam. If I waited to insulate until after the new roof deck sheathing was installed, I'd have to wriggle in there on my belly with the spray foam hose in tow and work in that cramped space. Being somewhat claustrophobic, I wanted to avoid that. Instead, could I insulate *after* the rafters were installed but *before* the sheathing was put in place? That would allow me to work out in the open, spraying the foam down between the bays of the rafters instead of working in the cramped, panic-inducing space of the new attic.

I would have to install some kind of barrier first in order to have something to spray the foam against. What if I stapled kraft paper to the bottom edge of the rafters, dropped in a layer of fiberglass batt insulation, and sprayed the foam against that? Problem solved. I felt pretty clever up there on the roof that September afternoon, working in the coolness of early evening as I carried out my plan. Standing on the rafters, I sprayed down into the cavities. After that, the construction crew installed the sheathing, and I never gave the dormer attic a second thought. Until I heard a tapping sound.

FIGURE 5.17 I install spray foam down into the cavities between the new rafters on the rear dormer roof. Do you hear ominous music in the background? Photograph by Sherri James.

It was a couple of months later, as I lay in bed one morning watching lazy snowflakes drift by the window. At first I ignored the tapping, dreamily connecting the sound to the solar panels that were heating up a bit: it was just snowmelt dripping on the window sill outside. I snoozed, but then I heard it again: drip. After 30 seconds, again: drip. Hmmm. I got up and looked out the window to see if the source was visible. No water that I could see. Drip. Yep, that was definitely water. It was time to put on some pants.

Without a source visible, I had to track the sound. It was somewhere toward the back wall and above my head. Outside? Maybe, but I couldn't see any evidence when I looked out there. The only other possibility I could think of was the attic. A leak in the new roof? I put on a headlamp and confronted my claustrophobia head-on. Up there, in the dark, I found the source of the sound. From the low end of one of the insulated rafter bays water dripped, landing on the old roof surface below. I reached up to feel the fiberglass batt insulation: soaked. One squeeze sent a small torrent running down my arm. *Oh no*, I thought, *what the hell is wrong?* I knew the possibilities. Either there was a leak in the roof or, worse, we had condensation buildup in the small gap between the top of the spray foam insulation and the bottom of the roof sheathing. I prayed for the leak.

Why was I praying for a leak? Because a leak could be fixed by finding the source and simply patching it up. If it was condensation, I faced a major redo project. I'd have to remove about half of the insulation I'd just installed and dry out the whole dormer roof structure with heaters and fans for weeks. Then I'd have to wedge myself into the attic to spray more foam between the rafters so that the foam covered the bottom side of the sheathing completely, filling in the cavity between each new rafter.

I pulled down a 6-foot-long piece of fiberglass batt. It was soaked. Six feet more got me to the ridge beam. Wet all the way up, although drier at the top. That made sense, since water would follow the laws of gravity, even on a shallow pitch, draining to the lower back edge of the roof. I tested more insulation in the other rafter bays. All wet. In the cramped space, I could feel my blood pressure rising. I poked a small drywall saw up through the layer of spray foam. The instant it passed through the foam, water began to trickle out of the hole. Then I cut a 6-inch square plug of foam. The plug dropped out of the hole, along with at least a quart of water. The stream of expletives that left my lips would have made a sailor blush. My heart sank; my mind raced. This was condensation, the worst possible problem.

It was the low point of our DER experience. We'd been hard at work for months, and we'd spent thousands of dollars. Had I not discovered this when I did, the entire back side of the house could have been catastrophically affected. I went through the equivalent of a grieving process before I could resolutely confront my error. First, denial: *"Hey, maybe this is just some water that got in from those storms before we put the sheathing on. Maybe I can just dry it out and we'll be okay."* Next, anger: *"What was I thinking of? What an idiot!"* Then bargaining: *"If only this will go away, I'll never make a mistake again. I promise!"* Then depression: A dazed lethargy crept into my body, denying me any pleasure in the project. Putting on the tool belt to bear the weight of our house crisis became a kind of dreary penance for my retrofitting sins.

I eventually reached the final stage in my grieving: acceptance. Luckily, Stalwart Construction felt my pain and dispatched a couple of guys to remove all of the fiberglass insulation from the dormer roof and cut a 6-inch wide swath down the cured spray foam layer in the center of each rafter bay. Before they left, they set up some small space heaters and fans that we would leave running for two months while the space dried out completely. They were in and out in a matter of hours, and I began to plan the fix.

In the end, I filled each bay completely with spray foam, right up to the back side of the sheathing, negating the possibility of condensation. The day I squeezed into the attic to do the job, I mentally prepared myself for the anxiety of working in a small space. Within 10 minutes I adjusted, relaxed, and felt fine. Why had I been so afraid of the small space to begin with? This wasn't so bad. Aside from the cost to my mental stability, the new materials and labor would run about $1,000, not including my own time.

It was a stupid and expensive mistake, and I could have avoided it if I'd vetted my original plan with a building science pro. Instead, I took the advice of some very well-meaning, but unqualified, folks on the matter. I certainly couldn't blame them, because I had made the final decision and it had turned out to be wrong. Luckily, it wasn't so wrong that it couldn't be fixed. I tell this story, though, to make a point. There really are right and wrong ways of building, and no matter how much DIY or construction experience you have, your instincts and wishful thinking can lead you astray. No matter what approach you think is best, run it by a pro before you ever put on that tool belt.

As I continued research for this book after our DER project was completed, a telling article was brought to my attention that made me feel (only slightly) better about my mistake. Titled, "Foam Shrinks, and Other Lessons" (*Fine Homebuilding Magazine,* February/March 2012), it detailed what building science pro and trusted writer Joe Lstiburek encountered when he deconstructed one of his 16-year-old DER projects. Some of the original retrofit work had performed remarkably well, but the 6-inch-thick EPS foam panels used on the exterior had shrunk markedly, allowing heat to escape from the building, and the plastic sheeting used as housewrap hadn't performed well either. The faulty materials were removed, and the re-retrofitted building features many layers of ISO sheathing with staggered, taped joints. I sincerely appreciated Mr. Lstiburek's "warts and all" approach in his article—it shows that the building science community is always improving the knowledge base that the rest of us can draw on for our own projects, and that mistakes often offer some of the most valuable learning experiences.

Chapter Six

RETROFITTING WALLS

WHEN WE MADE THE DECISION TO STAY IN TOWN, RATHER THAN move to the country, it was time for some brutal honesty about our house. The worst problem was the leaky exterior, which let too much inside air escape and too much outside air slip in. The single pane windows and wooden doors contributed to the problem, too. Light peeked in through gaps around the doors, most of which required vigorous slamming to fully shut. This had made for some not-so-comical misunderstandings in our house, since door slamming usually indicates that someone is angry about something. Our doors turned the simplest statements into pronouncements of rage: "I'm headed to the farmers' market!" *Slam!* "I'm taking the kids to school!" *Slam!* "Honey, I'm home!" *Slam!* "The pizza is here!" *Slam!* Our neighbors probably thought that we needed some good marriage counseling.

✈ The Law of Unintended Consequences ✈

We had made a small improvement to our walls years ago by having cellulose insulation blown into the empty wall cavities. The first thing we noticed after that insulation was installed was how much quieter things were inside the house. The level of street noise was reduced quite a bit. The house became somewhat easier to heat and cool, and we saved a little on energy, too. Building on that success I fixed some of the old, broken storm windows. I also restored the beautiful little arched dormer windows so that they looked like new. I installed new weather stripping on the doors, caulked around trim, and used little foam cutouts to try to seal some of the air leaks around electrical outlet boxes in the walls. We felt more comfortable, although we still felt the need to keep the thermostat turned down in the wintertime to economize. The energy savings really began to mount up—to about 15 percent. Soon after we completed the wall insulation and other weatherproofing improvements, though, natural gas rates went up. Not long after that electricity rates rose, too. Our measly 15 percent savings was wiped out, and we still had a house that felt sticky in the summer and frigid in the winter.

As we began planning our deep energy retrofit, I got to thinking about how air sealing can be even more important than insulation in terms of energy efficiency. And that made me realize that the insulation we'd had installed years ago might actually have made our walls *more* leaky, not less. You see, the company we had hired to insulate our walls prided itself on being able to blow in the insulation without making any visible holes in the *outside* surfaces of the house. Instead, they pried off pieces of aluminum siding and drilled lots of small holes through the old redwood siding and pine sheathing boards underneath. Through those holes, they blew the cellulose insulation into the wall cavities. Afterward, they carefully reinstalled the pieces of aluminum siding. The result looked nice and neat. However, it had left hundreds of little holes in my house, hidden from view behind the aluminum siding. Problem was, that aluminum siding *wasn't* air sealed. Like all "loose hung" siding material, our siding was a rain screen for the house, but it did nothing to slow *air* flow. I'd gotten a couple of thousand bucks' worth of insulation, but the job had probably opened a couple of thousand bucks' worth of draft-producing holes at the same time. It was the law of unintended consequences: fix one problem and create five more.

⋟ No More Holes ⋞

The DER fix for our walls was a drastic, once-and-for-all approach that solved multiple problems. First, we pulled off the old, dented, peeling aluminum siding and recycled it. We reaped enough money from the siding recycling to keep us in Friday afternoon beer for a while.

Removing the aluminum siding exposed the "holey" redwood siding beneath it. Just as we had on our roof, we applied a curtain wall over the damaged redwood siding. (For an explanation of the curtain wall concept, see "A New Protective Shell" in chapter 3.) We used long screws to fasten 2×3 studs to the walls, connecting through to the old studs inside the wall. This approach allowed us to avoid removal and disposal of the old redwood siding. It also created a thermal benefit because the new curtain wall studs contacted the old lap siding only at the points where it stuck farthest out, leaving an air gap between the back side of the studs and the face of the old siding, as shown in figure 6.4.

We turned that gap into a thermal break by applying closed cell spray foam between the new exterior studs. The foam, applied wet, covered the old siding face but also expanded into the spaces behind the new studs (see figure 6.4). The benefit was small—we would have gotten more of a thermal break by installing foam sheathing—but it was better than no thermal break at all, and required no extra work or materials (see the sidebar "Thermal Bridging and Thermal Breaks" in chapter 5 for a detailed explanation of the thermal break concept).

Leaving the old redwood siding in place was also a smart choice because the siding was painted, most certainly with toxic lead-based paint. Had we removed the siding, we would likely have disturbed that toxic paint. Instead, we encapsulated it, keeping the lead away from human contact for good. We would neither encounter lead paint dust during demolition, nor transfer the lead paint to a landfill where the lead could potentially leach into water supplies.

Once the foam was sprayed on and cured, the holes from the old cellulose insulation installation were sealed for good. Next, I installed OSB sheathing and standard housewrap. After that, we turned our attention to replacing all of the old windows and doors. Here we chose top of the line, triple pane, krypton gas–filled windows with insulated vinyl frames. I originally balked at the idea of vinyl, but once I had a chance to see and feel how these particular windows worked, I overcame my bias for metal clad wood windows. Wood windows, just like wood studs or wood rafters, act as fairly good conductors of heat. Insulated fiberglass or vinyl framed windows perform better than wood, both in terms of energy efficiency and durability, and modern versions of both are beautiful and virtually maintenance-free. With the krypton gas between the window panes, my new windows had superior thermal ratings and, I figured, they had the added benefit of keeping Superman from ever breaking in.

We pulled out the old windows, frame and all, to make space for the new construction windows to be installed. Following the install, I had to do some extra work on the interior side of the window openings, because our walls had been made thicker by the exterior curtain wall approach of our DER. The installers aligned the new construction windows flush with the outer plane of the new wall, so the curtain wall retrofit materials extended the sill on the interior to nearly 10 inches deep. Finishing those interior spaces required new trim and sill material, as well as fixes to the plaster.

FIGURE 6.1 Installing OSB sheathing is the step that follows application of spray foam in our exterior wall retrofit. Housewrap will follow, and then windows, doors, siding, and trim. Photograph by Sherri James.

This was work I was perfectly happy to do myself, and on the positive side, we ended up with deep sills that would accommodate all manner of plants, kids' projects, and objets d'art. And we'd have some serious energy efficiency when we were all done.

We selected new doors fabricated using fiberglass shells filled with closed cell foam, much like the foam we were spraying onto the house. Again, while solid wood doors have aesthetic appeal, they're unfortunately good at conducting heat. They're also susceptible to expansion and contraction from hot/cold and wet/dry cycles, which can eventually crack the wood or pull joints apart. Fiberglass doors

FIGURE 6.2 I remove trim as I prepare to take out one of the old single pane windows in our living room. Even with an exterior retrofit process, you can't escape doing some work from the interior side. Photograph by Sherri James.

do expand and contract in heat and cold, but they're made to be somewhat flexible so they're not as likely to crack or sag over time.

On the west side of the house, we took a different approach. Five years ago, before we had decided to go whole hog with a DER, I had replaced the windows there with a high-quality, double pane, metal clad wood type. Ditto the doors: they'd been replaced with new, metal clad wood versions with double pane glass. So we had to decide whether to replace the semi-new windows and doors or keep them. Since I had installed those windows as new construction windows, I knew they were properly air sealed and insulated around the frames. I couldn't stomach replacing windows and doors that were so new from either a cost or an environmental standpoint, so I decided to leave them in place. That presented a different, but not difficult, construction challenge in terms of the retrofitted walls: I'd have to build exterior inset trim boxes with sills and carefully install flashing and sealant materials to avoid water infiltration.

With the windows and doors complete, the final step was putting on new exterior siding. I chose engineered wood siding due to its green qualities, but also for its ease of installation. I have installed plenty of fiber cement siding over the years, and I dislike the risk of breathing the dangerous silica dust that's produced when the siding is cut. Not to mention that the "cement" part of fiber cement requires enormous amounts of energy to produce, so it's not particularly green. The engineered wood siding cuts and installs like regular wood, but the sawdust from cutting it is less dangerous than fiber cement dust. Plus, the engineered wood siding is made from sustainably harvested trees, and it has a 50-year warranty.

We wrestled with the decision about whether to replace the front façade of our house. Its whitewashed brick is unique in our neighborhood, and we couldn't imagine the house without it, much the same way we couldn't imagine it without its signature blue paint. I'd seen some retrofits where old brick is removed from the exterior walls, foam insulation is added, and then the house is finished off with siding or faux brick. I wasn't sure, however, that retrofitting a single-story wall that included two big bay windows and a door would offer much in the way of energy-saving benefits. The wall comprised less than 7 percent of the total exterior area of the house. It also already had loose cellulose insulation installed from our prior attempts at energy efficiency. In the end, we decided that the consequences of leaving the brick intact, from an energy efficiency standpoint, would be small, so the front brick façade would stay.

Your retrofit will probably include some hard-to-quantify components like our front wall. There are no easy answers, because it can be hard to put a dollar value on aesthetics or history. Like me, you'll have to do some fuzzy math to arrive at a solution that strikes a balance you can live with for the long term.

➤ Designing Your Wall Retrofit ◀

The exterior curtain wall approach worked well for our specific situation. We could leave the interior of the house virtually

A DER with a View:
Tobie and Bob Johnson, Oak Harbor, WA

FIGURE 6.3 Tobie and Bob Johnson's Retrofitted Home. Photograph by Ted Clifton.

Tobie and Bob Johnson have both served their country for decades. Bob is a Vietnam veteran with 38 years of service, and Tobie served with the National Guard as an intel sergeant in Desert Storm. Bob has also worked as a general contractor specializing in masonry. In the 1980s, the Johnsons renovated a 100-year-old, two-story home. After Desert Storm, though, Tobie's health problems made it difficult for her to navigate the stairs, so they began looking for a one-story home. "No more stairs," Tobie said, "and while we were at it, we wanted a view."

When they found the perfect view in Oak Harbor, Washington, it happened to belong to a not-so-perfect house. "It was an ugly 1960s ranch with a pink bathroom," Tobie recalled. At first I said 'No way,' but Bob liked it for the big workshop." There was no insulation in the walls, the wiring needed updating, and the ceilings were low. Calling the old house a challenge was an understatement, but with the help of contractor Ted Clifton, Tobie and Bob made a plan to transform the ugly ranch.

The plan called for applying nailbase insulation panels to the exterior walls, and SIPs were used where the house was bumped out to enlarge it. They paid diligent attention to air sealing and insulation and added variable-speed ventilation fans to address indoor air quality. High-efficiency, mini-split heat pumps were used for heating and cooling. Along with the energy efficiency upgrades, Tobie wanted the home to include "age-in-place" and Universal Design elements so that they could stay in the home "until we're 80 if we want to," she said.

The results? "We're not cold anymore, and we use very little heat," Tobie said. Their pre-retrofit energy bills have been cut in half, even though they've turned up the thermostat for comfort. Since they often lose power in Oak Harbor, they had the house wired for a generator, but they haven't bothered to install it yet. Now the home retains its temperature for long periods of time, so even after a couple of days without heat they're comfortable. Their home now works for them on many levels. With all of the aesthetic upgrades, including Bob's custom masonry work on the exterior, the house is finally worthy of the view.

untouched, with the exception of trimming out the new windows and doors inside. The stud and spray foam curtain wall process also suited our semi-do-it-yourself work flow: I could work alone to install the exterior studs, spray foam insulation, OSB sheathing, house wrap, and siding. Also, since the spray foam would expand into all of the gaps and cracks on its own, I wouldn't have to visually find every hole in my house to air seal it. A full coating of spray foam automatically accomplished what would be a very difficult job to do manually, one crack at a time. I wasn't sure that I'd be quite as effective at air sealing the house without the spray foam.

When you can include a retrofitting project as part of necessary maintenance and upgrades, the retrofitting part won't seem like a big economic burden, especially when you factor in the long-term benefits. Thus, one of the best times to retrofit exterior walls is when you're replacing your home's siding. If you have the economic resources to replace windows and doors at the same time, the cost of the retrofit materials will only be a fraction of the total cost. In contrast, if you would have to remove relatively new finish materials in order to retrofit, the costs can be hard to justify. As with many things in life, timing matters.

That said, as with a roof retrofit, a wall retrofit can be approached in many different ways depending on your climate, your preference for an interior or exterior approach, your budget, and your local codes and covenants. Are you planning to undergo a gut remodel, or do local historic rules prohibit major changes to the exterior of your home? Choose to retrofit from the interior. Do you want to live in the house while it's being retrofitted or are you due for lots of exterior maintenance anyway? Choose an exterior retrofit. Since you'll be adding a load to the existing structure and affecting the way moisture acts in the system, get some advice from a structural engineer and a building science professional before you settle on a final plan.

Exterior retrofits—using the stud and spray foam curtain wall, exterior gut, structural insulated panels (SIPs), nail base insulation, or foam panels—can work for walls as well as they do for roofs (see chapter 5 for more information on these materials). Interior retrofits, which require partial or full removal of interior finish materials like plaster or drywall, are viable, too. Walls can be riddled with air leaks, so whatever technique you choose, pay extra close attention to sealing up the holes. Windows and doors are important here, too. The number, type, and installation technique of windows and doors

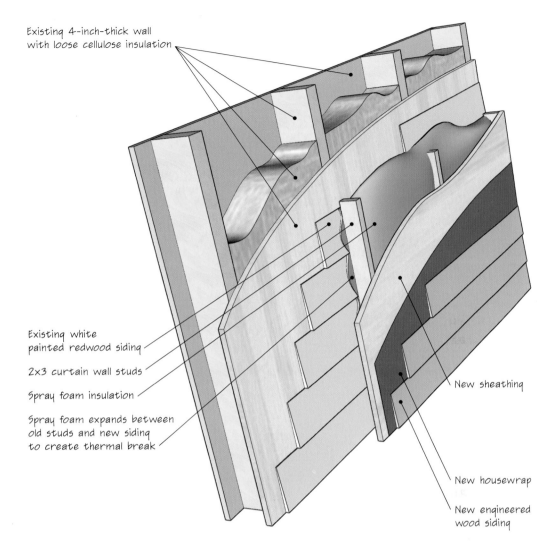

Existing 4-inch-thick wall
with loose cellulose insulation

Existing white
painted redwood siding

2x3 curtain wall studs

Spray foam insulation

Spray foam expands between
old studs and new siding
to create thermal break

New sheathing

New housewrap

New engineered
wood siding

FIGURE 6.4 The Wilson spray foam retrofit approach added retrofit materials directly over the old siding. Illustration by Matthew Baker.

should be carefully integrated into the DER plan to ensure that they don't become weak spots in the building envelope.

⊷ Exterior Wall Retrofits ⊶

If you choose an exterior retrofit, you'll start by deciding whether or not to remove the original siding and/or sheathing. If your siding is vinyl or aluminum, or any "loose hung" siding, it will need to be removed. Some structurally sound lap or panel siding can be left in place and the retrofit materials added over it. Masonry finishes present their own set of issues. In very old homes, brick and stone were sometimes used as a structural wall, so these cannot be removed without compromising the structure of the home. In other homes, masonry materials are applied as a "veneer" over the sheathing of a standard stud wall.

Whether or not to remove a brick or stone veneer will depend on a couple of things: if you choose to retrofit over the existing masonry, it must be in good condition, without major cracks or faults. Second, because it can be difficult to attach exterior retrofit materials properly to the masonry surface (see "A Masonry DER Solution" sidebar), extra care must be taken to ensure that retrofit connections are solid and sound. Choosing to remove masonry veneer can eliminate several inches of thickness from the exterior wall, which can then be filled with retrofit materials, leaving the original dimensions of the home relatively intact. Stucco can usually be left, assuming the retrofit materials can be attached in a way that ensures long-term structural integrity.

Most exterior retrofit methods focus on adding insulating and air sealing materials to the exterior surface of the old wall. Those materials thicken the walls, moving the exterior plane of the building outward by several inches or more. Gut retrofits give you the

FIGURE 6.5 This Las Vegas home is undergoing an exterior gut retrofit. All exterior finish materials and sheathing were removed, and the wall cavities were overfilled with spray foam. Once the foam cured, the excess was cut away. This ensured complete filling of the cavity. The house now awaits new sheathing, housewrap, and finish materials. Photograph courtesy of Building Media, Inc.

A Masonry DER Solution

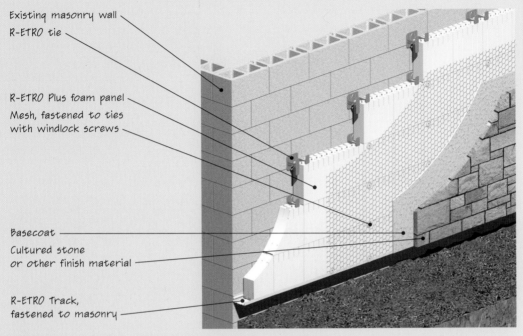

Existing masonry wall
R-ETRO tie

R-ETRO Plus foam panel
Mesh, fastened to ties
with windlock screws

Basecoat
Cultured stone
or other finish material

R-ETRO Track,
fastened to masonry

FIGURE 6.6 The R-ETRO masonry retrofitting system. Illustration by Quadlock Building Systems, www.quadlock.com.

As more and more homes are deep energy retrofitted, more and more companies are creating products to solve common retrofitting challenges. Quadlock, a manufacturer of insulated concrete form (ICF) products (see chapter 9, figure 9.2) came up with R-ETRO, a bracket and insulating foam block system, which addresses concerns of retrofitting over masonry materials. First, a track is attached at the bottom of the wall and a course of light-weight, EPS foam blocks are laid in place. Then a row of plastic brackets is inserted into slots in the top of the blocks and attached to the masonry. The next row of blocks has identical slots in the bottom, which slide over the top flange of the plastic bracket, and the process is repeated until the wall is completely covered.

The basic system is designed to be finished with stucco, but a version with plastic strips embedded in the foam blocks every 12 inches allows for lap or panel siding to be installed.

FIGURE 6.7 The R-ETRO system being installed on a brick home. Photograph by Quadlock Building Systems, www.quadlock.com.

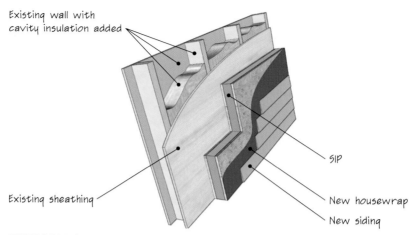

Existing wall with cavity insulation added

Existing sheathing

SIP

New housewrap

New siding

FIGURE 6.8A A SIP wall retrofit.

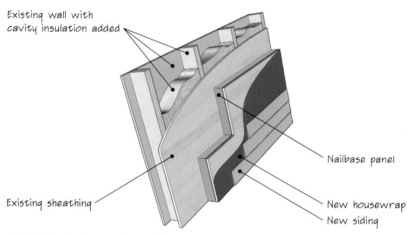

Existing wall with cavity insulation added

Existing sheathing

Nailbase panel

New housewrap

New siding

FIGURE 6.8B A nailbase wall retrofit.

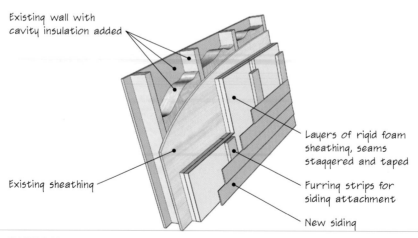

Existing wall with cavity insulation added

Existing sheathing

Layers of rigid foam sheathing, seams staggered and taped

Furring strips for siding attachment

New siding

FIGURE 6.8C A rigid foam sheathing wall retrofit.

Exterior wall retrofits can be accomplished using many different materials. SIPs, nailbase, and rigid foam sheathing are some of the materials available. Illustrations by Matthew Baker.

option of using the existing wall cavity for insulation and air sealing, without changing the outer dimensions of your home. By completely removing all exterior siding and sheathing, the wall cavity is exposed, any old wiring or systems within the wall are fixed, and the cavity is filled with spray foam. Spray foam is the insulation of choice in this approach, because other insulation materials lack the high R-value, air, and moisture-blocking qualities of spray foam. This is especially important in older homes, since 2×4 wall construction only leaves a small space in which to install insulation. That insulation has to have a very high thermal resistance per inch so that the final wall assembly performs in a highly efficient manner. Finally, new siding materials are installed. This approach keeps the bulk of the construction mess on the outside of the house, allowing occupants to live in the home during the retrofit.

Using SIPS for exterior wall retrofits is not do-it-yourself-friendly, since SIPs are so large and heavy. Each SIP is manufactured separately to a specific size and shape so that it will fit in a particular position on a house. Openings for windows and doors are typically cut in the factory, so SIPs need to be carefully specified so that they fit correctly when installed. Once the siding is removed, the SIPs are simply set in place on an installed bracket or ledge and attached to the house, with special long fasteners, through the old sheathing and into the studs. Small cans of insulating spray foam sealant are used to spray between panels, filling the gaps, to ensure a tight air seal. Once the panels are installed, housewrap and finish materials

FIGURE 6.9 Installing rigid foam sheathing to the exterior walls of a home can be an economical way to approach a deep energy retrofit. Here, exterior furring strips are being installed that will accept the fasteners for new lap siding. Photograph used by permission of National Grid and David C. Legg.

can be applied as in a new house. Nailbase material is installed similarly, except that the nail base material is usually cut to shape and size on the job site before being applied to the exterior wall.

Rigid foam sheathing can be used as well (see "Rigid Foam Sheathing" in chapter 5). Multiple layers of rigid foam insulating sheathing are applied to the exterior wall, staggering edge joints from layer to layer and carefully taping seams for a good air seal. Openings for windows and doors are extended with plywood boxes, and new windows and doors can be installed at the outer plane of the bumped out wall or at the plane of the existing wall (see the sidebar "Innies vs. Outies" later in this chapter) before new siding and trim are applied.

▬ Interior Wall Retrofits ▬

Interior retrofits work best when you're gutting the house for an interior remodel anyway. In the case of older homes, wiring and plumbing are likely not up to current code standards, so the safety and reliability of those systems are in question. Replacing wiring and plumbing can be very disruptive, since much of it is hidden in walls and floors that would have to be wholly or partially removed in order to gain access to the old wires and pipes. That's a big reason many people choose to do a gut remodel at the time they purchase a home, before they move in. Living in a home during a major remodel is nearly impossible due to the dust, noise, and general mayhem. Remember, too, that living in a remodel can expose a family to hazards like lead dust from old paint, so it's generally advisable to move out during such a project.

An interior gut renovation starts with removal of plaster, drywall, or other finish materials along with existing insulation. Wires, pipes, ducts, and other "stuff" in the wall may also be removed and brought up to current building standards at this point. Next, wall cavities are completely filled with expanding spray foam. Some spray foam contractors may recommend a "hybrid," spray foam and loose or batt insulation method. In this approach, 1 to 2 inches of spray foam is applied, and then loose or batt insulation is used to fill the rest of the wall cavity. While this is less expensive than the full-foam cavity fill, I don't recommend this approach in a retrofit unless the wall cavity is 6 inches deep or deeper. Since many older homes will have been built using 2×4 studs, the cavities will be too shallow to ensure enough insulation and air sealing using the hybrid insulation method. That's why, in the interior gut retrofit approach, a

FIGURE 6.10 New spray foam insulation is used to superinsulate the exterior walls as part of an interior gut retrofit of this older home in Massachusetts. Next, the homeowners will install new finish materials. Photograph used by permission of David C. Legg.

FIGURE 6.11 Fiberglass insulation shows through holes cut in the wall of this 20-year-old Florida home. Because the home's finish materials and wiring were in good shape, a partial gut retrofit approach was chosen. The fiberglass insulation was piped into each cavity. The holes will be patched and then the walls will be repainted. Photograph courtesy of Building Media, Inc.

full-foam cavity fill is necessary. However, this can be a great way to insulate in a new 2×6 wall (see chapter 9). Once the spray foam is installed, the final step is applying new interior finish materials. An interior gut is one of the best ways to retrofit an older home, especially if the home's exterior materials are in good shape or are of historical value, or if neighborhood covenants prevent changing the exterior aesthetic of the home.

Interior retrofits can also be done without a total gut. If a home is newer and its electrical wiring is up to date, but it lacks insulation, holes can be cut out of the interior finish materials to allow for blown-in insulation to be installed. In order to access the entirety of every cavity formed by each stud, holes are cut at increments along the wall (usually 16 inches apart, because standard wall construction uses a stud every 16 inches) in each wall cavity. This is done at several levels in each cavity so that the cavity can be completely filled and visually inspected so as not to leave voids. Dense pack fiberglass or cellulose is piped into the holes, and then the holes are patched and the interior refinished.

Another interior approach, called a double wall, can be used if a homeowner isn't concerned about losing interior space. A new, non-structural wall is built along the interior side of all exterior walls, leaving an air space between the old interior finish surface and the back of the new wall. An air sealing barrier (like plastic sheeting) is installed between the new and old walls, new wiring and other systems are run in the new wall, and then insulation is installed into the new wall cavities. Finally, new interior finish materials are installed. Few people are willing to lose interior square footage, but this approach can work if you're retrofitting a large, very inefficient home (see the chapter 7 sidebar, "Passive House, Texas Style," for more on this method).

⚬ Either Or? ⚬

The perfect retrofit for your home may not be wholly exterior or interior, but a combination of both. For example, you may decide to fill interior wall cavities with blown-in insulation, yet retrofit with rigid foam sheathing on the exterior for a good thermal break. Or maybe your exterior retrofit allows you to gut to the interior finish materials, use fiberglass batts, and then resheath with insulated sheathing before finishing out the exterior. Every project will demand a different solution, so spend plenty of time in the planning process to make sure you cover all your bases.

⇴ Windows and Doors ⇷

A large portion of any deep energy retrofit budget will be new, high-efficiency windows and doors. Older windows are typically single pane and wood framed, offering little in the way of thermal protection other than keeping heated air from directly escaping. Older doors are usually wood or steel, both of which have a serious negative effect on energy efficiency. Window and door replacement have lots of other benefits, aside from offering better thermal efficiency, the most important of which is air sealing. Not only will the new units themselves be tighter, but having them installed to current best practices ensures that they will be properly integrated into the building envelope. That said, there are lots of manufacturers out there that make dubious claims about their windows and doors, so it pays to educate yourself a little before making any major decisions in that department.

⇴ Choosing Windows ⇷

Shopping for windows can be frustrating. The maze of technical specifications and marketing ploys can make your head spin, but if you start by thinking seriously about what the most desirable window would accomplish you'll be on your way to making a sound decision.

New construction vs. replacement windows. One major decision is whether to install new construction windows or replacement windows. New construction windows require removal of the old window, frame and all, before installation. The upside of this is that it allows the installer to properly air seal and insulate between the new window frame and the rough opening of the home's original structure. A new construction window also affords the opportunity to add flashing materials to discourage water intrusion. Replacement windows require removal of the sashes only; the windows are then installed within the existing window frames. The new glass of the replacement window will improve the thermal properties of the glass itself, but any air leaks between the old frame and the home's structure will still be present. Thus, new construction windows will provide better energy efficiency because they can be properly integrated into the building envelope by sealing and insulating between the edges of the window frame assembly and the framing of the house.

U-value. First, you want windows and doors that keep the heat in or out, depending on the season, so you want good thermal

Innies vs. Outies

FIGURE 6.12 An "Innie" window installation (left); an "Outie" window installation (right). Photographs by Sherri James.

Nope, I'm not talking about belly buttons. I'm talking about the plane in which new construction windows are installed (or how existing windows are incorporated) into a wall retrofit. "Outies" are installed in the plane of the exterior trim and siding, while "innies" are installed in the plane of the sheathing, behind the bumped out materials. The outie creates a deeper sill on the interior, while an innie creates a deeper sill on the exterior. Which one is best?

Turns out that building scientists and builders have been arguing about this for decades. Generally speaking, builders are most familiar and comfortable with proper outie installation techniques and less so with innie installs. That means outies will result in a better overall installation and performance, since the installer is less likely to screw it up. On the other hand, others note that perfectly acceptable flashing and installation techniques exist for innies as well, and that any builders worth their salt would be able to competently install either. The upshot? You may have some of both, like my project, and you'll want to make sure your builder is comfortable installing both. The longevity of your windows and your home's exterior wall structure depend on it.

performance. This is typically expressed in doors as an R-value, just like in wall or roof insulation. With windows, it's expressed as a U-value. Why? Because that way it's more confusing for homeowners, and window salesmen can pull the wool over their eyes more easily. What does that "U" stand for? While the "R" in "R-value" stands for "resistance," the "U" is simply a symbol that stands for overall heat transfer. Simply put, U-value is the inverse of R-value ($U=1/R$).

That means, whereas *high* R-value is important in wall insulation, *low* U-values are important in windows. Lower U-values are achieved in windows by using multiple panes of glass with empty spaces between them. That space is usually filled with argon or krypton gas. Double pane, gas-filled windows are common, but triple pane windows are also available, boosting thermal performance. Triple pane windows can cost 20 to 25 percent more than similar double pane windows, so making sure that you'll benefit from choosing triple pane windows is important before you break the bank over them. If you live in a very cold climate and have a home with lots of windows, triple pane, gas-filled windows can help save you significant amounts of energy (and, as noted in chapter 4, triple pane windows are more comfortable to sit next to on a cold winter night than double pane windows—which may be a benefit worth paying for). Even the type of gas—argon or krypton, typically—will have an effect on thermal performance. Make sure to get a second (or third) opinion before buying triple pane windows, and be sure to get those opinions from someone who is not trying to sell them to you. This is a great question for your trained home energy auditor, who has the tools necessary to help quantify the savings of one type of window over another.

Window frame considerations. The way in which glass panes are mounted in a window frame is important, too. Traditionally, metal spacers are inserted between the panes

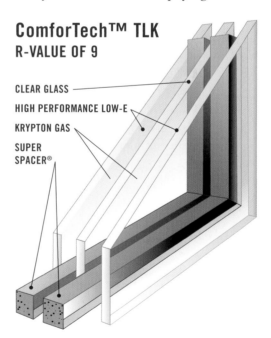

ComforTech™ TLK
R-VALUE OF 9

CLEAR GLASS

HIGH PERFORMANCE LOW-E

KRYPTON GAS

SUPER SPACER®

FIGURE 6.13 The "Super Spacers" in Pro Via triple pane windows are made of low-thermal bridging foam, not metal. Illustration courtesy of Pro Via.

of glass. Metal is an excellent thermal conductor, so heat is easily wicked through the edge of the interior solid glass pane, through the metal spacer, into the exterior solid glass pane, and to the outdoors. In the wintertime, this leads to a "cold edge" on the glass pane that often causes warm, humid interior air to condense near the edges of the window panes. This condensation often results in water beading up and running down the panes onto the frame. If the window frame is made of wood, it can become damp, which can lead to expansion. When the wood dries again, it contracts. Over time, this can lead to cracking of the wood and/or mold and mildew growth. In extreme conditions, the wood eventually rots and fails altogether. This "cold edge" problem led to the development of foam and butyl spacers that inhibit the conduction of heat between the panes. Called "warm edge" technology, it helps to avoid condensation and heat transfer through the spacer, extending the life of the window and making it even more energy efficient than a comparable window with metal spacers.

Frame type has an effect on how a window functions from an energy efficiency standpoint. While wood windows may have an aesthetic appeal, they have drawbacks, including somewhat higher thermal conduction and sensitivity to moisture, like the cold edge condensation mentioned earlier. Metal or metal clad windows might solve some of the moisture problems, but they still suffer from high thermal conductivity. Vinyl or fiberglass window frames, especially frames that are insulated, offer the best in energy efficiency, low maintenance, and stability over time, due to the fact that they resist both thermal conduction and moisture. They also never need painting, so that's one little job you can permanently delete from your "honey do" list.

Emissivity. The amount of sunlight that radiates through a window (or indoor heat that radiates out) affects the protective qualities of the window, too. In hot climates, the amount of sunlight allowed in can be controlled by adding a "low-e" (short for low emissivity) coating to the outside of a window pane. This coating, applied in the manufacturing process, blocks a certain amount of light from entering the house and also helps prevent radiant heat from transferring from a warmer pane to a cooler pane. That helps keep the window's U-value lower and stops a certain amount of the sunlight entering a house from hitting an interior surface and warming it. This keeps indoor air temperatures cooler so the air-conditioning has to work less to keep the space cool. In cold climates, the low-e coating can be applied to the interior of a window pane to block heat from radiating out from the inside. Different low-e coatings can be applied to windows that face different compass directions, customizing them for lots of sun on the south side of a house, or much less on the north.

The Solar Heat Gain Coefficient (SHGC) of a window is a measure of how much solar heat is transmitted through the window. If you live in a hot climate, you'll want a lower SHGC so that less heat enters your home. If you live in a cold climate, you'll want a higher SHGC so that more solar heat can enter your home. The extra heat gain during winter months can help offset some of your home's heating costs. In either case, the coatings can also limit the visual light that is transmitted, meaning a severely tinted window, which has a low SHGC and admits little in the way of solar heat, may also look too "dark."

Fixed vs. operable windows. Finally, think about which windows need to open and close and which can be fixed. A fixed pane window, with no operable parts, will naturally keep air movement at bay, while operable windows that rely on seals and latches to prevent air movement when they're closed will be more susceptible to air leakage. Those operable windows come in two basic types: casement/crank windows and sash/double-hung windows. Good quality casement windows have a single latch that controls several mechanical arms along the length of the window. When the latch is pulled down, the window is cinched tightly against the foam rubber gasket in several places, ensuring a tight air seal. Double-hung sash windows are designed to slide in a track. A foam rubber seal in the track isn't feasible because the window would catch against the rubber when moved. So even when tightly latched shut, double-hung sash windows won't have the high-quality air seal of casement windows.

You'll want enough operable windows in your home to take advantage of good weather when you have it. I like to have operable windows in all rooms, but not all of the windows in a room need to operate. A window with access partially blocked by a nearby appliance or piece of furniture may work best as a fixed pane window. Properly placed operable windows can help in cross-ventilation, which can help to cool your home without turning on an air conditioner. Consider, too, that operable windows can be used as emergency exits. Everyone will have a different plan and preference.

As you weigh all these factors, keep in mind that saving money in the short term by buying stock windows from a big box home improvement store—with its well-meaning but potentially less knowledgeable staff—could end up costing you money in the long run. Many of the better window brands are available only via wholesale to professional installers who have been certified by the manufacturers as competent in proper installation. When you buy high-quality windows, you'll also gain access to professionals who can help design a whole-house solution for your window needs, weighing all of the options available. Keep that in mind—paying more for professional-grade windows is likely worth the investment.

⊷ Choosing Doors ⊶

As with windows, it's wise to choose doors that have low thermal conductivity, good air sealing, long-term stability to stand up to heating/cooling and wet/dry cycles, and low maintenance requirements. Your basic choice of materials includes wood, metal clad wood, insulated metal, and fiberglass. And if you want doors that have glass panes in them, all of the same issues will apply as with windows.

Wooden doors are typically the most expensive and require the most maintenance. Well cared for, wood can last a long time. However, since wood expands and contracts depending on temperature and humidity levels, wood doors have the tendency to crack at joints and weaker points in the panels. This expansion and contraction also has an effect on how the door fits in the frame, possibly allowing gaps to form where the door meets the weather seal. To avoid this, wood doors need to be refinished every couple of years to keep them looking good and functioning correctly. If damaged, a wood door can easily be patched, sanded, and refinished. Another factor to consider is wood's somewhat high thermal conduction rate. It's not the best choice from an energy efficiency standpoint, although it does rank above metal on this front. Metal clad wood doors have a metal skin on the exterior, wood on the interior. The metal exterior will protect the wood part of the door, which will give it a longer lifespan. A metal clad door is less energy efficient than an insulated door, but it will provide the "real wood" aesthetic on the interior.

Metal doors are typically the least expensive. They consist of a wood frame that supports metal panels on the interior and exterior, with closed cell foam insulation filling the space between the metal panels. While they're inexpensive, metal doors are difficult to fix if

FIGURE 6.14 Conrad of Pro Via installs the new foam core fiberglass entry door that looks, quite convincingly, like real wood. The beautiful art glass in the door has the same triple pane construction as the rest of the highly efficient new windows in our home. Photograph by Sherri James.

they become dented. However, an insulated metal door performs better than a solid wood door from an energy efficiency standpoint. While most folks think of metal doors as very durable, the truth is a bit different. Since metal doors are made of steel, they're especially susceptible to rust and corrosion from weather, which can shorten their lifespan dramatically. This is especially true in a coastal environment, where salty sea air can quickly attack and eat steel.

Fiberglass doors have most of the advantages and fewer of the drawbacks of the other types of doors. While they do tend to be more expensive than metal doors, they're usually not as expensive as wooden doors. They're constructed much like metal doors, but the panels are made of fiberglass. During manufacturing, fiberglass can be pressed into molds, colored, and finished to look very much like wood. Fiberglass is more dimensionally stable than wood, so it will retain its shape and finish over time without the constant maintenance of a solid wood door. Thermally speaking, an insulated fiberglass door outperforms wood, metal clad, and metal doors. All in all, I prefer insulated fiberglass doors over other types for all of those reasons.

As with windows, the overall energy efficiency of a door is affected by the way it operates. Just as sash or sliding windows have a less effective air seal than casement windows, large sliding glass patio doors have a less effective air seal than French doors or standard operating single doors. This is because the locking and sealing mechanisms of French doors are able to pull the door up tight against a foam rubber gasket, minimizing air leaks. If possible, opt for French door operation over sliding glass patio doors.

While it might be tempting to install your own windows and doors to save some money, you don't want to compromise your retrofit because of it. Whatever type of windows and doors you choose, installation can have a major effect on how well they function. That's why it's absolutely critical to work with a contractor who is well known for attention to detail when installing windows and doors. Most professional grade window and door manufacturers offer their own installer certification programs, since they have a lot to lose in terms of reputation if their high-quality products are installed incorrectly. National, independent certification programs, like those from the American Window and Door Institute and the American Architectural Manufacturers' Association, educate installers in best installation practices—check out the Resources appendix for links to help you find a certified installer in your area.

⇥ Finishing Up ⇤

The last part of an exterior wall retrofit is to replace the siding and trim. Here, the options are endless—wood, engineered wood, brick and stone veneers and their engineered counterparts, stucco, vinyl, steel—you name it. Most siding is meant to be decorative and to work

Insulated Siding Materials

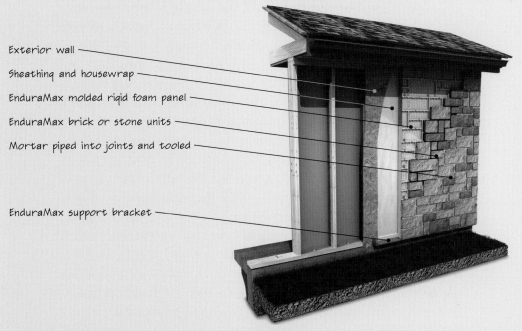

Exterior wall

Sheathing and housewrap

EnduraMax molded rigid foam panel

EnduraMax brick or stone units

Mortar piped into joints and tooled

EnduraMax support bracket

FIGURE 6.15 The EnduraMax masonry system starts with a molded foam panel, resulting in a brick or stone look while adding insulation value to the wall. Illustration courtesy of EnduraMax.

As a nod to energy efficiency, siding manufacturers have started introducing insulated siding materials into the market. Most commonly, vinyl siding is manufactured with foam insulation laminated to the back side. The siding manufacturers make big claims about how this siding helps with energy efficiency, without the homeowner having to go to the trouble and expense of retrofitting. Unfortunately, while the siding can offer a modest improvement thermally (about R-3), the foam that fills the space behind the siding actually interferes with what vinyl siding does best—acting as a rain screen. Also, because vinyl siding is a loose-hung product, air is able to flow around edges and connections, compromising the potential R-value of the insulated siding material.

One promising product that integrates foam insulation and does markedly improve a building's thermal envelope is EnduraMax, a masonry system. EnduraMax starts with a molded EPS foam panel that is attached to an exterior wall over the housewrap. The indentations in the panel accept a variety of proprietary manufactured modular stone and brick, which are numbered so that an installer knows exactly which sized stone fits in which indentation. The stones are pressed in place and held by the foam while the installer applies mortar to the joints. The resulting masonry finish is not only beautiful and durable, but also adds R-13.6 to the wall's insulation value.

as the first defense against the weather as a "rain screen." Siding sheds rain and repels snow and hail, but it will not exclude all wind-blown water, moisture, and air from penetrating a house. Beneath the siding the housewrap, sheathing, and general air sealing techniques and products do the bulk of that work and must be installed correctly for the house to function properly. Can a siding material help with energy efficiency? Sure, but its effect is typically less than that of the materials beneath, which include all of that new insulation and air sealing you've just installed as part of your deep energy retrofit.

Still, it's worth considering the green aspects of your siding choice (see "DER Materials" in chapter 3) to keep your project's environmental impact to a minimum. Also, think about a product's warranty—does the manufacturer stand behind its product? A low-maintenance product will help you avoid the time and expense of refinishing a product periodically. What about the ease of installation? A higher quality product might cost more to purchase, but then save money on installation labor, evening out the total cost. If it's a durable material, you'll save down the road, too, by avoiding replacement. If you are using a paint or stain, make sure it's durable and low in VOCs (volatile organic compounds) for the safest, greenest bet. As a final pass, the siding installer and painter are the ones who have the chance to seal up any remaining exterior gaps with caulk, so be sure that they're willing to take on the task.

FIGURE 6.16 As the controlled chaos of our one-man retrofitting operation proceeds, I continue applying spray foam. Luckily, this is the back of our house, which isn't visible from the street. Otherwise our neighbors would have drummed us right out of town. Photograph by Sherri James.

On the Wilson deep energy retrofit timeline, my exterior wall retrofit started once the Stalwart crew had finished the framing on the house and addition and the roof installation. Their contract completed, they moved on to their next renovation down the street. The job was now eerily quiet, with no one around talking, singing, and cracking jokes. It was just me and some awfully cool late fall winds that would whip up late in the day. I soldiered on—made a measurement, climbed down the ladder, cut a 2×3, drilled the pilot holes, climbed up the ladder, attached the stud, made a measurement, back down the ladder—in what seemed an unending cycle.

When the first snow flew, I had finished the basic exterior retrofitting on the main house. We were now cozily ensconced in a winter coat of closed cell spray foam insulation, new windows and doors, OSB sheathing, and housewrap. The engineered wood siding and trim lay in a carefully wrapped pile in the yard. That would have to wait for spring, when I could install it myself. Much of our original home equity line of credit was spent, so hiring someone to finish this job was out of the question. We'd be on the hook for the rest of it. A quick check of the housewrap instructions showed that I had one year from its installation to get the siding materials installed, or I'd have to rewrap the house. I kept repeating to myself, "Sure, no problem, I can do that."

FIGURE 6.17 New windows and doors and the exterior foam curtain wall are complete, but new siding and trim are still to come as the Wilson DER goes into hibernation for the winter. Photograph by Sherri James.

The new retrofitted "skin" on our house kept most of the outside noise from entering the house. Occasionally, though, one sound would pierce the frigid winter night air. The mercury would dip into the teens or single digits, and a wind would kick up, tugging at corners of the housewrap. Here or there a piece would come loose and flutter like a kite, shrieking and hissing, reminding me of the big jobs that lay in wait for me when spring came.

Chapter Seven

RETROFITTING BASEMENTS FOR MORE ENERGY SAVINGS

THE WINTER AFTER OUR RETROFIT BEGAN, I HAD MY HANDS FULL, catching up with my regular work that I'd put off while I was busy with the DER. When spring arrived, I was eager to shake off my cabin fever and install the siding and trim. Spring turned into summer as I finished that siding work, and when autumn came, I found myself with a new contract to produce online how-to videos. I hit on the idea to shoot most of those videos as I finished out the bath, kitchenette, and living areas of the addition. I turned my attention to those interior details and put the retrofit work on the back burner.

By the time we got around to retrofitting the basement, our DER had been under way for more than two years. Our energy bills had dropped drastically, we were much more comfortable, and the air in the house was fresher than it had ever been. Except, that is, during the summer, when a swampy smell would still rise from the basement. Or we'd have a good, hard rain, and the sump pump would kick on, and a swampy smell would rise from the basement. Or for no readily apparent reason at all, a swampy smell would rise from the basement. With the main house tight as a drum above ground and the new super-efficient addition mostly finished out, it was time to tackle that dreaded basement.

≫ Why Basement Retrofits Matter ≪

How much could it matter, though? Aren't basements underground, where the temperature is never below 45°F (7°C)? That's what I'd always been told. And doesn't heat rise? That's another one I knew from elementary school. So my house couldn't possibly be losing

GET YOUR PANTS ON!

20°F

98°F

INSULATION

68°F-70°F

INSULATION

HEAT

45°F

NO INSULATION

FIGURE 7.1 Living in a house with an uninsulated basement is like standing in a hole without your pants on. Illustration by Jeff Wilson.

much heat through the basement. That's what I thought until I met Erik Kiilunen and he told me the story about the guy with no pants.

Erik lives in Calumet, Michigan, and when he told me the story, thankfully, he *was* wearing pants. In the summertime in Calumet, the breezes off Lake Superior blow through the Upper Peninsula pines and perfect white clouds scud through an impossibly blue sky. In the wintertime, though, the snow lies so deep that they have to cart it out of downtown in dump trucks. Calumet, where the average *high* temperature in January is only 22°F (−5°C), is where Erik started a business retrofitting houses to help keep folks warmer. Calumet is a place where you don't have to convince people of the benefits of deep energy retrofits: they understand it in a visceral way.

Still, folks in Calumet had the same assumptions as I did about basements, until Erik told them the guy-with-no-pants-story. Erik tells it best standing in front of an easel while wielding a bright blue marker, illustrating as he goes. "Let's say you have a guy," he begins, "and you give that guy the warmest down-filled parka, mittens, and a hat." His Sharpie squeaks across the page, and the protagonist comes to life. "But all he gets to wear on his lower half are his boxer shorts." With a flourish, Erik gives the blue guy a pair of inky underwear.

Now the story gets interesting. Erik explains that it's 20°F (–7°C) outside, and we ask the guy to stand in a hole in the ground. Assuming that the temperature inside the hole, below soil level, is 45°F (7°C), our guy starts out pretty comfortable, although his bare feet feel a little cold. "Let's say that you and I go inside where it's warm, and leave the guy out there," Erik continues, "and come back out in a couple of hours." At this point, Erik asks the guy if he'd like another coat, hat, and mittens, but the guy shakes his head. "No. He's gonna want some pants, because that 45°F (7°C) hole, while it's warmer than the 20°F (–7°C) air, is still pulling the heat right out of his lower extremities, and he's freezing his tail off."

The same is true with your house. People often overstuff their attics and walls with insulation but not their basement or crawl space, due to the mistaken belief that buried foundation walls don't matter because temperatures underground are mild and "heat rises." Problem is, only one kind of heat, warmed air, actually

FIGURE 7.2 This thermal image shows how basements and foundations can be a major source of heat loss. The dark spots in these images show cooler surface temperatures, while the bright spots show higher surface temperatures, indicating heat loss. Note that the brightest area on this home's exterior is the foundation, indicating major heat loss there. Images courtesy of FLIR Commercial Systems, Inc.

prefers to rise due to *convection*. Heat itself only has one rule—move from hot to cold (the second law of thermodynamics). Whether it's up, down, backwards, or sideways, heat will move from a hot spot to a cold spot until both spots are the same temperature.

Yes, it was the laws of thermodynamics that were wicking heat out of my basement. While it's common practice nowadays to waterproof and insulate concrete slabs, foundations, and basement walls, it just wasn't done back in the 1940s. Outside the block walls and concrete floor of my old basement there was no insulation, just good old-fashioned dirt. Heat from inside my house was rushing out of the furniture, air, interior walls, human bodies—you name it—through the floors, into the basement, and then through the highly conductive masonry surfaces of the basement walls and floor into the cool soil beyond. With nothing to block the heat loss, I was paying to heat the ground around the outside of my house. According to Erik, that's where up to 30 percent of our total heating energy was heading in the wintertime.

✈ Figuring Out Our Retrofit Details ✻

Once we completed work on the addition and how-to videos, we returned to the business of deep energy retrofitting the house. It was time to kick the ravenous, energy-sucking monster out of my basement. In a sense, we were lucky, because our basement already had foundation drains and a sump pump. Otherwise we would have had to deal with remediating drainage problems in the basement as well as insulating and air sealing the cold masonry surfaces to isolate them from the indoor space. I'd been trying to decide on a retrofit approach, and I'd kicked around several possible ways to mitigate the negative effects of the laws of thermodynamics in my basement. I knew that we would be retrofitting from the interior of our basement rather than from the exterior. And I knew that closed cell spray foam would definitely be in the mix but I still didn't have a firm plan.

The basic approach of an interior retrofit is to fur out the basement walls and floor (to attach strips to the walls, which hold the fasteners of finish materials and between which insulation can be added), insulate, and then add finish materials. The drawback of this technique is that you lose a little bit of interior square footage. The advantage is that you don't have to tear up your yard the way you would with an exterior retrofit. The most readily available material for furring out a basement wall is wood. However, wood is susceptible to soaking up moisture, which can lead to mold and mildew trouble. As explained in chapter 5 (see sidebar "Thermal Bridging and Thermal Breaks"), wood isn't ideal as a thermal break either. Steel studs are an alternative, but steel is very conductive and would wick heat out of the basement rooms as well. This was the crux of my dilemma—I couldn't decide what kind of furring material to use.

That was when I met Erik Kiilunen. Turns out that, as a retro-fitting contractor in Calumet, he had crossed paths with the same predicament. That had led him to design a solution and start a fledgling business. While wandering the aisles at the International Builders' Show in Orlando one January, I spotted Erik's "EcoStud" Product and immediately knew that it was what we needed in our basement retrofit. No, EcoStud isn't a troupe of environmentally friendly, half-dressed male dancers. EcoStuds are building materials that look like steel studs but are made from recycled plastic. They're not used for load bearing, or structural, purposes, but they are great for constructing interior walls and furring out existing walls. EcoStud offers a standard "track and stud" product that works just like common metal stud systems, but they also have a series of "Z" furring products that are designed to accommodate a variety of rigid foam board thicknesses in retrofits. This was an ideal product to use in a basement retrofit. Plastic won't soak up moisture and won't harbor mold or mildew. It has better thermal characteristics than steel, so it would wick less heat. And to boot, EcoStuds are thin. If I used EcoStuds to fur out my basement walls, I would be able to completely fill the cavities between furring studs with closed cell spray foam, which would slow the transfer of heat dramatically. Finally, I'd figured out a way to put some "pants" on my house.

Work started with the demolition of old finish materials that had been installed over our home's 70-year history. On the walls in the finished part of the basement, someone had attempted a previous retrofit using wood furring strips and a thin layer of ½-inch white foam boards, followed by gray particle board paneling. When Sherri started tearing out the paneling, she noticed a stamped label on the back side: "Warning: Not for use in damp locations such as bathrooms or basements." It had warped and buckled due to condensation and humidity over the years. It was also a host for mildew and mold and, undoubtedly, was one of the enduring sources of the

FIGURE 7.3 My daughter, Sylvie, gets into the act, helping me demolish the remaining finish materials in the basement as we prepare for the retrofit. Photograph by Sherri James.

swampy smell. Many homeowners have unwittingly compromised their indoor air quality by installing this type of paneling, which was often treated with formaldehyde in order to make it unpalatable to biological attackers. Unfortunately, formaldehyde "off-gassed," meaning that it leaked out of the paneling into a house, poisoning the occupants for several years after installation. Once off-gassing was complete, the formaldehyde no longer protected the wood, and the paneling was then attacked by mold and mildew.

Sherri, wearing a respirator, tore out most of the moldy paneling, furring strips, and old foam panels. Sylvie and I worked together to finish up, once Sherri had done the dirtiest part of the demolition. Underneath, the block walls were covered in mold and mildew, another source of our "eau de swamp" perfume. Over the years, humid air had infiltrated the open space between the old paneling and the block wall and condensed when it hit the cool masonry blocks. Airborne mold and mildew spores found the damp environment good habitat and took up residence. We were now shutting down that mold farm, which we hoped would alleviate much of the swampy smell.

Next we had to deal with the floor, which appeared to be nearly as old as the house itself. It was a tongue-and-groove pine floor that had been built level over the sloping concrete slab. (The slope allowed any water that seeped in to move quickly to the floor drains.) I was hauling some of that floor out to the curb when my neighbor, Art, called me over. Art and Kate live across the street, and they've been in the neighborhood longer than anyone else I know. "So you're finally tearing out the old dance floor?" Art asked, with a twinkle in his eye. He went on to tell the story of how our home once served as a popular weekend gathering place. The owners would invite neighbors in, down the basement stairs, and onto the red painted pine floor to dance the evening away. I imagined the old radio crackling out big band tunes as couples waltzed and fox-trotted their way around the room. In the summertime the metal framed basement windows would have been propped open to invite in evening breezes, with a chorus of crickets from outside accompanying the strains of Frank Sinatra, the Dorsey Brothers, or Benny Goodman.

I felt a pang of guilt at disposing of history this way. I showed Art the black mildew stains on the old pine and the places where moisture had conspired with mold and rot to eat away at the wood. I told him about our retrofitting plans to help bring the house up to 21st century energy efficiency standards. How our indoor air quality would be much better. How much more comfortable we would be. And the music? There would be music, I promised, since the main end use of the finished side of the basement would be as a music room and recording studio for our family of budding musicians. Winter had caught the singer-songwriter bug, and she needed a place to record her creations. Sylvie had picked up the bass guitar. Both girls play piano and sing, taking after their mother and me in the music department (Sherri plays piano and a mean jazz/blues alto saxophone). The wooden dance floor would go, but the music would play on.

Once the basement was cleared of debris and cleaned of mold and mildew, the retrofit could begin. Our plan was to use the EcoStud track and stud system on the walls and apply spray foam insulation between the studs, all the way up to cover the sill plate and band joist. Then we would install 2-inch XPS foam boards to the floor using EcoStud's plastic "Z"-shaped furring strip. That would take care of the moldy smell from the walls and floor. Then we added special floor drain check valves and a sump pump cover to seal off the drain system and eliminate the swampy smell. All of those efforts would also slow or stop the movement of radon into the space. Last, having addressed all of the potential moisture and radon hazards, we could install finish materials that would make the space comfortable and homey.

Passive House, Texas Style

FIGURES 7.4A AND 7.4B Nicholas Koch's Passive House retrofit in Texas (top) and a view of the taped layer of OSB that was applied to the old interior wall finish (bottom). New double-wall framing is also in place, ready for insulation and finishing. Photographs courtesy of egreengroup.com.

Nicholas Koch is the founder of E Green Group, an Austin, Texas, construction firm committed to building sustainable, ultra low energy homes. When confronted with a fixer-upper that had more renovation challenges than you could shake a stick at, Nicholas and his wife hatched a bold plan: to create the first "Passive House" remodel in Texas.

Passive House is a very strict building standard for new construction, requiring an extremely tight air seal and superinsulation so that the resulting home needs little in the way of heating or cooling. The "passive" part refers to the fact that homes built to this standard can often be heated entirely by passive solar means and cooled merely with fans or air cooled by tubes buried in the earth, without energy guzzling "active" heating and cooling like most homes use. The Passive House

⊱ Start with Moisture Management ⊰

Let's face it: many peoples' basements are like the black sheep of the family. They're useless spaces that suck up loads of energy resources and never really pull their own weight. And most of the time, they smell bad, too. Respectable basements would at least make themselves useful and maybe clean up once in a while! To redeem our basements, most of us need to undertake a basement deep energy retrofit.

standard originated in Darmstadt, Germany, as "Passivhaus" but is now gaining recognition in the United States and other parts of the world due to its success in creating extremely energy efficient homes in many different climates.

Instead of applying the standard to a new home, Nicholas applied it to the deep energy retrofit of his older home. "We were pregnant with our first child and we were tired of moving, so we wanted to build a home that we really loved," said Nicholas. "Everything I read about Passive Houses said that they were too expensive and difficult to build, so I took that as a challenge to create the first Passive House retrofit in Texas."

The home they retrofitted was a dilapidated 1950s home that had been abandoned and become a flophouse for drug users and vagrants. The old place was sided with asbestos siding, and the walls and ceiling had little in the way of insulation. Their retrofit started with a double wall, interior plan: first, for the tightest air seal possible, OSB sheathing was installed over the old interior finish of the walls, ceiling, and floor. All of the seams were carefully taped and sealed with a mastic coating to ensure a super-tight air seal. Then, an entirely new, non-structural

wall was built around the interior perimeter of the house, leaving a 3-inch air space between the old and new walls as a thermal break. Into the new wall all new wiring, plumbing, and fiberglass batt insulation were installed. Then, a new interior finish was applied.

On the exterior, cellulose insulation was blown into the old wall cavities before the old asbestos siding was encapsulated with ¾-inch XPS rigid foam sheathing, which was finished off with stucco. The result: the first Passive House renovation in Texas, and a high-performance building heated and cooled by a single, small ductless mini-split heat pump. The Kochs have turned an eyesore into a fully functioning member of their community. The home's modern interior is light and airy, and the perfect place to raise their growing family. Nicholas also proved that Passive House standards could be successfully applied in Texas—as a result of his achievements his company has been hired to retrofit 250 homes built in 1950 on the nearby Fort Hood army base to Passive House standards.

See the Resources appendix for more information on the Koch project and Passive House standards.

There are several approaches to retrofitting an existing basement or crawl space, but the first task in any retrofit is mitigating moisture. If your basement is always dry, even during rainstorms, you likely have good exterior foundation waterproofing and foundation drains. On the other hand, if you experience a wet or damp basement, your foundation may be neither waterproofed nor properly drained. Without foundation drains, water can be allowed to sit against the foundation walls and the pressure of gravity can force water through even the thickest concrete or block. But good water management

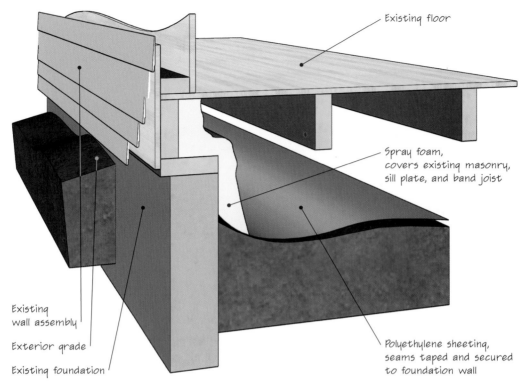

Existing floor

Spray foam,
covers existing masonry,
sill plate, and band joist

Existing
wall assembly

Exterior grade

Existing foundation

Polyethylene sheeting,
seams taped and secured
to foundation wall

FIGURE 7.5 This is one possible approach to creating an unvented crawl space. Illustration by Matthew Baker.

starts above grade: bulk water management should include gutters
and downspouts that move water away from the foundation, and
the soil surface around the house should always slope away from
the foundation. Planning and implementing a moisture management strategy can be a sizeable project in and of itself, but it's a
necessary precursor to any basement or crawl space retrofit.

Retrofitting a Crawl Space

Crawl spaces are best retrofitted to become part of the conditioned
space, within the building and thermal envelopes of the house. In
older homes, vented crawl spaces were usually built, but there are
few benefits to such an approach. In an unvented retrofit, the dirt
floor of the crawl space is first sealed with a layer of polyethylene
sheets, which are carefully taped at the seams. Then the perimeter
of the crawl space foundation is insulated using spray foam or carefully sealed foam boards. All vents are sealed, as well. Then a couple
of small vents are installed in the floor of the living space to allow
conditioned air to circulate. That conditioned air will help to dry

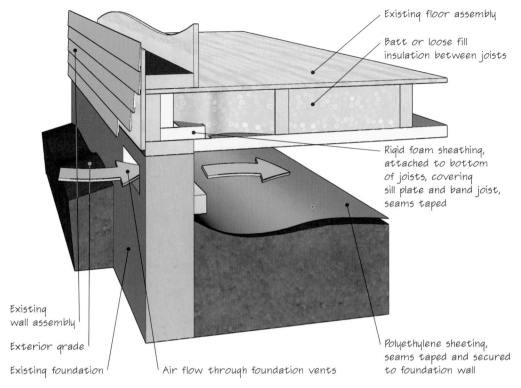

Existing floor assembly

Batt or loose fill
insulation between joists

Rigid foam sheathing,
attached to bottom
of joists, covering
sill plate and band joist,
seams taped

Existing
wall assembly

Exterior grade

Existing foundation

Air flow through foundation vents

Polyethylene sheeting,
seams taped and secured
to foundation wall

FIGURE 7.6 This is one possible approach to creating a vented crawl space. Illustration by Matthew Baker.

out any moisture that invades the crawl space, avoiding mold and rot problems in the wood joists that support the floor of the living space.

In some regions, including flood-prone areas where water must be allowed to exit a home's crawl space after flooding occurs, vented crawl spaces are still the rule under local building codes. In others, such as very dry climates, it's not necessary to condition the crawl space. Instead, you'll want to thermally isolate the living space from the crawl space. This is done by first filling the joist cavities with batt insulation, and then installing rigid foam sheathing boards to the underside of the floor joists, wrapping the sill plate and band joist (see figure 7.6) and carefully taping or otherwise sealing the joints between the foam boards. Another option is to use spray foam, covering all of the floor wood that's exposed in the crawl space, including joists, the underside of the subfloor above, the sill plate, and the band joist; this will air seal and insulate at the same time. Insulating the "ceiling" of the crawl space in this way allows air to circulate through the crawl space but prevents heat loss from or cold air infiltration into the living space. This approach will also keep any naturally occurring radon from entering the living space.

⇒ Basement Retrofit Strategies ⇐

Basements and their foundations come in all shapes and sizes, so the details of each basement retrofit strategy will be different. But all retrofits start with a basic choice: work from the exterior, or work from the interior? What is right for you will depend on your particular situation. I cover the basics below and describe some of the techniques I used for our basement retrofit. For a list of technical books and web links about basement retrofitting, see the Resources appendix.

⇒ Retrofitting from the Outside ⇐

An exterior basement retrofit can be a monster project. It requires the removal of soil to expose the entire basement foundation, so that a waterproof membrane can be applied to the masonry on the exterior. Foam boards are added against the membrane. Foundation drains are installed, and then the soil is backfilled against the foam boards. Sometimes a sump pump and well are installed inside the basement to ensure that any water that does seep in can be pumped out and away. This approach is expensive and disruptive due to the fact that all landscape plants and hardscape features, such as fences, decks, or patios adjacent to the house, might need to be removed for the duration of the job and then reinstalled. Major soil excavation can be required, as well. Properly executed, this method works to dry out a chronically wet basement, so it can potentially be worth the headache.

⇒ Retrofitting from the Inside ⇐

If you have a chronically wet basement but decide that a major basement and foundation retrofit isn't financially feasible, it is possible to "divorce" the problem basement from the rest of the house. This is just like the vented crawl space retrofit (see figure 7.6). The ceiling of the basement, along with the sill plate and rim joist, is sealed using spray foam or carefully lapped and taped rigid foam boards. This method isn't ideal because of the possibility that moisture from the floor above—from a kitchen or bathroom, perhaps—might enter the sealed floor cavity and not be able to dry or escape. Then the damp wood structure can potentially rot, causing structural failure of the floor and joists. Still, carefully planned and executed, this method can help solve heat loss through a wet basement without the necessity and expense of completely solving

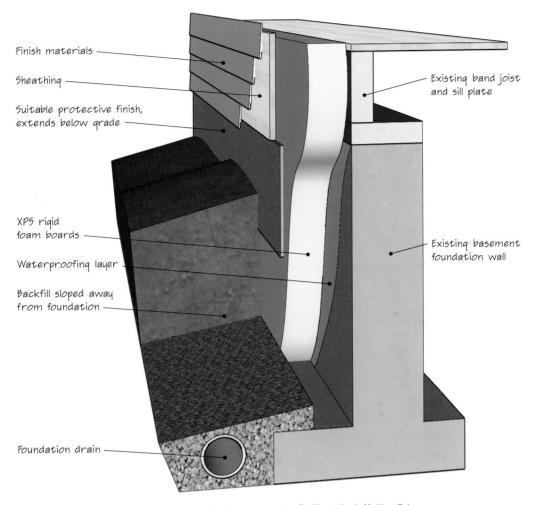

Finish materials

Sheathing

Suitable protective finish,
extends below grade

XPS rigid
foam boards

Waterproofing layer

Backfill sloped away
from foundation

Foundation drain

Existing band joist
and sill plate

Existing basement
foundation wall

FIGURE 7.7 This is one approach to an exterior basement retrofit. Illustration by Matthew Baker.

moisture issues. It's a good, second-place alternative to a full exterior basement retrofit.

As I said before, any basement retrofit where the aim is to create livable, conditioned space must start with solving moisture and water problems. Otherwise, retrofit and finish materials will be compromised by water damage, mold, and mildew. But what if your basement is already finished? How can you tell if moisture issues were resolved prior to the basement renovation? Was insulation installed, and if so, was it installed properly? Moisture problems will present themselves to you as musty smells, water stains, mildew stains, mold, and warping or buckling of finish materials. Lack of insulation might be indicated if the basement temperatures are markedly different from the rest of the house, despite being heated and cooled. Your HERS report and both interior and exterior thermal images of the foundation and basement walls can also indicate whether or not insulation was installed. If, as with our original "finished" basement, you're experiencing many of these symptoms, you'll need to remove and discard the existing finish materials. Once mold and mildew get a foothold in porous, natural materials like wood, it can be nearly impossible to get rid of them—especially in a damp basement where materials will experience some level of dampness at all times.

One more caveat about finished basements: before choosing to retrofit a basement, it should be tested for radon. Especially if the finished space is intended to be used on a daily basis for many hours over a long period of time (as in a bedroom or home office, where eight hours or more each day can be spent over many years), because repeated, prolonged exposure to radon has been shown to cause cancer. Radon test kits are commercially available at big box home improvement centers and are easy to use, or the test can be done by a professional home inspector. If radon is found in large amounts, radon remediation should be addressed before any retrofitting for energy efficiency starts. This isn't an empty warning—the EPA puts radon second only to smoking as a leading cause of lung cancer, so make radon remediation a priority.

That said, once old finish materials are removed down to the masonry surface of the basement walls and floor slab, all surfaces should be cleaned and mold and mildew remediated. It's not only important to clean the surface, but also to kill any mold or mildew spores so that they won't simply grow back. This can be done with common household bleach (1 cup to 1 gallon of water, sprayed on and left without rinsing), but there are many commercially available mold removal solutions and natural approaches that can be used as well. If bleach is used, be sure to ventilate the area and wear goggles, rubber gloves, and a ventilator. Then, let the surfaces dry completely before starting retrofit work.

Retrofitting Basement Walls

The basic approach is to build an interior double wall and floating floor by first adding an air- and moisture-sealing layer, followed by an insulating layer, and then finish surfaces. In theory, this is simple. In practice, it can be difficult to keep humid air from sneaking around the insulating layer and condensing on the cool masonry surfaces behind it, encouraging mold. That's why, except for very

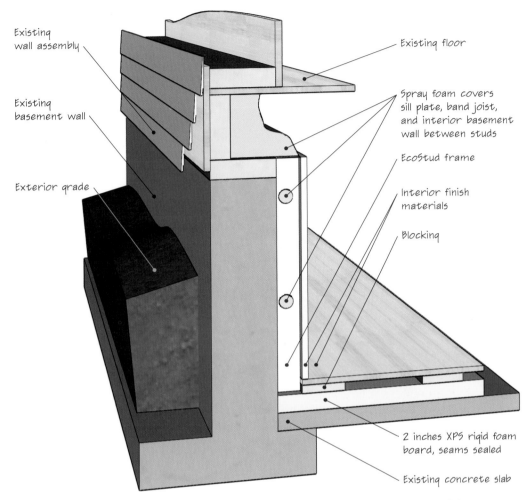

Existing wall assembly

Existing floor

Existing basement wall

Spray foam covers sill plate, band joist, and interior basement wall between studs

EcoStud frame

Exterior grade

Interior finish materials

Blocking

2 inches XPS rigid foam board, seams sealed

Existing concrete slab

FIGURE 7.8 This illustration shows the elements of our basement wall retrofit. Illustration by Matthew Baker.

dry climates, I steer people away from building a simple double wall and filling it with loose-fill or batt insulation. I prefer spray foam or carefully sealed foam boards because they discourage moisture problems from condensation, instead of air-permeable insulation types in basements.

The first step is to install a framework to which finish materials can be attached. In my basement, I used the plastic EcoStud track and stud system, and it worked very well. It's a good project if you have some DIY experience. One track is laid on the floor, secured with construction adhesive, and another is screwed to the underside of the joists above. Then plastic studs are cut to size and then snapped into grooves that are spaced every 8 inches along the tracks. I spaced the studs at the standard 16 inches apart, skipping every other slot in the tracks. At this point, the EcoStud system feels a bit flimsy. It's actually pretty easy to remove or add a stud because they're so lightweight and flexible. Once the spray foam was installed it would act as an adhesive, binding the whole system together.

FIGURE 7.9 I install the EcoStud track and stud. The tracks, installed on the floor and ceiling, have slots cut in them, allowing the stud ends to pop right in and then stay put without fasteners. Photograph by Sherri James.

FIGURE 7.10 After installing the EcoStuds, I spray Foam it Green spray foam between them, 2 to 3 inches thick. Once cured, the spray foam acts as an adhesive, gluing the whole wall together and to the block basement foundation walls. Photograph by Sherri James.

Before spray foam, though, I ran the electrical wiring through the EcoStuds. Since the EcoStuds have predrilled holes for things like electrical and plumbing, this was a piece of cake. Next, I spray foamed the wall cavities from floor to ceiling, making sure to completely fill the sill plate and band joist area at the top of the basement walls. Not only does the cured spray foam act as a great insulator and sealer, but it also works like an adhesive, bonding to the old masonry walls, wood sill plate and band joist, and plastic EcoStuds. Fully cured, all the separate parts become one solid unit, ready for finish materials.

I laid the foam on fairly thick so that it would be at least 2 to 3 inches deep in any one place. This was especially important at the top of the basement walls where they extended above the ground. Those portions of the walls were conducting heat, not into the 50°F (10°C) dirt, but often into the 20°F (–7°C) winter air outside. At the sill plate area, my exterior retrofit and interior basement retrofit would overlap, making for a nice, comfortable basement. It would also help keep heat from moving into the basement from the rest of the house on its way outside, following the laws of thermodynamics. Paying attention to the aboveground portion of foundation walls is especially important in any basement retrofit project.

I chose to use spray foam, but rigid foam sheathing boards can also be used on walls. Instead of the track and stud system, Z-furring is used to attach the foam boards to the masonry surface. Sealing between the boards with spray foam is important to keep humid air from flowing through the cracks and condensing on the wall behind it. Close attention should also be paid to the sill plate and band joist to make sure the foam board completely covers all of the surfaces and is well sealed between each piece. Another wall solution for masonry surfaces is the Quadlock R-ETRO system, which uses special plastic brackets and proprietary EPS foam blocks. See "A Masonry DER Solution" in chapter 6 for more on this product.

Retrofitting Basement Floors

For our floor renovation, I'd decided to use EcoStud Z-furring and 2-inch thick XPS foam panels from my local home improvement center. The foam panels would be allowed to "float" above the concrete but would be held in place by the edges of the Z-furring and edge sealed against the surrounding panels and the walls with spray foam. This would allow any moisture that happened to percolate up through the concrete floor to drain down to the floor drains. In each

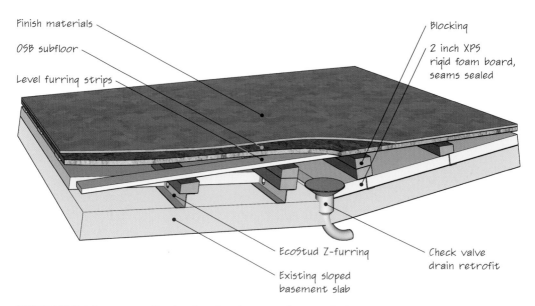

Finish materials

OSB subfloor

Level furring strips

Blocking

2 inch XPS rigid foam board, seams sealed

EcoStud Z-furring

Existing sloped basement slab

Check valve drain retrofit

FIGURE 7.11 This is a cross section drawing of our basement floor retrofit. Once insulation materials were installed on the sloped concrete floor, I added a level, finished floor above it. Illustration by Matthew Baker.

of the three floor drains in my basement, I installed a special check valve (see the Resources appendix for more information) that allows water to flow into the drain but doesn't allow sewer gases or radon to seep back out. I also decided to replace the 20-year-old sump pump and seal that opening with a proper sump pump cover. This means that the final source of swamp smell, the old drains and sump well, would be closed off from allowing sewer gas and radon from getting into the basement.

In some situations, very minor water intrusion, either through walls or wicking up through floor slabs, can be handled by installing a layer of drainage mat material as part of a floor and wall retrofit. Drainage mats are made of a waterproof plastic that is pressed with a dimpled design. It is manufactured in rolls that are rolled out and installed against the masonry of the basement floor and walls. Then insulation and finish materials are installed over it. The dimples create an air space and small channels between the concrete floor surface and the mat where water can drain. Since the mat itself is waterproof, moisture isn't allowed up into the finish materials. Properly integrated with a floor drain system, this waffle-textured mat material allows water to flow behind insulation materials, into the floor drains, and away from the basement. Proper installation is key and a drain mat won't handle large amounts of water, but it's a good solution if you're at all concerned about minor water

FIGURE 7.12 In this basement floor retrofit, a textured drain mat was first installed, and then a layer of 2-inch XPS foam board. The drain mat allows minor water intrusion to flow to the floor drain without contacting finish materials. Photograph by Greg Pedrick, NYSERDA, deep retrofit pilot project.

intrusion in your basement retrofit. For more information about drain mats, see the Resources appendix.

Completing the Transformation

Winter, our songwriting teenager, was excited to see the retrofitted basement come together. She wanted to have a hand in designing the room she hoped to spend a lot of time in, so we let her pick the paint color and some of the finish materials. I consulted with her on where pieces of furniture might go and the lighting plan. For the finished floor I used a similar approach to the old red dance floor. I allowed the foam board insulation layer to follow the slope of the old concrete slab and then used blocks to build a level, ¾" OSB subfloor surface above that. Then we finished it off with some recycled content carpet and cork flooring, a pine ceiling, compact fluorescent recessed lighting, a slate fireplace with a small gas-log heater, and a deep red paint on the walls—Winter's pick.

While the red was a little shocking at first, we realized that it worked, not only to help make the room a vibrant, creative space, but also as an homage to the red dance floor of our neighbor's, Art and Kate's, era. We also moved in an old log bed that Sherri and I had built during our "salad days" out of pine trees felled by a big ice storm in Tennessee. Its presence makes the music room a comfortable and private guest room when friends and family come to stay.

FIGURES 7.13A AND 7.13B Here's the scene in our basement before the retrofit (top) and after (bottom): pictures worth a thousand words!

Chapter Eight

RETROFITTING HOME SYSTEMS

BACK IN *2001,* WHEN WE FIRST FOUND OUR HOUSE AND TOLD OUR kids we would be moving, Winter (then age two) shouted, "YAY! We're movin' to Ohio and we're gonna live in a tent!" When we stopped laughing long enough to explain that we would actually be moving into a nice little house, Winter seemed a little disappointed. Her confusion was understandable. While researching places we might like to live, we had spent several nice weekends camping in the local state parks near our prospective new town. To Winter, Ohio had become synonymous with some great frontier where people camped out, roasting hot dogs and marshmallows over a fire every night. "It's still pretty cold there," Sherri consoled her, "so we'll probably be more comfortable in a house." Disappointed, Winter resigned herself to regular-old-house living.

Friends from Nashville helped us move into our new house at the end of March. It was Winter's third birthday, and I don't think that we've ever topped the birthday present of a new bed in a new bedroom in a new house. We went to bed tired but excited to start a new life in our cozy little house, unaware of what it had in store for us now or in the years to come.

The next morning, we woke up cold. "Terrific," I thought. "Only day two in this house and we've already got a problem with the heating system." Sherri and the kids wrapped up in down comforters, and I headed for the furnace in the basement. No fans ran and no flame roared, although power and gas seemed to be working fine in the rest of the house. I prodded and probed the decades-old hulk of a furnace with my multi-tester and found the culprit: a faulty relay. I called several local plumbing and heating supply houses in town looking for the part. Phones rang and rang, but nobody picked up.

It was Saturday, and I was having my first small-town experience. With no phone success, I visited the corner hardware store, where the clerk told me I would be able to get the relay at Economy Supply, the pro supply shop across town. Today, I asked, hopefully? Oh, no, not until Monday morning. Plumbing supply places around here aren't open on the weekend. My other option would be to try my luck in Columbus, a three-hour round trip by car. Resigned to waiting it out, we started a fire in the fireplace, gathered as many comforters and sleeping bags as we could find, and camped out in the living room.

Winter had been right after all—it was more than a little like living in a tent in Ohio. Was it a bad omen? Nope, just a reminder of how homeownership and parenthood both come with responsibilities, some of which can present themselves at rather inopportune moments. It certainly wasn't the only time I'd spend a Saturday repairing something or other around my house. And looking back on it, maybe that little job was actually the first step in our deep energy retrofit journey, because it started me thinking about how to fix all of the other problems with this old house.

➤ Our Rolling Systems Retrofit ◄

In a sense, the deep energy retrofit of our home systems has been going on for years as we've replaced one old appliance after another. Several years before launching the DER, we'd replaced our old, corroded, tank-style water heater with a tankless, natural gas–fired unit, which significantly reduced our gas bill. Not long after that, that old furnace died completely, beyond repair. We carefully selected a new HVAC system that delivered notably better efficiency and comfort, and we paid a premium. The new system was properly sized to our old, leaky house, with a 97 percent efficient natural gas furnace and a super-efficient (16 SEER) air conditioner. Another early system improvement was replacing all but a few of the incandescent lightbulbs in the house with compact fluorescents and LEDs. After we started the actual DER project, it almost became a joke: when is the next appliance going to fail? First, it was the old stove, which we replaced with a convection oven that reduced cooking times and temperatures by 25 percent. Then it was the refrigerator, more than 10 years old, which we replaced with a small, Energy Star–rated model. After that the washing machine gave up the ghost, and its replacement was a front loading water and energy miser.

Our dryer was a recent failure. Replacing it meant making a hard choice: stick with natural gas or go electric? Natural gas dryers

Recycling Refrig-a-saurs

FIGURE 8.1 Another refrigerator is recycled at JACO Environmental. Photograph by Jeff Wilson.

Michael Dunham, director of energy and environmental services at JACO Environmental, had a career as a rock concert promoter cut short by a freak surfing accident. "After about two years of recovery, I ended up with one leg shorter than the other," he recalled, "and I decided it was time for a new profession." That's how Michael ended up becoming the "Fridge Guy."

JACO Environmental is a state-of-the-art refrigerator and air conditioner recycling plant in Stow, Ohio. One of more than two dozen around the country, these plants are remarkable because they are able to completely shred an old appliance while separating it into its constituent parts, ready for reuse. The "demanufacturing"

process goes like this: consumers sign up for an appointment and a truck arrives to remove the offending appliance. Usually the homeowner is given a rebate check for $30 to $50 as a modest incentive. The refrigerator is then trucked to a JACO plant where the refrigerants—which are powerful greenhouse gases—are carefully removed from the compressor and refrigerant lines and sent out to be destroyed. Then the compressor is cut out, loaded into a bin, and sent to another company for its own demanufacturing process. Finally, the rest of the shell is dropped into an enormous, wailing machine and completely shredded.

The appliances are shredded in a "negative nitrogen" environment, inside the sealed machine. This allows for capture of the greenhouse gases embodied in the foam insulation of the walls and doors of the refrigerators. Like the compressor gas, that gas is stored so that it can be destroyed later. Using a series of vortexes in the wind tunnel–like operation, other materials are automatically sorted into bins. Steel, aluminum, copper, plastic, and foam powder from the insulation are all separated and sent out for reuse in other products.

In all, more than 95 percent of each appliance is recycled, providing raw materials for a new generation of super-efficient appliances. In the process, thousands of tons of dangerous, old-school chloroflourocarbon (CFC) greenhouse gases are removed from the environment. JACO Environmental had taken the multi-material complexity of a fully manufactured appliance destined for a landfill and rendered it useful again. Check the Resources appendix for a link to see if JACO Environmental offers appliance recycling in your area.

are generally considered cheaper to run, but our situation is unique because of the grid-tied solar panels we'd installed. We weren't using all of the solar power we were generating. Instead, we were selling it back to the utility company at a loss. Since our new washer's super spin cycle wrung the clothes out so well, less energy was required for drying laundry. We decided to buy an energy efficient electric dryer and use it during the day to take advantage of that solar power that would otherwise flow out to the grid. The last appliance to die was our dishwasher. Its replacement is super-efficient and very quiet, and it uses less water and detergent than the old beast. With that, we had completed the random rolling retrofit of our old appliances.

As I described in chapter 3, we'd already made a start on improving the efficiency of electronic devices, too, and we'd used a Kill-A-Watt meter to test for "vampire loads" (also known as standby power). These continuous power draws, although small, add up to serious inefficiency over time. As a matter of fact, until 2010, when most countries enacted rules to limit an appliance's standby power to 1 watt (½ watt by 2013), that load could account for as much as 10 percent of a home's overall energy use. Thus, you could potentially see significant energy savings when you replace pre-2013 appliances and electronics with newer devices. You can also manage the load yourself by plugging devices into a power strip that you can switch off when they're not in use.

New concerns related to home systems arose once we sealed the building envelope of our house. One of those issues centered on our indoor air quality and how fresh air circulates through the house. Pre-DER, our leaky house supplied a limited amount of fresh air through all of the energy-sucking cracks and gaps. Once the building envelope was sealed up those avenues for fresh air were gone. In our now-airtight home, use of household cleaners, off-gassing of paints and carpets, contaminants tracked in on our shoes from outdoors, and even plain old humidity and carbon dioxide could become an indoor pollution problem. We could let in fresh air by leaving a window open year-round, but that direct loss of energy to the outdoors was exactly what we had just fixed with the insulation and air sealing of the exterior shell. Instead, we installed an energy recovery ventilator, or ERV, (for details on this and other types of ventilation systems, see chapter 3.)

Our ERV is 95 percent efficient, recovering 95 percent of the energy in the outgoing air. I've set it to run all day, while we're generating free solar energy, and to come on intermittently at night. If we leave on vacation, we turn it off. One of the fringe benefits of the ERV is that it now supplies fresh air to our basement and exhausts air that contains radon at the same time. Between our basement retrofit, which discourages the poisonous gas from entering the space in the first place, and the ERV diluting what radon sneaks in past the retrofit, the radon levels in our basement are now negligible.

As we replaced things, we also looked for opportunities to automate for energy efficiency. We added common sense items like a programmable thermostat with humidity controls and vacation settings. We installed timers on bathroom exhaust fans so that they run long enough to exhaust stale air and humidity but then shut off automatically. Exterior LED lights are on dusk-to-dawn motion sensors. This type of off-the-shelf automation is available at a very low cost and pays itself back quickly.

We've squeezed each of the various systems in our house to make sure they're as energy efficient as possible. This all adds to the bottom line energy savings of our DER. Then we've automated what systems we can using inexpensive, off-the-shelf automation. In the process, we've made sure that our comfort and indoor air quality is radically improved, taking advantage of our now properly air-sealed and insulated home. Air seal, insulation, and finally systems—they're the pillars upon which a good DER stands.

Implementing Your Systems Retrofit

 "Home systems" refers to the various ways energy is used to do work in your home. HVAC, water heating, lighting, appliances, electronics, home automation, and energy monitoring all contribute to overall energy use. Breaking down the work done in your home into systems makes it easy to isolate and test each area for inefficiency. Knowing which systems use the most energy can help you decide where to attack first to get the biggest benefit.

If the idea of completely replacing all of your home's systems at once leaves you financially shell-shocked, you're not alone. Don't worry—it's not necessary. Our random, rolling home systems retrofit occurred as much by happenstance as by planning, but it's that planning that's really important. While a few of your home's worst energy-wasters will need to be replaced right away, the rest can be allowed to die a natural death. If you've planned for those system failures in advance, then you'll be ready to replace an old unit with a highly efficient one. That will not only spread the financial strain out over time, but it will mean you're completely ready to deal with a system's eventual failure without needing to panic and buy the first, inefficient appliance or system you come across.

⊶ Heating and Cooling Systems ⊷

Heating and cooling make up about 46 percent of the average homeowner's energy costs. Depending on your climate and habits, you may use more heating than cooling or more cooling than heating. That makes your furnace and air conditioner—your HVAC system—the prime energy waste suspect. It will also likely be one of the largest single expenses after your extensive, DER building envelope improvements.

Your HVAC system is one of the most critical pieces of the deep energy retrofit puzzle. This is one place where you'll really want to do your homework before purchasing a system. Don't wait until your old system fails to begin the search—most bad HVAC decisions

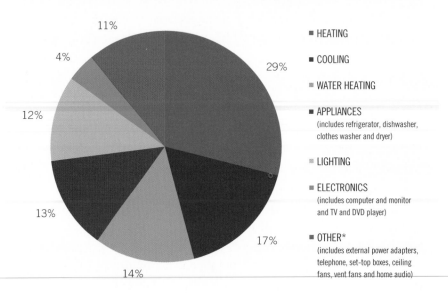

WHERE DOES MY MONEY GO?
ANNUAL ENERGY BILL FOR A TYPICAL SINGLE FAMILY HOME IS APPROXIMATELY $2,200

- HEATING
- COOLING
- WATER HEATING
- APPLIANCES
  (includes refrigerator, dishwasher, clothes washer and dryer)
- LIGHTING
- ELECTRONICS
  (includes computer and monitor and TV and DVD player)
- OTHER*
  (includes external power adapters, telephone, set-top boxes, ceiling fans, vent fans and home audio)

FIGURE 8.2 Ever wonder how your energy bills break down by system? Here are some interesting statistics to help understand energy use in your home. Source: US Department of Energy.

are made when you wake up on Saturday morning to a cold house and all of the parts stores are closed. Having to make a split second decision on such a critical system almost guarantees a mistake that you'll have to live with for a very long time.

Many HVAC systems are sized incorrectly to the homes in which they're installed. If your HVAC unit is too small, your unit won't keep you warm or cool enough for comfort. Too large, and you'll experience huge temperature swings as it cycles (turns on and off), trying to keep your house at an even temperature. You can compare the performance of an HVAC system to that of a car engine. A properly sized system is like a car traveling at an even 55 mph on the highway. The car gets better gas mileage than it would in stop and start traffic because it doesn't have to repeatedly come to a stop and then accelerate again, which burns up extra fuel. The constant stopping and starting is also much harder on a car's engine than driving at a steady speed, so it will wear out sooner.

A properly sized HVAC system will run more constantly at a lower, even speed. Without having to stop and start so much, its working parts will last longer and provide greater efficiency. You'll also be more comfortable because the temperature will remain even over time, whether heating or cooling. Low-speed operation of the air conditioner has the added benefit of continually removing moisture from the air, dehumidifying better than a unit that constantly cycles on and off. This gives you a much more comfortable, lower humidity level in the house. In our house, we've found that we can be quite comfortable at 77°F (25°C) to 78°F (26°C) during cooling months in a house with 55 percent relative humidity or lower. Higher than 60 percent relative humidity, you start to feel "sticky." Then you turn the temperature down, making the air conditioner work harder, wasting energy. More than 70 percent relative humidity and mold can easily begin to grow.

Undersizing of an HVAC system is rare, but oversizing is quite common. This results in a more expensive system that will break down more often and will be more expensive to operate than an optimally sized system. Right-sizing of HVAC units is a must, and any HVAC installer worth his or her salt should be capable of doing exhaustive "Manual J" calculations to ensure that you're not over-paying for an oversized unit. "Manual J" refers to a publication by the Air Conditioning Contractors of America (ACCA) that calculates heating and cooling "loads" in the house to help right-size heating and cooling units. If your system will include ducts, then an ACCA

Manual D calculation should be done to ensure that your ducts don't interfere with delivering the right amount of conditioned air to each room. Many computer applications now exist to make this calculation easier for HVAC installers to accomplish with a greater degree of accuracy than doing the calculations by hand. If you've already had a home energy rater do a complete energy audit on your home, your HVAC contractor can use that information to help size your equipment properly. Better yet, introduce your home energy rater and your HVAC contractor and have them work together to find just the right solution.

Once a proper system size is figured, there are still many decisions to be made. Generally speaking, the more efficient the HVAC unit, the more expensive it will be in its initial costs. That means that the calculations have only just begun. As the homeowner, you'll need to weigh the costs and benefits of paying a bit more for a high-efficiency unit now against higher utility bills into the future with a less efficient model. In our case, I had to pay a 25 percent premium to get a high-efficiency HVAC system over a standard model. At the time, I calculated about a seven-year payback on that initial extra investment, but I hadn't really thought about the better comfort that we would experience with the more expensive unit. The standard HVAC didn't include things like a variable speed fan or dual speed compressor on the AC, so it wouldn't have maintained the lower humidity levels at higher indoor temperatures the way the high-efficiency HVAC does. That means that we're saving even more money, since we're more comfortable at a higher temperature in the summer with the high-efficiency model. We'd have had to keep the less efficient AC cooling more to have the same comfort level.

It's also important that your HVAC unit is installed in the right place. Some units are installed in attics, while others are installed in basements, garages, or special closets. The compressor and condenser parts of the air conditioner or heat pump will be installed outside, but the rest of the system, including the ductwork, should be installed inside the thermal envelope in a conditioned space. This will keep the system from having to compete with the outdoor air temperature to heat or cool your house. Many contractors traditionally install HVAC equipment in attics, but if your attic is the vented variety or if your system is installed outside the thermal envelope, it should be moved within the thermal envelope to a well-insulated, air sealed, conditioned space.

Decoding Efficiency Ratings for HVAC

- **AFUE** stands for annual fuel utilization efficiency. Used in rating furnaces or boilers for efficiency. A higher number denotes better efficiency. For example, if a furnace has an AFUE rating of 93, then 93 percent of the energy in the fuel consumed becomes heat, with the other 7 percent lost to the exterior, through the exhaust vent.
- **SEER** stands for seasonal energy efficiency ratio. Used in rating air conditioners (or the cooling cycle in heat pumps) for efficiency. A higher rating denotes better efficiency. This rating denotes equipment efficiency over an entire cooling season.
- **EER** stands for energy efficiency ratio. Similar to SEER, but denotes efficiency of equipment at a single moment, under precise conditions. SEER has mostly replaced EER as a more reliable indicator of overall equipment efficiency.
- **HSPF** stands for heating seasonal performance factor. A rating of the heating efficiency of air-source heat pumps. A higher number denotes better efficiency.
- **COP** stands for coefficent of performance. Also used as a measure of performance of heat pumps for heating. A higher number denotes better performance.

Going All Electric?

Many people take the opportunity of a DER to go all electric, removing fossil fuel–powered appliances like furnaces, boilers, and water heaters, and replacing them with electric units. While this may or may not result in dollar savings for the homeowner, it will likely result in a lower carbon footprint in the long run. Even if your electricity is generated from coal, most states have now passed minimum renewable energy generation rules for utilities (in Ohio, 12.5 percent of our energy must come from renewables by 2025). That means your all electric home will actually get cleaner over time, while natural gas and heating oil appliances will get dirtier as they age and lose efficiency. All electric homes also avoid the danger that back drafting of flue gases can pose. Finally, you may find that incentives for high-efficiency electric geothermal or air-source heat pumps, combined with incentives for solar power, add up to an "extreme, deep green" that's hard to resist.

Choosing an HVAC System

What's the best HVAC system for your situation? That will depend on many factors, but here are some choices and guidelines. Whatever your choice, make sure to check thoroughly for federal, state, local, and utility company financial incentives for very high-efficiency HVAC installations (see the Resources appendix for links).

Electric resistance heating: Baseboard or stand-alone plug-in heaters are the most common examples of this type of heating system, although some standard (non-heat pump) electric central heating systems use it, too. In most cases, electric resistance heating is the least efficient, most expensive way to heat a home. However, if your home's thermal envelope is on the extreme-efficiency end of the DER, or if your home uses little energy for heating, it may be hard to justify more expensive equipment.

Furnace: Typical furnace choices include natural gas or oil. Look for AFUE ratings greater than 90, a variable-speed fan, and high-quality thermostat and humidity controls. New units should have a sealed combustion unit with both air intake from and exhaust to the outdoors.

Boiler: Natural gas, oil, or electric boilers heat water, which is then piped through radiators or tubing loops embedded in floors (radiant floor heating). Look for AFUE ratings greater than 90, high-efficiency pumps, and sealed combustion units.

Air conditioner: The Energy Star program demands a minimum SEER of 14 to receive its endorsement. But for a DER, you should seek out no less than a 16 SEER unit or better if your budget allows (models up to 27 SEER are available). A variable-speed fan and compressor, humidity controls, and environmentally friendly refrigerant are all important.

Air-source heat pump: This type of HVAC unit is more efficient than a standard furnace and air conditioner and will both heat and cool. It's helpful to think of a heat pump as an air conditioner that has the ability to work in reverse. An air conditioner works by using a refrigerant to absorb the excess heat in your home. That refrigerant takes the absorbed heat outdoors where it is "dumped" into the outdoor air. In the wintertime, a heat pump works in reverse to absorb heat from the outdoor air and "dump" it into your home. Heat pumps are most efficient in climates where there is a need for both wintertime heating and summertime cooling. They are less efficient in very cold climates; however, the latest technology in mini-split, ductless air-source heat pumps stays effective even when temperatures drop well below zero. Energy Star minimums are 8.2 HSPF and 14.5 SEER, but for maximum DER effectiveness, strive for higher ratings.

Geothermal heat pump: This type of heat pump is the most efficient form of heating and cooling on the market today, but it's also the most expensive, because deep wells or trenches must be dug to accommodate long loops of tubing. Water or coolant runs through the tubing, which is embedded in the constant temperature environment of the soil. This even temperature alleviates the problem of declining efficiency in air-source heat pumps as outdoor air gets colder. With a geothermal heat pump, heat is drawn from underground during wintertime and dumped underground during the summer. Minimum efficiency ratings, depending on system type, should be an EER of 16 to 20 and a COP of 3.5 to 4.1. Many geothermal heat pumps offer a domestic hot water option. This option uses the waste heat from the air-conditioning cycle, which would usually be dumped into the ground via the water loops, to pre-heat domestic hot water. Any time the air-conditioning cycle is being used, water is heated as a by-product, for free.

Ductless mini-split heat pump: These small air-source heat pumps are very efficient and a good option when there is no existing duct system in the house or when an addition requires additional HVAC capacity. A small compressor/condenser is mounted outdoors, and a small air handling unit is installed in each room. Choose a model with high SEER ratings.

Technology has brought about some other HVAC options that can help with efficiency and comfort. With several thermostats in different zones of the house, automated dampers can be installed in your ductwork to restrict or allow air flow through the system to different areas. This makes your duct system more efficient by only delivering heated or cooled air to the rooms where it is needed. This not only saves money but also helps to keep your house at a more even temperature. Creating heating zones used to be very expensive because it required installing separate HVAC units for each zone. Now, automated damping systems make it possible to create zones using one central HVAC unit, relatively inexpensive dampers, and remote thermostats. This makes it easy and affordable to retrofit into an existing system.

High-tech thermostats that include humidity sensors are also much more common today, giving homeowners better control and heightened comfort. Installing a humidifier for use during the heating season can help with comfort, but beware: a deep energy retrofitted home won't dry out the same way an unretrofitted home will, so a humidifier can cause too much humidity. As a matter of fact, the first time my furnace came on after the DER air-sealing and insulation of our home, our humidity levels spiked up to more than 70 percent. I was puzzled at first, but then remembered the humidifier I'd installed, which had automatically come on when I fired up the furnace. Once I removed the humidifier, humidity levels in our house leveled out for a comfortable 50 to 55 percent all winter long—no humidifier needed.

Whatever type of HVAC system you decide to have installed, make sure your contractor returns to perform scheduled cleaning and maintenance to ensure the unit is functioning up to its potential. Learn how to change filters on ducted systems, and do so regularly. This will help guarantee a long, useful life, protecting your investment.

– Adding a Ventilation System –

Public health officials consider poor indoor air quality (IAQ) a health hazard that can cause or exacerbate asthma, cancer, and other serious health problems. As you implement your DER and eliminate all sources of "accidental" ventilation, it's important to provide ventilation mechanically by using intake/exhaust fans, a heat recovery ventilator (HRV), or an energy recovery ventilator (ERV).

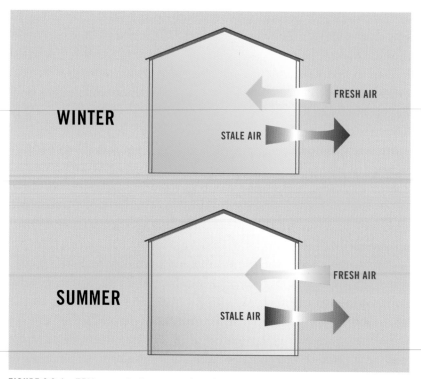

FIGURE 8.3 An ERV prevents the energy from heating or cooling from escaping the home while it exhausts stale air and admits fresh air from the outside. Illustration courtesy of UltimateAir.

If you live in a very mild climate, a simple exhaust fan and fresh air intake will solve an air-quality problem. If you live in a cold or hot climate, though, where you spend the bulk of your energy bill on heating and cooling, the simple exhaust fan will not only exhaust stale air, but it will also exhaust the energy that was used to heat or cool that air. That's why opting for an HRV or ERV might be a better choice. These integrate with the existing duct system in your house to constantly exchange stale air for fresh air. As they do so, they recover the energy used to heat or cool the indoor air and keep it inside the thermal envelope. An HRV is used in heating-only climates, recovering the heat from the exhaust air to heat the incoming fresh air from outside. An ERV works in both heating and cooling climates, recovering the heating energy or cooling energy in your indoor stale air to help heat or condition the incoming fresh air, depending on the season.

Some run at low speed year-round, while others are tied into your HVAC system and will run only when your furnace or air conditioner runs. Many will offer some form of air filtration option as well, removing pollen, dust, and other airborne irritants. Another nice option is a mode that switches off the energy recovery between certain outdoor temperatures, pumping naturally cool air into your home on perfect spring and fall evenings when the house is hot and stuffy but the outdoor air is cool and comfortable. This can save even more money by avoiding the need for expensive air-conditioning during "shoulder seasons."

⊶ Water Heating ⊷

After air heating and cooling, water heating is the next largest piece of your energy bill. Like your HVAC system, you expect your water heater to do its job and stay out of the way. It's not something you think about until you jump into the shower, expecting that warm cascade of water down your back, but instead get an icy surprise. Like planning for your HVAC unit to fail, having a plan for the day your water heater quits is important so that you don't just grab the first inefficient water heater to fix the problem.

When should you replace that old water heater? A good rule of thumb is that if it's more than 10 years old, you should replace it with a new one, especially if the old water heater is an electric resistance tank model. A 10-year-old water heater might only be working at 50 percent of its brand-new efficiency due to corrosion and mineral build up on the heating elements and tank interior.

Negative Pressure and Back Drafting

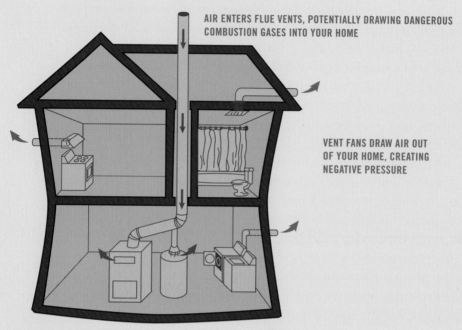

AIR ENTERS FLUE VENTS, POTENTIALLY DRAWING DANGEROUS COMBUSTION GASES INTO YOUR HOME

VENT FANS DRAW AIR OUT OF YOUR HOME, CREATING NEGATIVE PRESSURE

FIGURE 8.4 How negative pressure can lead to back drafting. Illustration by US Environmental Protection Agency.

When you exhaust air from your house—through bathroom or kitchen vents for example—the air pressure inside your house can become lower than that outside. This is called "negative pressure," and if the pressure difference between outdoors and indoors is large enough, outdoor air may be pulled into the house. Negative pressure becomes a problem if air is pulled into your home through combustion exhaust vents of furnaces, water heaters, and fireplaces, because the air may mix with dangerous flue gases, such as carbon monoxide. This is called back drafting. An ERV fitted with a pressure sensor can actually adjust the air pressure inside a home to maintain a very slight positive pressure at all times. If your home has a fireplace, furnace, or appliances that burn fossil fuels, be sure to get a pressure sensor.

Also, over the decade since that water heater was put into service, water heater technology has improved markedly. Options for new water heaters include standard tank-type models in electric or natural gas, tankless models in electric or natural gas, newer air- or ground-source heat pump models, and "hybrids," which typically combine two different types of water heaters to balance efficiency and comfort. Solar water heating is another option, and many solar water-heating systems can be integrated with radiators or radiant floor heating systems to help control heating costs, as well.

Your choice of a new water heater will depend on which type you're replacing, your climate, the types of fuel available to you, how much hot water you need, and your budget. Remember that a low "off the shelf" price doesn't guarantee that your choice will be the most economical—don't forget to consider installation costs, energy use over time, and the expected lifespan of the unit. As usual, a little research and basic math will go a long way in helping you make the best decision.

One basic decision is between natural gas and electric. Natural gas is relatively cheap right now, but electric water heaters are a bit safer, since they don't produce combustion gases or require a flame for heat. The easiest thing to do is to replace your current water heater with a new model of the same type. That way there's no extra expense in the installation process due to running a new natural gas line or more electric capacity when you switch from one type to the other. It's also a no-brainer to choose an Energy Star–rated water heater and to check the handy Energy Star label for the expected long-term energy use of each water heater you're considering. Using those labels, which clearly display a water heater's projected yearly energy use in dollars, you can easily figure out which models cost the most to operate over time in just a few minutes.

Standard tank units are common but offer little in savings. As a matter of fact, you won't find a standard electric water heater with an Energy Star label, since they're such big energy hogs. Some standard gas-fired units will have the Energy Star label, but so much newer technology exists in water heating today that a serious deep energy retrofitter will ask for more than a run-of-the-mill unit. At the very least, buy a superinsulated standard, gas-fired tank-style model with an Energy Star label.

Step up from there to a gas-fired, whole house tankless water heater. Tankless (or "on demand") units don't have to keep a tank of water hot 24 hours a day, so they run only when hot water is being used. The heart of a tankless water heater is a heat exchanger made up of many loops of metal tubing, through which water flows. When a tap is opened somewhere in the house, a flow sensor turns on a high-capacity gas burner (if you're standing next to a tankless water heater when someone uses the hot water, it sounds like a little jet engine). Water is instantaneously heated as it passes through the heat exchanger and heads to the open hot water tap. Once the tap is closed, the burner shuts off, waiting for another tap to open. Tankless models require a larger gas line to the unit and are more expensive to purchase than a tank heater, but their 20-year lifespan can pay for the extra expense. The energy savings—up to 50 percent if you're converting from a standard electric water heater and 30 percent from a standard gas water heater to a gas tankless model—can add up quickly.

Tankless water heaters are old news, though, when you consider newer air-source heat pump water heating technology. These electric water heaters are efficient enough to earn the coveted Energy Star rating. Essentially, air-source heat pump technology transfers heat from the surrounding air into the water in the tank, which is then used for household needs. The air surrounding the water heater is cooled and dehumidified as a by-product of water heating, which can be an added benefit if the water heater is installed in a slightly damp basement. While air-source heat pump water heaters work in all climates, they're ideal in climates with long cooling seasons, because the unit is doing double duty, acting like an air conditioner while heating water. This can lighten the load for your home's AC unit during the dog days of summer.

Interestingly, some ductless mini-split air-source heat pump HVAC units offer water heating as an option. During hot months when the unit is used for cooling, the waste heat generated in the process is used to heat water in a tank. This is similar to options offered in conjunction with a geothermal HVAC system. If you've installed, or will be installing, a geothermal heat pump HVAC system, consider adding super-efficient water heating to the system. This idea has been used to begin development of water "pre-heaters" that use the waste heat from your refrigerator for the same purpose. Again, these technologies are especially effective in hot-humid climates, since they have the benefit of using waste heat that would increase a home's cooling loads to perform a task that needs to be done anyway—in this case, making sure you never have to go without hot water.

Cool Energy Saving Gadgets

Aside from thinking about what kind of water heater you need, there are some other options that will help save energy and water. One is the Metlund D'MAND circulation pump. This little pump retrofits under the sink on the fixture farthest from the water heater. Walk into that room (typically a bathroom is chosen), and the pump is activated by a motion sensor. It immediately, quietly, begins pumping the cold water in the hot water line over into the cold water line and back to the water heater in a circulation loop. This is just like turning on the hot water tap and letting the water run down the drain until the hot water reaches the tap. In this case, though, that water is saved, and fed back to the water heater. Once the sensor in the pump "feels" the hot water reach the pump, it shuts off. When you turn on the hot water, it's already at the fixture, hot and ready to go. This saves a lot of water—it's estimated that 3 to 7 gallons of water are lost every time we wait for hot water to reach the tap. Over time, that really adds up.

Another nifty energy saver is one I first discovered while covering a plumbing and heating trade show for HGTVRemodels .com. I was stopped dead in my tracks when I saw the glint of copper on a table across the enormous show floor. As my producer protested, I beelined over to the other side of the convention center. There, carefully chained and locked to the table, was a valuable 3-foot piece of 2-inch diameter copper pipe, around which had been wound about 20 feet of ½-inch copper tubing. It was a heat exchanger, but I'd never seen anything like it before. This heat exchanger was clearly made to fit on a shower drain. I'd often wondered about the potential for this type of heat exchanger while taking a shower (some people sing in the shower; I think deep, deep energy retrofit thoughts).

Showers account for nearly 40 percent of hot water use in a home—the largest single use of hot water in the house. But what happens to all the heat in the water? It goes right down the drain, out of the house, into the sewer. That's where drain water heat recovery units come in. A drain water heat recovery unit uses heat from the drain water to preheat incoming cold water before it reaches the shower valve, recovering heat that would otherwise be lost. It's not high technology, but old technology reapplied to tap a heretofore untapped energy resource. If you're remodeling an old bath or installing a new one, consider installing a drain water heat recovery unit to stop your energy dollars going down the drain.

Solar water heating is also a possibility, although usefulness and payback times vary widely depending on where you live. The sun shines most during the spring, summer, and fall, but I need hot water during the winter, too. During the summer, a moderate- to small-sized solar water heating system could easily take care of our

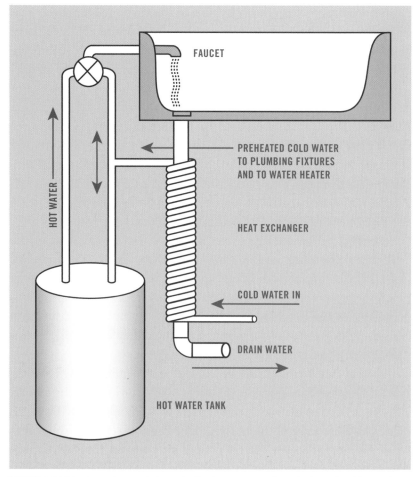

FIGURE 8.5 This shows how a drain water heat recovery unit works in a plumbing system. Illustration by US Department of Energy.

needs, but during the winter, I wouldn't be able to produce a fraction of that hot water from solar. That would make the system's initial cost outweigh future benefits. For more about this, see chapter 10.

So heating water in your home isn't just about making cold water hot. By thinking of water heating as part of your home's systems, you might be able to compound efficiencies by making various appliances do double or even triple duty. As home technology advances, we'll almost surely see waste heat from our refrigerators, air conditioners, and heat pumps redirected to better use in preheating domestic hot water supplies. Also, considering how much heating energy that literally goes down the drain, tapping into that source with a drain water heat recovery unit will be tempting, too.

⚊ Appliances ⚊

Appliances are items for which most of us feel completely qualified to select replacements without seeking professional advice. Choosing the smallest model that will do the job is a good start. Be sure to check the bright yellow Energy Star tags, which aim to compare "apples to apples" when it comes to energy efficiency performance in common household appliances like refrigerators, dishwashers, clothes washers, and dryers. By quickly referencing the Energy Star tag, we can immediately know how each appliance stacks up against its rivals. If we can also cross-reference that information with reliable third-party ratings on reliability, repair costs, and consumer satisfaction, we can make reasonably good choices on replacing appliances as they fail.

As I mentioned earlier in this chapter, I highly recommend the "rolling replacement" plan. Unless your appliances are well into their second decade, let them fail before you replace them. That will give you time to plan for the best replacement possible and ensure that the replacement saves you money on energy and upkeep over time.

Deep energy retrofitting requires that we delve a bit deeper than simply choosing energy efficient appliances. Rethinking the number of necessary appliances might be a good start. For example, do you really need more than one refrigerator? Many Americans swear by that second refrigerator or freezer in the garage, mostly to keep beverages cold or to store the excess from those super-sized warehouse club deals. I might argue that paying to store large amounts of perishable food in a second refrigerator or freezer is risky and expensive. What happens when the power goes out for three days? Now the extra freezer is a liability, since it will require purchasing, running, and maintaining a generator to keep the food from spoiling. I'd say that allowing the corner grocery store to hold that liability is a better choice. Simply live within the confines of a single, smaller refrigerator, and let the grocery store pay for the energy and upkeep of the extra refrigeration.

While the big appliances like refrigerators get our attention, don't forget to consider smaller appliances, especially smaller appliances that you use every day. In my house, we've replaced the electric drip coffee maker with an insulated French press. A traditional electric drip coffee maker uses some energy to boil the water, but even more to keep the carafe hot after brewing. By using an insulated French press, I only use energy to boil the water. After that, my coffee stays hot for hours without added energy. Microwaves are energy savers, too. They use less energy for small warming jobs in the kitchen than a stove top or full-sized oven. Ditto toaster ovens: if the item you want to cook will fit into your toaster oven, use it.

➤ Lighting ➤

Next on the list is lighting. You'd have to live in a cave to have missed the revolution in lighting over the last few decades. Since energy-wasting incandescent bulbs were fingered as culprits in our energy gluttony, they've been systematically demonized and nearly removed from modern life. This has mostly been done by government rules and regulations, which has some folks riled up about "lightbulb socialism." Who do those feds think they are, telling me what kind of lightbulb to buy? But that kind of thinking misses the point: It's not big government, but poor math skills that have kept the incandescent bulb on the market. The problem is that, while that incandescent bulb only costs 50 cents on the store shelf, using incandescent bulbs costs many hundreds of dollars (in energy costs) more over the long term compared with much more efficient compact fluorescent (CFL) and light-emitting diode (LED) bulbs. This also costs society in wasted energy and excess pollution from having to generate that extra power. In the end, if individuals can't make those basic calculations, we'll have to enforce them collectively through good laws.

That doesn't mean that those laws were perfect from the get-go. The first compact fluorescent bulb alternatives had a bad reputation for their poor color quality, long startup times, and flickering. Manufacturing processes improved, creating bulbs that offer more pleasing, instantaneous, flicker-free light. However, the mercury content of CFLs is an environmental concern. It makes the bulbs dangerous to dispose of in landfills, since the mercury can escape and contaminate groundwater supplies. That's one reason that LED lighting is a better alternative. LEDs are generally more energy efficient than even CFLs, they last a very long time, they're generally dimmable, and they're extremely sturdy compared with CFLs or incandescent bulbs. While the first LED bulbs had similar light quality issues to CFLs, those coming on the market now offer a variety of color temperatures that mimic the "soft white" and "warm white" light we we're used to from incandescent bulbs but at a fraction of the energy use. Though expensive when they were first available, LED prices are continuing to drop precipitously, making them the odds-on favorite to knock out CFLs and really lead the lighting revolution forward.

But is replacing your lightbulbs all you can do as a deep energy retrofitter concerned with lighting? Not hardly. The first place to look for more light with less energy when you're remodeling is from daylight. The best, most pleasing, and cheapest light comes from the sun, so finding ways to get that light into your home will obviate the need for artificial light in the first place. For more information on day lighting, see "Passive Solar Design" in chapter 10. Use of reflective and light colored surfaces can also cut down on the amount of light that each fixture needs to deliver to a space. While rich, dark colors in some rooms can create a cocoonlike ambience, using lighter colors in spaces where light is critical, like kitchens or offices, can help distribute light more evenly in that space. Another strategy in workspaces is to use small task lighting, like desk lamps, to light only the immediate area where work is being done instead of large, room-filling fixtures. A smaller bulb in a smaller fixture can be used up close for reading or countertop food prep, for example, instead of the scattershot approach of lighting an entire room from ceiling-mounted fixtures.

Since there's so much more to energy efficient lighting than simply replacing bulbs, it's best to make a lighting plan for each room before your retrofit begins. That way you'll be able to maximize the use of the strategies described here for the greatest energy savings possible.

⚊ Electronics ⚊

One of my favorite writers, Wendell Berry, refuses to use a computer when writing his novels, essays, and poetry. Berry talks about this in his essay, "Why I am NOT Going to Buy a Computer." Essentially, he argues that a computer, for him, is not worthy as a tool because it uses so much energy while not making the task of writing well one bit easier. While I humbly tapped away at a laptop to create this particular piece of unworthy literature, I still take Mr. Berry's point and apply it in my own way. Our lives are more and more cluttered with electronic devices, few of which provide usefulness as tools for better living. On the contrary, most of these devices waste inordinate amounts of our time which could be better spent reading a book, talking with our families and friends, playing music on an acoustic instrument, making a pie, or any other more soul-nourishing activity than one more round of Angry Birds.

That leads me to my first energy-saving tip when considering the purchase of just about anything, electronics especially. Just ask yourself one question: "Will this purchase make me, my family and friends, my community, my country, or my world better off?" And by "better off" I mean: will it make you a better person, give your family a truly richer life, or make the environment you live in cleaner and safer? For me, the middle ground between Wendell Berry's position and full-blown consumerism allows for a computer, a mobile phone, and a television. I can credit my computer for freeing me from a daily commute to work, my mobile phone for freeing me to leave my desk to walk my kids to school, and my television for enlightening my family through foreign and independent films and documentaries.

If you use electronics, it's important to choose the most energy-efficient tools. Again, look to the Energy Star label. Energy Star–rated electronic devices aim to be 40 to 50 percent more efficient than non-Energy Star–rated devices. The label not only ensures energy efficient operation but also has strict rules about vampire loads. However, relying on that label alone will only get you so far. Look a little deeper, and you'll find even more energy savings. For example, the most efficient laptop will beat the most efficient desktop computer most of the time. Since laptops are becoming more and more powerful from a computing standpoint, it makes sense to switch to a laptop for your computing needs. Go even further. Make sure that the power-saving options are enabled, which will put the computer to sleep but not completely off when you're not actively using it. While it's common for people to leave their computers on overnight, fully turning off your computer when you're done with it for the day can save even more. A general rule of thumb for printers is that inkjets use less energy than laser printers. Between using the Energy Star label in new purchases and shutting the printer down when it's not in use, printer energy use can drop markedly.

With televisions, newer LED technology offers big energy savings over older models. At the same time, new restrictions on acceptable levels of standby power usage have been going into effect. Ditto other home entertainment equipment—DVD players, sound systems, docking stations, and more are all becoming more miserly. The key with electronics is to employ a critical eye when purchasing devices, as well as smart habits during their charging and use. Plug them in to charge, and unplug them after. A central power strip with a switch will help on that account—plug all of your electronics charging cords into one strip and simply switch it off when not in use.

◄ Home Automation ►

Home automation used to be the province of the wealthy, who could outfit their homes to be controlled by a large, central computer hardwired to various switches and mechanical controllers. Back in the 1990s, one of my contractor friends showed me a $2 million gut remodel job on an old southern plantation home. He laughed when he showed me the master bath: "The lady of the house can dial her spa bath tub from the airport and tell it to be full and up to temperature by the time she gets home. Not sure why you would need that, but if you've got money to burn, I guess this is one way to do it." All of that technology put into the service of automatically running a bath seems ridiculous, but put in the service of helping to run your home for peak energy efficiency makes increasingly more sense as that technology gets cheaper and simpler to install.

Start out with the simplest and most widely available automation. Programmable thermostats allow you to control your HVAC system for a variety of situations. First, a programmable thermostat can be programmed to "setback" temperatures (lower temperatures in the winter and higher temperatures in the summer) so that you won't waste energy heating or cooling an empty house. You can set back the temperature during the night or when the family is away at work and school. Then, for example, you can set the thermostat to automatically heat the house back up just before you wake up or return from work. The US Department of Energy estimates that a 10°F (6°C) to 15°F (8°C) setback for eight to 10 hours at a time on a daily basis can save up to 15 percent on your energy bill. The thermostat can also be set to "vacation mode." This allows you to raise or lower the temperature in your home for the number of days that you'll be gone on vacation. I like to set my thermostat at 55°F (13°C) if I'm vacationing during the winter months—that's low enough to save a lot of energy on heating, but still warm enough to keep the pipes from freezing. The same is true for summer vacations: I set my AC to cool my house just enough to lower the humidity so that mold won't grow, but no cooler. A programmable thermostat makes sure that the house is always comfortable when you're in it without wasting energy when you're not.

Lighting automation is another way to employ simple, off-the-shelf energy savings. Dusk-to-dawn sensors coupled with motion sensors on an LED exterior fixture can save enormous amounts of energy compared with a standard fixture and incandescent bulb left on all night. You still get the security and safety of outdoor lighting, but you don't have to be there to switch it on and off, so it's only in use when necessary. Most home improvement centers now carry motion sensor and timed lighting switch options for interior use in homes, too. One of the added benefits of using switches like these, aside from the energy savings, is that you won't have to hassle your kids to turn off lights when they leave the room.

Timed switches for exhaust fans are another inexpensive but effective use of simple home automation. It's important to exhaust moist or stale air from kitchens and baths, but it's easy to forget to shut exhaust fans off, wasting energy. A timer switch will allow you to simply touch a button to select a range of on times from 10 to 60 minutes, after which the fan will shut off.

Want something more high-tech? Whole-home automation systems use powerful processors and wireless technology to control many home systems from one central touchpad. This type of automation also will allow you to control your home using an app on your smart phone or tablet. Essentially, whole-home automation can offer all of the automation I mentioned above, plus even more, and allow you to program it all from one place. Most systems will include HVAC, lighting, security, video, and audio controls, while some may even include automation of things like window blinds or sprinkler systems.

This type of automation is helping to bring the "smart home" idea closer to your home. Whole-home automation offers many convenience items like controlling door locks or audio and video, but it also can have a positive effect on energy efficiency. Imagine a home where, from your tablet's touch screen, you could set your HVAC's programmable thermostat. Did you leave for your vacation and forget to turn down the heat? No problem. Your smart phone will allow you to fix that by logging onto your system and making the adjustment remotely. Automation can also be integrated with an energy monitoring system to control window blinds that can be raised or lowered to block out unwanted sunlight during cooling periods. Or as the technology advances, smart homes will be linked with the smart grid to help manage energy use on a neighborhood-by-neighborhood basis. I describe this home of the future in more detail in chapter 11.

Whether you choose simple, off-the-shelf automation or go "whole house," home automation will help you to achieve deeper levels of energy savings with your deep energy retrofit.

► Energy Monitoring ◄

Most of us have very little idea where we use energy. We simply pay our utility bills, mumbling epithets at the utility companies while we write the check. Since there's only one number on our bills, the overall use of energy for a given period of time, there's no way to look at your bill and figure out where that energy is being used in your home. Aside from some educated guessing—air-conditioning, heating, refrigeration—we're clueless where most of it goes. That's where energy monitoring comes in.

It's estimated that by knowing exactly where energy is used in a home, the homeowner can save as much as 20 percent by simply adjusting habits in minor ways. Considering that most weatherization steps, like weather stripping doors or caulking around windows, aim at 10 to 15 percent savings, energy monitoring has serious potential as part of a deep energy retrofit strategy. Energy monitoring can be as simple as using a point source meter, like the Kill-A-Watt, to see how much that extra refrigerator in the garage is costing you, or as complicated as a multi-sensor, home automation integrated system like Crestron's Fusion EM system, which carefully monitors and automates systems for optimal energy performance. Either way, monitoring how your home uses energy can help you to adjust your habits and make better choices when the time comes to purchase new systems or appliances.

Chapter Nine

ULTRA HIGH-EFFICIENCY ADDITIONS

IN THE LOVE-HAZE OF THE EARLY RELATIONSHIP WITH OUR 1,000-square-foot home, we glossed over the challenges of shoehorning two adults, two children, two businesses, and two workshops into such a diminutive space. We're "small house people" who actually enjoy the benefits of living in a home that requires less housework, less maintenance, and less energy than the average American home. As we moved in, Sherri expertly organized what fit into the house and donated the rest to a local thrift store. The storage space above the dilapidated garage, measuring in at 8 feet by 9 feet, became a dual office, with two desks, a file cabinet, and some wire-rack storage.

At the beginning, I would have called it "cozy." There was something nice about backing up in my small office chair and accidentally running into my wife's chair. "Sorry, love," we might say to one another, and go about our business day. Over time, though, our passive-aggressive tendencies began to rear their ugly heads and a simple chair-bump could elicit a scornful sigh or a wrinkled brow or, on occasion, both. One fateful day, Sherri was working at her desk, concentrating on a sensitive bit of e-mail correspondence with a new gallery she hoped to land for her artwork. I was at my desk, cradling the paper shredder in my lap, feeding in out-of-date but financially sensitive documents. The grinding of the shredder as it labored under the strain was unmistakably irritating. Sherri glanced up and frowned, then returned to her computer screen. A minute later, she shot me a withering glare, but I kept on shredding. She put up with sonic assault for about 50 pages before she burst out in frustration, "Do you have to keep

FIGURE 9.1 The old garage, just before demolition begins—the back wall is rotting away, the concrete slab is cracked and uneven, and there's no insulation to speak of. Photograph by Sherri James.

running that awful thing? Can't you see I'm trying to get some *work* done? Have you gone *crazy*?"

Thoroughly chastened, I bundled up the shredder, the offending documents, and my pride and trundled down to a dark, musty corner of the basement where I could shred the remaining papers out of earshot. As I shredded, I ruminated on the stress our way-too-small office was introducing into our relationship, as well as all the structural problems with the garage. It was a moment of anxiety, but also of clarity: there was no workable solution except to tear down the garage and start over.

⊁ A Hard-Working Addition ⊰

A replacement addition would allow for a bigger office that would be heated and cooled, part of the indoor conditioned living area. The garage below wouldn't need to be heated and cooled, but superinsulating it would allow us to "semi-condition" the space. On a cold winter day we could heat the garage a little so that we could work out there comfortably, but otherwise leave it unheated.

So we started designing the addition in earnest. Aesthetics played a role in the design, as well. Its size had to be proportionate to the main home, and the appearance would need to complement the house's Cape Cod style: too many additions ignore simple rules of the existing aesthetic, and traditionally styled homes end up looking like a cubist painting. We also had property setbacks and lot coverage rules to adhere to from our city codes office. Not to mention considerations of our budget. What would happen if we ran into trouble paying for all of this? How could we ensure that building a new addition wouldn't end up costing us the house if our fortunes took a nose dive, as often happens in the career of a minor TV-and-Internet personality?

By confining the design within all of these criteria, it nearly created itself. To comply with local building codes we expanded the garage footprint just 6 feet toward the property line on the north side of the house. This added about 125 square feet to the original garage space, making for a nice workshop. For the second story, we made the decision to raise the roofline (as described in chapter 3), which suddenly gave the upper level twice as much usable floor space. That left room for designing the space as a small, self-contained loft apartment, which we could live in now, and rent out once the kids left home.

On a large piece of graph paper, I carefully drew out the concept. When we stood back and compared the new drawing to the old photos of the house, the new addition looked much better and more balanced than the old, narrow garage. The old garage looked like a haphazard add-on, much too small to balance the larger façade of the house. The drawing of the proposed structure made much more sense aesthetically, and it solved all of our problems elegantly. If times remained good enough for us to make the payments, Sherri and I would move into the new loft apartment "suite" and turn our old bedroom into an office. If times got tight, we could lock the door between the house and the apartment and rent it out until our good fortune returned. The new design would alleviate our space issues in an economically responsible way.

Naturally, when it came time for the actual construction, we followed through with the same energy efficiency principles that guided our house retrofit. We started with an insulated foundation and slab. Moving up, we had the crew construct exterior walls that were thicker than ordinary walls (with 2×6 studs instead of the standard 2×4 studs) to provide ample space for extra insulation. In order to get the advantage of spray foam in the wall cavities without all of the cost, we opted for a "hybrid" insulation system: first, 2 inches of spray foam was sprayed against the back of the exterior sheathing, then R-13 fiberglass batt insulation was installed in the remaining space (for more about this technique, see chapter 5). That compares with standard construction methods that offer no air seal and less than half the insulation value of our walls.

Our window installer used the same triple pane, krypton gas–filled windows in the addition as in the main house. The three exterior man doors were insulated fiberglass models with the same high-efficiency glass (for more on these features, see "Windows and Doors" in chapter 6). After some careful searching, I found a garage door with an R-19 insulation value. Not perfect, but a far cry from a standard, non-insulated door. If I was careful to superinsulate the space between the downstairs garage workshop area and the upstairs loft apartment, I should be able to stay comfortable in the workshop during the wintertime without much extra heat and without adversely affecting the efficiency of the upstairs.

The vaulted ceiling and roof structure were constructed using 10-inch rafters, which left room for 4 inches of spray foam insulation for an R-28 value, followed by R-19 fiberglass batt, for a total of R-47. With the superinsulated foundation, walls, and roof, and the careful attention to doors and windows all the way around, we would have one tight, comfy little space.

Doing a little math, I figured that we would be adding about 350 square feet to the original size of the house, bringing it to a whopping 1,350 square feet, which is only about half the size of the average American home. However, we were fortunate not to have to add a heating and cooling system or change out our existing system for a new one, thanks to calculations we made and the advice of our home energy auditor (see chapter 2 for more about this). We opted to run two ducts from the existing HVAC system into the new addition's upper level and hope for the best. In the future, if we found that the new space was too hot in the summer or cold in the winter, we could add more HVAC capacity to that space using a small, ductless mini-split heat pump.

The exterior finish materials for the addition matched the newly retrofitted main house: engineered wood siding and trim, recycled rubber faux slate on the front roof and white TPO membrane on the shallow rear pitch. Half-round faux copper gutters and some art glass in the windows and doors would also help tie the new addition stylistically to the existing house. On the inside, we opted for as many "green" finishes as possible: locally made tile, locally harvested cherry flooring and trim, LED lighting, recycled glass countertops, and low flow plumbing fixtures were among them. We even installed a reclaimed bottle window of Sherri's design into the interior. The finished product was a reflection of our "live lightly" ethic, but also a reflection of our personal styles and tastes.

⊱ Redesign, Bump-Out, or Addition? ⊰

I've talked with many homeowners who deep energy retrofitted their homes following an initial decision to put on an addition. Their reasoning was like this: if we're going to go to all of the expense and trouble to create a wonderful new space in our home, why not improve the old space at the same time and get the hassle over with all at once?

That said, it's important to understand that building an addition is a major financial commitment, just as a deep energy retrofit can be a major expense. I don't recommend undertaking both unless you're absolutely sure that your house needs an addition. However, if you are building an addition, I highly recommend that you go the extra mile to build that addition using the best energy efficient practices out there. It's possible that this may raise the overall price tag for the addition. Since the operation of a high-efficiency addition will be markedly less over time, however, any additional costs may pay for themselves in energy savings. And what about your family's comfort? Remember that all of the benefits of a deep energy retrofit also apply to new construction.

On the other hand, it's not necessarily true that a highly efficient building must cost more to build. Often, buildings designed by building science professionals can integrate very high energy efficiency standards without adding to the initial construction costs. That's because the extra cost in insulation, for example, results in a lower cost for smaller HVAC equipment. Or because a building science–designed wall assembly uses less lumber and labor to build. By careful coordination of all of a building's many elements, savings can be gleaned by ensuring that they work together, and that can result in no additional up-front costs for the homeowner.

But aren't current building practices better than they used to be? Yes, to a degree, but many contractors work under a philosophy of delivering the minimum that building codes require, and no more. This allows a contractor to present the lowest possible bid on a project, without anything "extra" inflating the costs. However, minimum code requirements don't address issues of efficiency, comfort, and health the way that stricter building practices do—issues you're solving by undergoing a DER with your existing home. Plus, if your new addition is built to lower standards, the new space will be less comfortable and harder to heat and cool than your original-but-now-retrofitted home is. That's why it makes sense to build any addition to very high energy efficiency standards.

Now that our addition is complete, my family and I can't imagine a better solution to the space problems we were facing in our house. That said, I advise you to think very carefully before you undertake any large remodeling or adding-on project. Every situation is unique, and there are many reasons homeowners wish for extra space: "The kitchen is too cramped, and we spend all of our time there." "We need to have a great room where the whole family can gather." "If we had space for an office, my work stuff wouldn't be cluttering the kitchen table." Just as there are plenty of reasons for needing more space, there are plenty of ways to solve those problems, not all of which include adding on to your home.

Once you've defined the space or design problems you want to solve, small-space guru Sarah Susanka, author of the Not So Big House series books, suggests working through a hierarchy of possibilities before settling on a plan. First, can you meet your objectives simply by reconfiguring the space within the footprint of the existing home? Take a fresh look at the space you already have and imagine ways to use it better. For example, a house with many small, cramped rooms can be opened up to create better flow and a more comfortable design simply by removing walls to create the kind of open floor plan more common in modern homes. An architect or interior designer can help you envision this—many now employ 3-D rendering so basic drawings can be transformed into realistic images that show exactly how a potential new floor plan will look from eye level.

After thorough consideration of the first approach, you may decide it's just not viable. If so, consider the second level of change: Would a "bump-out" offer just enough extra space? Bump-outs require cutting through an exterior wall, which involves more money and mess than working within the original building envelope. However, bump-outs don't require the expense and mess of a new foundation the way an addition will. Bump-outs can usually extend as far as 3 feet out from a home and can be up to 12 feet long. That might be just enough space to expand a kitchen, make room for a tub in a bathroom, or add a window seat. Bump-outs are "hung" onto the side of a home either by cantilevering (adding extensions onto the existing floor joists) or by using brackets to hold the weight of the new building materials. Often, a home's existing roof line can be extended to include the bump-out. If a bump-out, along with some creative reimagining of your existing floor plan, can achieve your renovation goals, you'll save a lot of money and time on your project by avoiding a full-fledged addition with a foundation.

Sarah Susanka's advice is well worth following. If you reach the conclusion that you don't need an addition after all, not only will you reap the benefits in lower energy and maintenance costs of living in a smaller home, but you'll have the opportunity to take the money you would have spent on creating more square footage and spend it instead on the details that make a space a truly great place to live. For example, with less area to fill, higher quality finish materials become more affordable and high-end, high-efficiency appliances may be within your reach. If you don't have an artistic bent, you could even spend a little of that money on a professional designer who can help you design an attractive space that meets your specific lifestyle needs. All in all, having a *smaller* space allows you to have a *higher quality* space, and a place you're more likely to be proud to call home.

✈ Addition Advice ✦

If you ultimately decide, as we did, that an addition is absolutely right for you, it still pays to keep it small and functional, for all of the reasons I outlined above. Your first step is to design it and draw up plans. An architect, engineer, or a competent general contractor can help with this design process, making allowances along the way for your budget, neighborhood covenants, property zoning and setback rules, and building codes. I highly recommend hiring professionals who have building science training so that they'll include the latest best practices and products to ensure your new space is as energy efficient and comfortable as possible. As I've mentioned before, they're also able to design the project so that the many disparate parts work together as a whole, coordinated system. This has the potential to save money both on construction and over the life of the building. For more information on hiring a pro for your project, see "Hiring Building Professionals" in chapter 3.

Basically, an addition consists of a foundation, walls, windows, doors, a roof, and working systems. Once you have a plan on paper for your addition, you'll face many of the same choices about construction techniques and materials as you would for a retrofit.

⊷ Foundations ⊷

Any building is only as strong as its foundation. A foundation for an addition might just be a simple concrete slab, or it might include a foundation wall, crawl space, or basement. Depending on the use of the addition, you might have more than one foundation type. For example, you may want a basement under part of an addition, but only a concrete slab where a new garage will be. Generally speaking, the deeper you go, the more expensive and complicated a foundation becomes. Each home's foundation will vary based on homeowner preference, regional climate, seismic activity, soil type, a property's susceptibility to flooding, budget, and many other considerations. Most likely, your architect or other building pro will design the foundation for your addition, but you can ensure that your new foundation integrates well with your high-efficiency addition by insisting that it be properly waterproofed and insulated.

Many remodeling contractors pay little attention to waterproofing and insulating the foundation for an addition, but that's a mistake. If you neglect to insulate and waterproof the foundation and slab under your addition, heat will simply move through the cool slab and right into the cool ground beneath, and groundwater and storm water will have an easy path into your new space. I recommend insulating foundations on almost all additions, even if it's going to be used as a garage. Garages often double as workshop space, and insulating the foundation will have a big effect on energy efficiency and comfort even if you heat or cool the space only occasionally. Our new garage, which is properly insulated all around, never dips below 48°F (9°C) even on the coldest winter day, and a small space heater is sufficient to take the chill out of the air when we work out there. That versatility makes insulation and waterproofing worth doing right in the first place: remember, it's almost impossible to go back *after* the concrete is poured and the foundation has been backfilled to add insulation or a watertight seal.

⊷ Walls ⊷

Moving up to the walls, aim for a superinsulated structure that goes "beyond code" to make sure that the new walls really do offer better insulation and air sealing than standard construction. Standard construction calls for 2×4 studs in the walls, which creates cavities about 3½ inches deep for some kind of insulation. Building with 2×6 studs instead will produce 5½-inch-deep cavities, allowing 2 inches of extra space for a higher insulation value. And if your

Building REMOTE-ly in Alaska

Way up in Alaska, home builders and building science pros face some big challenges. The biggest is that although outdoor wintertime temperatures can drop to -30°F (–34°C), folks like to keep indoor temperatures up near 70°F (21°C). The resulting 100°F (55°C) temperature difference between indoors and out wreaks havoc with wall systems, making it difficult to build a wall in this environment of extremes that performs well thermally without resulting in mold and rot of the wooden structural elements inside the wall.

The issue at hand is the problem of "dew point" occurring within a wall structure. Dew point is a temperature below which water vapor, suspended in air as humidity, condenses on a surface to become water droplets, or dew. Imagine a wall with its exterior exposed to a frigid winter night, and its interior basking in a heated living space. As you travel from the interior of the imaginary wall toward the exterior, the temperature begins to drop as you leave the warm living space. If the dew point is reached within the open wall cavity, humidity will condense on the interior face of the exterior sheathing, resulting in a wet wall cavity.

To combat this problem, in 2002 the Cold Climate Housing Research Center (CCHRC) in Fairbanks began to develop the Residential Exterior Membrane Outside-insulation TEchnique (REMOTE) wall system. This system includes 4 to 6 inches of rigid foam sheathing applied to the exterior of a building, over a water- and airtight membrane. The system was monitored for moisture content and energy use over time, and the result was some basic standards that can be used to reliably develop wall systems that will work in nearly any climate. The REMOTE system, with its very thick exterior rigid foam insulation layer, ensures that the dew point temperature will occur somewhere within the solid mass of foam sheathing, where humid air cannot reach and condense.

A decade and many REMOTE wall studies later, a recommended standard has been produced: for the coldest climates, placing at least two-thirds of a wall assembly's insulation to the exterior of the membrane-protected sheathing (as rigid foam boards) and one-third of the wall assembly's insulation within the cavity itself (as batt or loose fill) protects the whole system from dew point–related condensation problems. And it results in a superinsulated wall system that can even stand up to Alaska's frigid climate.

contractor uses *advanced framing techniques* (a method of spacing 2×6 studs farther apart than in standard construction practice to decrease wood use and increase insulation in a wall) in your new 2×6 wall, less lumber will be used than a standard 2×4 wall. Also, while standard construction results in corners that cannot be accessed for insulation, advanced framing uses an open corner design that allows for easy insulation installation. Whatever design is chosen for your wall assembly, aim for at least a well-sealed R-30 wall assembly insulation value and you won't be sorry later when those miniscule heating and cooling bills start coming in.

An insulation value of R-30 can be achieved by using insulation within the wall cavity, on the exterior, or a combination of both. Within the wall cavity, fiberglass, cellulose, or spray foam can be used. On the exterior, rigid foam sheathing panels can be layered to add insulation value and a thermal break (see chapter 5 for more on thermal breaks and rigid foam sheathing). It's likely that your wall will be designed with a hybrid of interior and exterior insulation strategies, since this approach gives the highest overall insulation rating, as well as a thermal break between structural framing and the outdoors.

For example, 2 inches of spray foam (R-14), followed by 3½ inches of batt insulation (R-13) within a 5½-inch-deep wall cavity, and then a 1-inch layer of XPS rigid foam sheathing (R-5) on the exterior would create an air-sealed R-32 wall assembly. Or a 2×6 cavity of blown-in cellulose (R-20) and 4 inches of ISO rigid foam sheathing (R-24) would create an R-44 wall assembly. Exactly how your wall assembly is built will depend on many factors, but your well-trained building science pro will be able to design a solution that makes the best use of insulation and air-sealing materials for your climate and budget. Getting this right is very important—get it wrong and your new wall assembly can experience moisture problems in the form of condensation, and it can ultimately fail (for more detailed information about condensation problems in walls, see the "Building REMOTE-ly in Alaska" sidebar).

Other options exist for superinsulated walls. SIPS are one solution that greatly simplifies wall building on the job site (see chapter 5 for more on SIPs). Also, Insulated Concrete Forms (ICFs) are another great way to build for ultra high efficiency. These concrete forms look like oversized, hollow toy foam building blocks (see figure 9.2). Once installed, they're filled with concrete. The foam blocks then remain in place to act as insulation on both sides of the concrete. Wiring is run by carving out channels in the interior foam with a hot knife or router. Choices for interior and exterior finish materials are the same as with a traditionally built home. As you can imagine, this results in a thick, well-insulated wall that creates a very solid and efficient home. ICF-built homes are also extremely quiet on the interior, too, since the massive walls block out exterior noise. While the initial costs of building with ICFs and SIPs are higher, the result will save lots of money on energy and maintenance over time.

FIGURE 9.2 Foam ICFs are stacked like toy blocks, then filled with concrete and left in place for a superinsulated wall. While not common, ICFs are gaining in popularity as a way to build very tight, well-insulated homes and additions. Photograph courtesy of Quadlock Building Systems, www.quadlock.com.

⚊ Roofs ⚊

Insulating ceilings and roofs is also very important with new construction. An air-sealed R-50 to R-60 insulation value is a good goal to strive for, and you can achieve it whether your addition has a vented, unvented, or cathedral ceiling roof structure. Your choice of roof assembly type will depend largely on the style of your roof and whether or not any HVAC or mechanical equipment will be installed in the attic space. If you're going to install a new furnace or air conditioner in the attic space, you'll want to opt for an unvented attic, keeping the entire space within the thermal envelope of the building. The specifics of your project may dictate the type of roof your project needs. The ins and outs of vented vs. unvented roof designs are covered in detail in chapter 5, and all of those considerations apply when building an addition. In the end, don't let a contractor or architect railroad you into accepting a vented attic without a serious discussion of the merits of unvented spaces— they're often doing this because of tradition, not building science. Hiring an architect, engineer, or contractor with building science credentials early in the design phase can ensure that you get the right roof assembly for your addition.

Whatever attic or roof type you choose, you'll need to plan for creating a thermal envelope that is properly sealed. While the insulation values in roofs will be higher than in walls, the basics of creating a superinsulated roof or attic assembly are similar. Spray foam, fiberglass, or cellulose can be used on the interior, while SIPs, nailbase, or rigid foam sheathing can be used on the exterior.

If you live in a hot climate, consider using radiant barrier sheathing to avoid heat gain. Radiant barrier sheathing can block radiant heat from entering the attic, helping to reduce attic temperatures and therefore reducing the load on your air conditioner during the summer. Radiant barrier sheathing costs about 30 percent more than standard OSB, but since it cuts and installs just like standard roof sheathing, there are no extra labor costs involved. This makes it one of the more economical ways to help reduce air-conditioning loads (see "Radiant Barrier Sheathing: A Space Blanket for Your House" in chapter 5).

In very hot climates, reflectivity of roofing is a serious issue, profoundly affecting cooling loads. The amount of sun reflected by a given roofing material is called the Solar Reflectance Index," or SRI (see more about SRI in chapter 5). A darker colored roof will absorb more of those rays, passing the energy into the roof assembly as heat that is conducted through the building materials and into the home. A lighter-colored finish material reflects more of the sun's energy away from the building. An essentially cost-free choice to reduce heat gain, lightening the summertime load on the air conditioner, is to choose a lighter-colored roofing finish material.

Once your new, ultra high-efficiency foundation, walls, and roof are built, you'll need windows, doors, and systems to complement them. All of these topics are covered in the associated chapters on deep energy retrofitting. The same advice on choosing new windows and doors for your DER will apply here, as will the advice on choosing HVAC, water heating, lighting, and all of the other systems for your addition. See "Windows and Doors" in chapter 6. For information on HVAC and other systems for your new addition, see chapter 8. Also, to ensure you're using the most eco-friendly materials in your high-efficiency addition, check out "DER Materials" in chapter 3. In the end, you'll want your new addition to have the same characteristics as your deep energy retrofitted house so that you'll maximize energy savings and comfort.

Today, nearly a year after finishing the major interior installations in our addition, I wish I could say that it was finished. On the contrary, the ceiling fans have yet to be installed and about half of the cherry baseboard and trim still sits unfinished. They're jobs that I swear I'll finish after this book is done (really, Sherri, I will!). The good news is that we've lived through three winters and three summers without needing to add extra heating or cooling capacity. Now Sherri and I have a comfortable, private space that doubles as a room where the whole family can enjoy a movie together. We also have a new, larger office where our old bedroom used to be. All of that and our energy bills have dropped by more than 85 percent. Despite the success, however, I still find it prudent to act with an abundance of caution by executing all shredding of documents in a dark, quiet, well-insulated corner of the basement.

Chapter Ten

RENEWABLE ENERGY: THE FINAL STEP

WHEN WORD OF A BIG FREEZE IN FLORIDA CAME ON THE EVENING news in January 1977, I wasn't quite 10 years old. My mother was concerned about my great-grandparents, who lived in Clearwater, so she called to check on them. They were fine, Great-Grandma Lisa said, but Great-Grandpa Murray couldn't come to the phone to chat because he was out in the yard. "Why," my Mom asked, "is he out in the yard at this time of night?" It wasn't a trivial question. Murray was well into his eighties at the time. With mild amusement, Lisa told the story of how Murray was out in the frigid dark trying to save his homemade solar heater.

My great-grandfather had long been interested in solar energy and how to capture some of that "free" energy to help heat our homes. He was a civil engineer and architect, but also a tinkerer. His question about solar energy was how it could be easily and elegantly captured by anyone with a modicum of skills and cheap, widely available materials. That had led him to collect and fill hundreds of discarded plastic milk jugs with water and stack them in a glass-enclosed rack against the side of the house. During the day, the sun would warm the water in the jugs. At night, a fan blew air across the warm jugs, collecting the day's stored heat before channeling it into the house through ducts. The jugs acted as a solar "battery," storing heat energy during the day for use when it was needed at night. The design met Great-Grandpa's requirements for simplicity, frugality, and ease of production. Normally this setup worked just fine in Florida. But in January of 1977 the region was pummeled by one of the worst freezes of the century. Citrus crops were ruined, and it was cold enough to freeze the water in my great-grandfather's hundred-odd plastic jugs. He knew that if the water froze, it would expand and burst the jugs. So there he was, out in the cold and dark, emptying jugs of water onto the frozen yard.

Great-Grandpa's contraption wasn't high-tech, nor was it his original idea. Using water, masonry, or other "thermal mass" like this has long been a common way to store solar thermal energy. He liked the idea of using commonly discarded items like plastic jugs because it had the potential to make harvesting solar energy easy for anyone, rich or poor. He was simply trying to ensure that "everyman" could keep his family safe and warm, no matter what.

Not long after the freezing-jug affair, my parents began to build the home of their dreams in Michigan. That home featured lots of passive solar design elements—plentiful southern windows and carefully sized southern eaves to assist in heating and cooling the house. Those eaves allowed sunlight in during the wintertime, but blocked it during hot summer months. It was a simple design element that cost my parents next to nothing, but is still saving energy and money for the occupants today.

⚡ Revolution in Renewables ⚡

In the years since my great-grandpa's experiments and my parents' passive solar home, solar and other renewable energy technology has come a long way. Passive solar design, solar thermal collection, and photovoltaic (PV) electricity generation are now commonplace. Likewise, wind generators regularly dot the landscape, cropping up like weeds across America's farmlands, ridges, and coastlines. Renewable energy has become less expensive at the same time that traditional forms of energy have become more costly. Solar and wind power are still clean and green, while the environmental toll and national security effects of traditional energy sources have made them more hazardous.

Lots of people are anti-renewables; they view the technology as very expensive, government-subsidized toys. If I had a solar panel for every time I heard someone say, "Solar and wind will never create enough of our power because they're too expensive and can't compete with fossil fuels," I could cover the entire Southwest with them. Technically, these folks are right: if most people continue to choose to live in energy-wasting, uncomfortable, unhealthy homes, solar and wind will have a hard time keeping up. However, if we embrace a nationwide boom in deep energy retrofits, which would dramatically shrink our need for power, then renewables have the capacity to supply the bulk of the energy we need for a prosperous, clean, and safe daily life. Dirty fossil fuels and nuclear can become the rarely used backups to clean, reliable renewable power. After all, scientists estimate that every day enough solar energy hits the United States to supply the energy we need as a society for a year and a half. Seems a crying shame not to take advantage of it.

I had originally chosen not to install solar panels on our old, inefficient home because I knew I needed first to invest in reducing our house's power requirements. But as the plans for our deep energy retrofit took shape, I realized that our deep energy retrofitted home would only require a fraction of the energy we were currently consuming, and solar after the retrofit might make sense. I'd also always thought of our house as poorly situated for solar panels because the house faces east-west, and not south. But imagining changes to our roofline for the retrofit allowed me to reconsider the use of photovoltaic panels on our home.

As we designed our deep energy retrofit and new addition, I realized our new, raised-pitch dormer roof would be a nearly flat rectangular area, tilted slightly to the west, and that it would be free of shade from surrounding trees most of the day. Solar panels mounted nearly flat on my new, nearly flat roof would offer excellent potential for generating electricity. I ran the idea by Geoff Greenfield, the owner of Third Sun, a local solar panel installation company. After taking some measurements and making some basic calculations, he agreed. With the available space on the main house rear dormer roof we could fit a 4kW PV array consisting of 18 solar panels. He calculated that the electricity generated from that system would cover at least 80 percent of the electricity needs of our home. If we decided to cover the proposed garage replacement addition roof with panels, too, we could add another 2kW of capacity. The panels would be installed on a low-profile rack system on the back side of the house. Only the very front rail of that rack system, at the peak of the roof, would be visible from the road, so the panels wouldn't unduly affect the curb appeal we'd worked so hard to protect. Soon Geoff's proposal arrived in my mailbox, including an installation plan, detailed calculations on how much energy the system could be expected to generate over its lifetime, and information on costs and incentives.

That last bit was very important. Since Sherri and I would be spending a big chunk of change to retrofit the old home for deep energy efficiency, and we had decided to tackle the garage replacement addition at the same time, funds were tight, to say the least. But since incentives would bring the original sticker price down from $32,000

Palo Alto Net Zero

FIGURE 10.1 Marc Porat's Palo Alto deep energy retrofit. Photograph by Sarah Cornwell.

Marc Porat takes energy problems personally. As an entrepreneur, he's the founder of Serious Materials and CalStar Cement, two companies aimed at reducing energy use in the building sector. As a father, Mark has had the wider problems associated with Americans' profligate energy use hit him particularly close to home.

to only $9,000 (see chapter 4 for details on incentives and financing), I could calculate a "payback time" of fewer than 10 years. The system would last for 30 years, so the last 20 years would be pure profit.

I gave a verbal green light to Third Sun, with the stipulation that we wouldn't sign the final contract until our State of Ohio grant application was approved. We also decided to install panels only on the main roof of the home, leaving the roof of the addition vacant for now. The system could be easily expanded in the future up to 7kW by simply adding panels. It would be "grid tied" and have no batteries for storage.

"I live in California, and I got a call early one morning from my son, who was in school at Columbia in New York," Mark recalled. "It was around 6:00 a.m. Pacific time. All he said was 'Dad, turn on the TV set.'" It was September 11, 2001, and the history-changing events of the World Trade Center terrorist attacks were unfolding. Marc, like millions of people around the world, watched in horror.

"A few years later I had another, similar phone call," he remembered, "but this time it was my daughter, in tears. She was in college at Tulane in Louisiana, and she was being flooded out of her house by Hurricane Katrina. I couldn't help but notice that these stories were two sides of the same coin." Porat's work in the energy efficiency field had helped him to make the connections between energy use and both national security and world climate change.

The imperative to face the energy issues contributing to those problems led Marc to start businesses aimed at drastically reducing energy use in the built environment. Eventually, it occurred to him that his own house had many of the problems he was trying to solve in his businesses, albeit on a smaller scale. With the help of Recurve, a San Francisco–based retrofitting company, Marc elected to deep energy retrofit his 1936 historic home in Palo Alto. The house was originally designed by artist and architect Pedro de Lemos, and in order to retain the home's sensitive historic details, the retrofit team worked from the interior. Wall cavities were filled with dense packed recycled cellulose insulation, and handcrafted wrought iron windows were improved with custom-made, magnetic interior storm windows that add thermal resistance but don't compromise the home's aesthetics. The HVAC system, lighting, and all appliances were replaced with high-efficiency models. A heat recovery ventilator was installed to provide fresh air and photovoltaics to provide power. As a nod to Palo Alto's arid climate, the retrofit included some advanced water-saving measures, including a gray water system to irrigate landscaping. Marc's efforts were rewarded with a true net zero home that is also a more comfortable and healthier place in which to live. In both his home and his businesses, Marc is on the front lines fighting for solutions to the world's energy challenges.

That last bit is an important advance in modern residential solar energy. In the "old days" of solar panel installation, power generated from the panels during the day needed to be stored for use at night or on cloudy days when the sun didn't provide enough power. That meant big battery banks, requiring not only a huge expense, but also a carefully constructed outdoor shed in which to house them. The batteries had to be stored outside because the main by-product of energy storage was hydrogen. Hydrogen is extremely volatile and easily ignites and explodes if allowed to build up in any quantity, so it had to be properly vented out of the shed. The battery banks also needed no small amount of maintenance to ensure that they were working correctly, and they usually had to be replaced at least once during the life of the solar panels. The battery problem was one of the main deterrents to early photovoltaic adoption. A battery bank could easily cost as much as the rest of the system, doubling the cost of installing a PV system. If you lived far from the electrical grid, where it could cost you thousands of dollars to have a line run to your remote home, a photovoltaic system's relatively large expense, including the battery bank, might be justifiable. Otherwise, there was no way solar power could compete with cheap fossil fuel–generated power from the grid.

All of that changed when grid-tied PV installations became the norm. These systems eliminate the battery bank and connect directly to a home's existing utility power line. When the sun is shining the panels generate power. That power is first routed to satisfy the needs of the home where it's generated. If the panels produce more power than the home can immediately use, the excess, instead of being stored in batteries, flows out to the grid, where it's mixed into the existing power "stream." Essentially, those electrons flow out to neighbors' homes, or wherever the closest electrical need presents itself. Whenever the home needs more power than is generating from its solar panels, it pulls power from the grid, like any other home. A new type of "smart meter" tallies up how much grid electricity flows into the home, and how much solar power flows out. When the homeowner receives an electric bill, one column shows how much electricity was bought from the utility and another column shows how much electricity was sold back.

This was how our system would be set up. While I wouldn't need to install batteries, I would have to comply with some rules and regulations to allow my system to integrate with the grid. First there was a bit of paperwork establishing my home as a small electrical generation plant, which I signed at the end of August. At the end of October, our grant funding was approved, and all of our solar ducks were in a row. When the system was ready to start generating power, inspectors from the utility company and the State of Ohio would make sure it was up to snuff, and then we could connect to the grid.

The panel installation happened quickly. The first day, a two-man crew spent a couple of hours installing the vertical supports, called standoffs, which connect the rack system that holds the solar panels to the roof. Once the standoffs were securely bolted into the new roof, it was my job to install all of the flashing to ensure that

FIGURE 10.2 The Third Sun Solar team installs the rail system for our photovoltaic panels on the dormer roof. Photograph by Sherri James.

none of the roofing penetrations would leak. Many times this job is done by the PV installer but, due to the unique qualities of our new roof, Third Sun had decided not to attempt it. Armed with official roofing manufacturer training (via excellent web video) and all of the proper primers, sealants, and tools, I spent the afternoon carefully installing "witches' hat" flashings to each of the 21 standoffs. This was a job I was glad to do, just to ensure it was done right; doing it wrong would mean a leaky roof.

The next day, the solar team came back. In a few hours they had hoisted the horizontal mounting racks and solar panels up the ladder and installed them. Then they wired the panels to one another, and fed the wires through the conduit and into the garage. When the crew left, we had solar panels, but they weren't generating any power yet. The holdup was that we had yet to install a garage door, which was a prerequisite to installing an inverter—the part of the system that prepares and conditions the raw power from the solar panels for use in the home. This electronically sensitive and expensive device can't be exposed to the elements. Delivery of the new garage door had been delayed, first to November and then to December. Finally the door arrived and was installed. Only then was the electrician able to hook up and commission our PV system. As part of the process, he installed a wireless monitor in the house, which displays a readout of current and past electricity generation. We watched it with anticipation: When our monitor picked up the

FIGURE 10.3 Each solar panel is first secured to the rack system and then wired to the panel beside it. Additional wiring is run from the panel assembly through a conduit to the inverter in the garage. Photograph by Sherri James.

wireless signal from the inverter and began to show power flowing from the panels into our home, it was an exciting moment. The Wilson family had gone solar.

Nowadays I rarely think about the solar panels on our house. The big difference is that I actually *look forward* to getting our electric bill. In December or January, we may owe as much as $35. By the time April rolls around that drops to zero. Then, during summer months, we actually get credits on our statement for all of the excess power we generate over and above our needs. The mailman appreciates my enthusiasm for getting bills in the mail, but several times a year, it's even better than that: each time the meter registers 1 additional megawatt-hour (1,000kWh) of power generated by our panels, I get a check for $250 from SolSystems, my

SRECs broker. That's totaled up to almost $3,000 so far, helping to bring "payback day" closer. I like to think of our solar power system as "inconspicuous anti-consumption." Folks walking by the house are far more apt to comment on the recycled rubber roof than to notice the solar panels.

⤜ Renewable Energy Choices for Your Home ⤛

"We think of solar power as 'dessert,' and energy efficiency as 'vegetables,'" an executive of a big solar installation company once told me. "You've got to eat your vegetables before you have your dessert." He went on to say that, when a homeowner signs a contract to purchase or lease a photovoltaic system from his company, the company automatically provides a home energy audit to determine major inefficiencies in the home. After that, a mitigation team arrives to install energy efficiency measures indicated by the home energy audit. Only then is the photovoltaic system installed.

Renewables should be the "final course" of your retrofit, installed only after you've finished all your efficiency improvements. It makes no sense to install solar panels on a house to create electricity that will be wasted anyway. If you've paged forward to this chapter in hopes of a "quick fix" to the problems of your home's energy use, you won't find it here. My advice is to first recover all the energy your home is wasting; then you'll find that renewables can generate all the power you really need. Those renewables can include solar, wind, or even small-scale hydro power.

Regardless of what type of renewable energy you decide to use in your deep energy retrofit, remember to maximize your savings by using all of the many financial incentives available to you. The Federal Renewable Energy Tax Credit will knock 30 percent off the top, but there are also plenty of other incentives in the form of tax credits, grants, rebates, feed-in tariffs, and low- or no-interest loans at the state, local, and utility company level. See the Resources appendix for more.

⇥ Solar Energy ⇤

Solar energy approaches can be "passive" or "active." Passive types are non-mechanical, and rely on building design to take advantage of light or heat energy from the sun. Active solar uses the sun's energy to heat a storage medium, like air or water, and then the stored heat is used for space heating or domestic water heating.

Utility Green Power Programs

Not enough space to put solar panels on your roof? Can't afford them anyway? There's still a way to use renewables at home by signing up for green power through your utility company. For a few extra dollars each month, utilities will purchase power from renewable sources as part of their overall power mix to offset the amount of power you use. For example, if you live in Oregon, you can sign up for the "Green Source" power options, which, for about 10 bucks a month, will source the amount of energy you use from renewables. While you may not see the exact electrons generated from the wind generator across the state, the entire system becomes greener by your purchase. Check the Resources appendix for details on specific programs and how to find out about the green power options in the state where you live.

Photovoltaic panels generate electricity from solar energy. Depending on where you live, one or more types of solar energy might work in your retrofit.

Passive Solar

Passive solar generally requires little or no attention from the homeowner, working "passively" in the background. It can be as simple as allowing enough daylight into a space to reduce the need for artificial light. Windows, standard skylights, compact "tube" skylights, or even small collectors with fiber optic cables can be used to bring daylight into interior spaces. During retrofitting, when windows are normally being replaced anyway, it's a good time to consider where a new window or skylight might help with day-lighting. However, it's important to balance the savings from lighting with the potential transfer of heat into and out of that window since even the best windows are inferior to a well-insulated wall when it comes to thermal transfer. You might save a few pennies on lighting, only to spend a few dollars on heating and cooling.

Passive use of solar energy for heating and cooling is accomplished in the design phase and usually includes south-facing windows (called the "aperture" in passive solar design) and specially designed eaves or awnings (called the "control") that prevent sunlight from shining in during hot summer months and allow the sun's energy in to help heat the home in the wintertime. To make the best use of that heat energy, so that it can work both during the

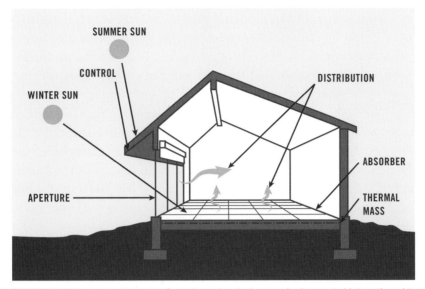

FIGURE 10.4 The basic elements of passive solar design can be integrated into a thoughtfully planned deep energy retrofit to assist in lighting, heating, and cooling your home. Illustration by US Department of Energy.

day and at night, an absorber is added to the system (usually a flooring material) that will collect, store, and evenly distribute the heat. The best absorbers are dense, heavy materials like stone, tile, or concrete, because they have very high "thermal mass," or heat storage capacity. They work like batteries, storing up daytime solar heat and radiating it back into the home at night. These kinds of features

FIGURE 10.5 A CanSolAir solar thermal air collector uses recycled aluminum cans in its design. The air inside the collector is heated by the sun, and that hot air is used to heat the home. Photograph courtesy of CanSolAir.

can be installed during a retrofit as well as during new construction. If you live in an area where the sun shines a lot during the wintertime and add south-facing windows with overhangs during your retrofit, you may find that the sun can provide most of your daytime heating needs for your superinsulated home.

The simple elegance of passive solar design is attractive, but it requires a lot of planning and careful calculation to ensure that the finished building performs well. Too much solar energy allowed into a space can quickly overheat it; too little can mean the money spent planning is wasted, because the space will need traditional heating anyway. At least some attention to passive solar design in your retrofit can help you live more amicably with the sun's energy: simply installing awnings on south-facing windows in the summertime can markedly reduce air-conditioning needs, for example. Increasing the number of windows in the south side of your home and decreasing the number of north-facing windows can help with heating in the winter, too.

Active Solar

When solar energy is collected in the form of heated air or water via panels, pumps, or fans, it's called "active solar." Basic active solar air heaters are constructed using a black-painted metal absorber plate behind a sheet of glass in an insulated collector. The simplest of these are nearly passive, with no fans or blowers. As the sun heats the absorber plate and the air around it, the warm air inside the collector begins to rise. It exits the collector through a duct in the top that feeds into the house. At the same time, cool air from inside the house is drawn into a floor-level duct that feeds into the collector. There, the cool air absorbs heat from the absorber plate, and rises to the top duct and back into the house. Movement of air in this way is called the stack effect or chimney effect. A more complicated version of this collector, like the one shown in figure 10.5, can include thermostats, duct damper controls, and fans to better control heat delivery. This type of system is less likely to overheat an interior space on a sunny winter day because it can be set to work only when interior temperatures are between certain levels.

More commonly, active solar thermal energy takes the form of flat, glass-enclosed panels through which run looping grids of black-painted metal pipes. Water or liquid antifreeze flows through the pipes, absorbing the sun's energy, and is then pumped through a heat-exchanger in a large insulated storage tank filled with water.

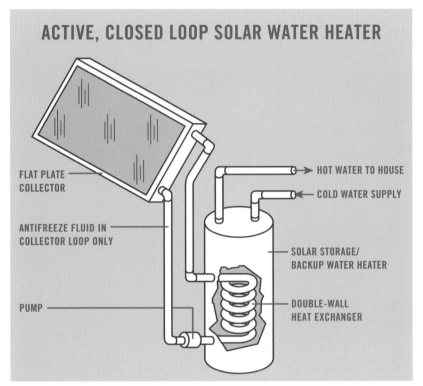

ACTIVE, CLOSED LOOP SOLAR WATER HEATER

FLAT PLATE COLLECTOR

HOT WATER TO HOUSE

COLD WATER SUPPLY

ANTIFREEZE FLUID IN COLLECTOR LOOP ONLY

SOLAR STORAGE/ BACKUP WATER HEATER

PUMP

DOUBLE-WALL HEAT EXCHANGER

FIGURE 10.6 In an active solar water collector, a coolant solution is heated in the panel and is pumped to a heat exchanger in a hot water tank inside the home. There, it heats the water in the tank before circulating back to the panel to collect more solar heat. The water in the tank can be used for domestic hot water or space heating. Illustration by US Department of Energy.

The water in the tank takes on the heat from the pipes and stores it for later use by the homeowner as domestic hot water or for space heating through radiators or in-floor hydronic radiant heating. It can even be used in forced-air central heating systems—hot water from the storage tank is pumped through a radiator inserted in the heating system, where air is blown across it, picking up that heat, and the warm air is delivered to the home through the duct system.

Active solar thermal makes the most sense in regions where the sun shines regularly year-round, like the desert Southwest, as opposed to places that experience lots of cloudy days. Active solar thermal collectors are very sensitive to cloud cover or shading. Their ability to collect heat drops off dramatically when the sun is not shining directly on them. The obvious problem is that, in many places, the sun shines least when its heat energy is needed most—during the winter. A system designed for a cold, cloudy region, which could deliver all of a home's hot water during the middle of winter, would be very large and extremely expensive. In those

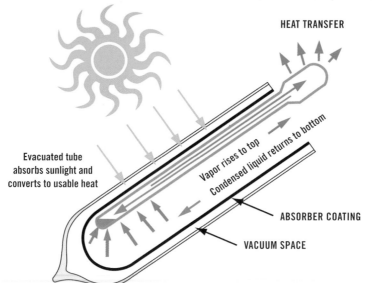

HEAT TRANSFER

Evacuated tube
absorbs sunlight and
converts to usable heat

Vapor rises to top

Condensed liquid returns to bottom

ABSORBER COATING

VACUUM SPACE

FIGURES 10.7A AND 10.7B An evacuated tube collector uses a vacuum tube to prevent the metal heating element from losing heat to the outside air through convection and conduction; this design makes it more effective than a standard collector. Images courtesy of Apricus, Inc.

places it makes more sense to install photovoltaic panels (which can generate some electricity, even when it's cloudy) to generate electricity that can then be used to power an efficient air-source heat pump electric water heater. Before investing in active solar thermal collection, be sure it makes sense for your home's climate.

Improvements in solar thermal technology are now making solar water heating more viable under less-than-ideal conditions.

Evacuated tube solar collectors use long glass tubes that hold metal collector tubes in a vacuum, which minimizes the amount of heat lost through convection and conduction back out to the environment. It's an idea similar to a vacuum bottle that keeps your coffee hot. This system is more efficient than standard flat-plate collectors and will work better than a flat-plate collector on a cloudy day. Due to that efficiency, when the sun *is* shining, an evacuated tube system will take up less space than a flat-plate collector with the same capacity. That said, evacuated tube collectors are more expensive than flat-plate collectors, and while they have helped to make active solar thermal practical for more parts of the country, the issue of too much heat in the summer and too little in the winter remains.

Photovoltaic Solar Electricity

Photovoltaic solar systems are increasing in popularity, partially due to the phenomenal drop in the cost of panels. As solar panel manufacturers all over the world have scaled up production, savings due to "economies of scale" have come into play, causing panel prices to plummet. The Chinese government has heavily subsidized its solar manufacturing sector, believing that panel manufacturing will be a big part of world economic growth in coming decades. Inexpensive Chinese panels have saturated the market, driving down profit margins, and forcing many less-subsidized solar panel companies in the United States out of business. While the lack of a robust US solar manufacturing sector and the jobs that accompany it is regrettable, inexpensive panels are a good thing for consumers.

When exposed to sunlight, photovoltaic panels generate direct-current electricity. That electricity runs through wires to an appliance called an inverter, which changes the direct-current electricity into alternating-current electricity, which is the type that can be used in your home. Panels can be mounted on roof surfaces or on stand-alone racks. Either way, panels function best when faced in a somewhat southerly or southwesterly direction and in direct sunlight, with no shade. Most mounting systems are fixed racks, but another type includes a small motor that rotates the panels so that they're always optimally faced toward the sun all day long. This type of "tracking" system is much more expensive to install than a fixed rack system, so careful calculations should be done to see if the added costs would deliver sufficient extra power to justify them.

Once the panels and inverter are installed, the system is connected to your home's electrical panel, feeding solar power into

Solar Air-Conditioning— A Hot Commodity

FIGURE 10.8 The evacuated tube solar curtain wall at the University of Cincinnati's Solar Decathlon Home. Photograph by Eric Stear.

your house. On the exterior, a grid disconnect switch and a new digital meter are installed. The meter has the capability of showing how much power is bought from and sold to the grid, and your electric bill will reflect those numbers. You'll only pay the difference when you use more power than you generate, and you'll get credits on bills when you generate more power in a month than you use. Those credits offset future electric bill payments. Some systems also have a small display monitor that shows how much power you're generating at any one time, as well as daily and lifetime totals.

Most PV systems have a useful lifespan of 25 to 30 years, and most need little or no maintenance. Snow sometimes collects on

The "too much heat in the summer and too little in the winter" solar thermal conundrum might be solvable in the near future. Technology called an "absorption chiller" uses heat energy instead of electricity to provide cooling that can be used in air-conditioning. The concept is actually fairly simple and is used in recreational vehicle refrigerators, where propane is burned to create the heat source in the absorption chiller system to keep food in the refrigerator cold. But that heat source doesn't have to be fossil fuel—it could be anything that delivers the minimum 190°F (88°C) needed to activate the system. Solar-heated water works just as well.

I saw this technology in use in a University of Cincinnati Solar Decathlon home. The Solar Decathlon is a competition put on by the US Department of Energy every two years. College students from 20 universities compete to design homes that are completely run on the sun's energy. The homes are designed and built during the two-year time periods between competitions, and then trucked to the National Mall in Washington, D.C. There, they are assembled, tested over several weeks, and judged in multiple categories, including effective use of solar energy, style, and cost. It's an event I attend as a video host and writer, and an event that never ceases to amaze with its creative use of both old and new solar technology.

While absorption chillers require 190°F (88°C) heat, flat-plate collectors can only reach 160°F (71°C). Evacuated tube collectors are more efficient and able to deliver the needed heat. The University of Cincinnati home used a large "fence" of evacuated tube solar thermal collectors situated on the south-facing patio of the home to heat water that was stored in a large insulated tank. That heat energy was then used in an absorption chiller to air-condition the house in the summer. The evacuated tube collectors also heated the domestic hot water and easily provided space heating for the home in the wintertime.

So when is solar air-conditioning coming to a home near you? Not tomorrow, but the technology is advancing. "Absorption-cycle heat pumps" are now on the market but are very expensive and only available in larger sizes, suitable for very large homes or commercial buildings. As the technology matures, keep an eye out for advances in it that will make plentiful summertime solar thermal energy useful for cooling smaller spaces, like the average American home.

the panels during the winter, which I find disconcerting, but once the sun comes out, the frames warm and snow melts off. Rain keeps the panels clean in all but the most dusty, arid places, where cleaning may be necessary once or twice a year. Once your system is installed, be sure to call your homeowners' insurance company and add the system to your policy. If you live in a hail-prone region, extra insurance protection may be advisable.

Contrary to popular belief, PV panels can generate a meaningful amount of power, even on cloudy days. Al Compaan, a physics professor and solar researcher at the University of Toledo, once told me that if two identical photovoltaic systems were installed,

FIGURE 10.9 This is our 4kW solar array installed on the new, nearly flat, rear roof of our retrofitted home. The system generates 90 percent of the electricity we use in a typical year. Photograph by Sherri James.

one in Miami, Florida, and one in Toledo, Ohio, the Toledo installation would generate 85 percent as much power as the Miami installation. That means the Toledo installation needs only 15 percent more solar panel area to equal the output of the Florida system. Thus, with the prices of solar panels continuing to decrease, solar energy is becoming viable in more and more places.

Including passive solar elements in your retrofit design may call for the expertise of an architect who is familiar with your climate and with passive solar techniques. If you envision adding active solar thermal and/or photovoltaic systems, a call to a local solar installer will get the ball rolling. The installer will usually do a free site evaluation and make recommendations on whether your home is properly situated for solar energy. They'll design a system based on the available mounting space and the amount of electricity you currently use. They can also assist you with lining up the many potential incentives and financing. Many solar companies now even offer leasing programs in which homeowners have no upfront costs at all, but receive a 20 to 25 percent reduction on their electric bills for the life of the installed system. At the end of the lease period, you can opt to renew your lease with new panels or have the panels removed at no cost. The solar installation company then makes its profit in the incentives, SRECs, and excess power generation. Even if you don't live in the sunny southwest, it can't hurt to talk with a solar installer to explore your options.

┅ Wind and Micro-Hydro Power ┅

Most houses that are candidates for deep energy retrofits aren't located in places where they can take advantage of small-scale wind generators and micro-hydro power. Wind power is unlikely to be useful in most of these settings for two reasons. First, in order for residential wind power to be viable, a home must be located in a region that experiences average sustained wind speeds of at least 10 miles per hour. Data from the US Department of Energy on average wind speeds at a height of 30 meters (about 98 feet) off the ground shows that most of the country doesn't meet these standards.

The second problem with residential wind power is the height issue. The DOE provides data on average wind speeds at a height of 30 meters because, at lower levels, obstacles like trees and buildings obstruct the wind's path, slowing it down. That's why you usually see wind generators mounted on towers or tall poles. Most neighborhoods have restrictions on the height of towers for safety and aesthetic reasons, so a home wind generator usually isn't an option. While rooftop mounting of a wind turbine might seem like a good idea at first blush, the vibration from its operation and the turbulence of the wind at roof height would make wind generation there annoying and unstable. That relegates wind generators to places without rules against raising high towers, like rural areas.

Engineers are trying to develop new wind generator designs that can be mounted closer to ground level. Vertical Axis Wind Turbines (VAWTs) are an example. They have twisted, helical blades that spin around a central, vertical shaft. These turbines are usually mounted closer to the ground because they require lower average wind speeds for operation. They also create less vibration than horizontal axis turbines, which gives them the potential for being mounted on rooftops. The current designs aren't yet perfect, however, since current VAWTs are still sensitive to stalling in gusty winds, and the particular stresses on their blades cause them to fail more often than standard horizontal axis wind turbines like the ones you see in fields or on ridgetops.

Similar problems, albeit problems much lower to the ground, affect micro-hydro power. Very few people live in areas where a small stream's energy can be harnessed, so micro-hydro power option can't be widely adopted. Even those with access to a viable water source face the problems of wildlife effects, water rights, and high system maintenance.

FIGURE 10.10 Vertical axis wind turbines (VAWT) like this one made by Urban Green Energy solve some problems of integrating wind power into residential areas by requiring lower average wind speeds for operation and markedly reducing vibration in their operation, making them suitable for rooftop installation. Photograph courtesy of Urban Green Energy.

As an idealist, I love the pure idea of wind and hydro power. As a pragmatist, I can't justify recommending them at the residential scale for the average homeowner. If your particular circumstances warrant the use of residential wind or micro-hydro power, good for you. There are lots of great resources out there to help you get started. For the rest of us, wind and hydro power will best be experienced at the utility-scale level. I had originally dreamed about installing VAWTs on the roof of our house, before a good friend gently reined in my enthusiasm with his good sense. Now I enjoy seeing big wind farms off in the distance or a convoy of semi-trucks with "long load" banners carrying enormous windmill blades down the highway. "There goes another windmill," I tell the kids as I point them out. "There goes part of the solution."

Chapter Eleven

THE GREENED HOUSE EFFECT

A FRIEND AND FELLOW DO-IT-YOURSELF ENTHUSIAST ONCE DESCRIBED his first foray into home sausage-making as a "self-inflicted wound." Turns out that it may just make more sense to buy sausage from the store, rather than go through the pain of such an endeavor. I empathized with him, on a grand scale. We dreamed, planned, and designed for nearly 18 months before breaking ground on our deep energy retrofit on the day after Labor Day in 2009. It was already December before I had wrapped my self-inflicted wound of a house against the weather, but there was still a laundry list of important tasks to be done stretching out into our future.

≫ Finishing the "Honey Do" List ≪

When I came out of hibernation a few months later as spring melted the last of the snow off the solar panels, installing trim and siding was next on the agenda. I had hoped to hire a crew to do it, but we

FIGURE 11.1 Using PacTool hands-free gauges allows me to install LP SmartSide siding on my own, saving me the expense of hiring extra workers. Photograph by Sherri James.

had officially run out of DER money, so it fell to me. I considered hiring a helper, but even that would stress our budget. It looked like Sherri would have to join the siding crew, so that I'd have someone to help hold up "the other end" of each piece as it was installed. That made me think back to our pre-DER home and the old, cramped office we shared: The experience of becoming her office nemesis left me wary, so I opted to look for a do-it-yourself solution.

I found it in an $80 pair of siding clamps that allowed me to install the engineered siding alone. The clever design held each course in place, hands-free. Then I could shoot siding nails to hang a piece, move the clamps up, and add another course. Up the ladder, down the ladder, back up the ladder, working my way to the top of each wall. In about eight weeks I trimmed and sided the entire exterior of the house in my "spare time." Sherri followed behind me, caulked and painted, and in no time our little blue house looked like new.

As the spring wore on, I attacked other jobs on the exterior. First, I replaced the old roofs on the new bay windows in front with standing-seam copper. I'd never fabricated a metal, standing-seam roof before, but with a borrowed metal brake and an online tutorial, I was able to fashion passable tops for the bay windows. The gutters came next. I found half-round, faux copper gutters online and hired a local crew to install them. A local woodworker fashioned trim pieces for the rounded dormers and the front door, adding enough relief detail to really make the finished façade eye-catching. In the backyard, I

FIGURE 11.2 Sherri paints the new siding, bringing back the "little blue house" just as our daughter, Sylvie, wanted. Photograph by Jeff Wilson.

found time to replace the end of the deck that I had removed to make room for the addition. With a cleaning and new waterproofing coat, the backyard entertaining space was back in business. One by one, tasks on my oversized "honey do" list were checked off.

While I finished up the outdoor tasks, Sherri installed fiberglass batt insulation over the spray foam in the interior of the

FIGURE 11.3 I learn to bend sheet copper into standing seam roofing on a metal brake for the bay windows. Photograph by Sherri James.

FIGURE 11.4 A finished bay window looks terrific with my standing seam copper roof and a decorative band of copper wrapped around the bottom. Photograph by Sherri James.

addition. We even put my father-in-law to work on that task when he came to visit. With the insulation installed, drywall was next. After the dust cleared, we launched into finishing the space, opting for as many locally made finish materials as we could. This included Seneca Hand Mold tile, which is fabricated not three hours' drive from our town. The clay they used to make the tile is dug within an hour of the factory. Visiting the plant, we were impressed by the enormous beehive kilns and lightly mechanized production line. Being predominantly human-powered, it felt like

FIGURE 11.5 The faux copper gutters we ordered through GutterSupply.com complement the EcoStar recycled rubber faux slate roof. Photograph by Sherri James.

FIGURE 11.6 I help out by adding batt insulation on the addition interior over the layer of spray foam I installed earlier. Don't let the photo fool you—Sherri did most of this work! Photograph by Sherri James.

something out of the 19th century. There, we were able to talk with the owner, Jim Fry, who told us that the recession had hit them hard, but they were staying afloat. He couldn't beat cheap imports on price, but he hoped that a trend toward using local building products would help sales of his hand-pressed and molded product. It was hard to be optimistic in a tough construction market, Jim said. We promised to spread the word about Seneca Hand Mold, and he promised to try to keep those good American jobs right here at home.

We laid and finished locally grown and milled cherry flooring and installed cherry bookshelves and trim. I put in LED recessed and track lighting. In the new bathroom, low-flow fixtures would keep our water use to a minimum. Sherri designed a one-of-a-kind bottle window that fit in the wall between the shower and the open living area of the loft apartment. The blue and green glass window was stunning, and it was a kind of monument to our lifestyle: a creative, frugal, unique way to make the space our own.

➤ Was It Worth It? ◄

Putting the finishing touches on the last bit of DER work in the basement was the final skirmish in the war on our home's energy efficiency problems. After that, we took a well-deserved break, getting away from the house for a visit with family out west. When we came home from that trip, we were pleasantly surprised: For the first time since we moved in a dozen years prior, the smell of mold didn't assault our senses on reentry. It seemed that we had finally kicked the condensation and mold problem in our basement. Another surprise came in the mail: our electric bill showed that, from April through September, our solar panels had produced more power each month than we had consumed. About the same time, we received a check for $500 from the broker that sells our Solar Renewable Energy Credits. The DER was paying off.

FIGURE 11.7 The new bathroom radiates beauty, elegance, and character with the Seneca Hand Mold tile and recycled glass countertops from Glass Recycled. Photograph by Sherri James.

Before the DER, our 70-year-old house consistently let my family down in both ways that we could measure and ways we couldn't. One look at a gas bill in February was enough to tell us that the house was inefficient. One sniff of the air inside the house during humid summer months was enough to alert us that the air quality was compromised by mold. One exceptionally cold or hot spell was enough to convince us that the old place was uncomfortable. The original HERS home energy audit revealed the things we couldn't always see or sense and pointed to larger problems of major air and moisture infiltration, lack of proper insulation, and some potentially serious indoor air quality problems. Now, at the end point of the DER process, our energy bills are down by more than 85 percent (despite adding square footage), we're far more comfortable in all seasons, and our indoor air quality has improved markedly. In all of the ways we had hoped, our DER is paying dividends.

⊱ Smarter Energy Tomorrow ⊰

It's also getting us ready for a new energy future. As things are now, most of the electricity generated in the United States is delivered to customers via the aging power grid. The grid consists of big, centralized plants generating power that is sent out via large transmission lines, feeding into substations and transformers. From there, local power lines come into neighborhoods and deliver electricity to businesses and homes. That setup has worked fine for the last hundred years, but now, due to lack of public investment in this critical part of our infrastructure, it's deteriorating, leading to more frequent and widespread power outages during storms and in times of heavy demand. It's also inefficient: at least 7 percent of the original power generated at a typical plant is lost during transmission, simply due to distance between the plant and the end user.

What's needed to ensure uninterrupted, efficient power for decades to come is a smart grid system that would replace the existing one-way, generator-to-home analog system with a multidirectional, energy-plus-information network that would allow real-time communication between generation, end users, and electricity markets. Basically, a smart grid would not only deliver electricity, but it would be able to monitor how that electricity is being used. It would also be able to sense disruptions in the grid and route power around the disruption to avoid blackouts. It would allow us to participate in the system by automating parts of our

FIGURE 11.8 Here are three views of the finished interior in the loft apartment (clockwise from top): looking into the kitchenette; looking down out of the sleeping loft to the living area; and looking up from the living area to the loft. Photographs by Sherri James.

electricity use and allow us to better sell power back to the grid from solar panels and wind generators. Here's how it might work in our smart home of the future:

First, a smart meter is installed, which not only monitors how much power I buy from the utility, but also how much solar energy I sell back to the utility from my photovoltaic system. (As a matter of fact, a smart meter was installed at my house when my solar panels were connected to the grid.) Then some appliances will have computer chips installed to allow the smart meter some degree of control over my HVAC, refrigerator, washer, dryer, and other large energy users. My utility will then offer me a financial incentive to sign up for a program that will allow their computers to remotely control some of those appliances to more efficiently manage power delivery throughout the day and over different seasons. For example, on the very hottest day of the year, I might allow the utility to remotely raise the temperature by a degree or two in my home to ensure they have enough power to go around without causing a blackout. Or I might allow them to defer the defrost cycle in my freezer until the middle of the night when there is less demand and power is more plentiful and cheaper to generate. I could use the system the same way to my advantage—for example, telling my dishwasher or electric dryer to start at 3:00 a.m., when power is cheapest. With a smart home on a smart grid, each homeowner would be able to customize an energy plan that fit his or her lifestyle.

The new smart grid will be able to more easily differentiate between expensive, peak-usage power and cheaper, off-peak power, and my smart home will then be able to communicate with energy markets to sell power from my solar panels at peak-usage rates and buy power at off-peak rates to maximize my savings even more. This automated market could also take advantage of the batteries in my plug-in hybrid or electric car to store power when it's cheap and sell it when it's more expensive. All of the smart grid advantages will amplify the savings of our DER by making even better use of energy in our home and our community. The DER makes our home "plug and play" when the smart grid finally reaches our town. Bring on the energy future; we're ready.

⚡ Small Ripples in a Big Ocean ⚡

In our small way, we're also making a difference in solving economic, environmental, and national security problems. Our DER put several local construction crews to work during a tough time. From pouring the new concrete foundation and slab on the replacement addition, to framing and roofing the addition and retrofit elements, to installing the photovoltaic system, our dollars went to help pay wages directly to at least 20 people. Indirectly, we helped support the jobs of their office staffs and the manufacturing jobs that produced the materials used in the project. Purchase of those materials helped to support jobs all the way up and down the material supply chain and out into the communities where those people lived, even helping to support the pizza shops and bookstores in their communities. Broken down to the individual level, it was small, but our economic effect was there.

FIGURE 11.9 Sherri's Blue Moon Bottles window installation in the new addition—her reclaimed bottle art is well represented in our home, with pendant lighting, tumblers, and even furniture made from recycled bottles. Photograph by Sherri James.

In the short term, the environment suffered a bit due to our retrofit activity. We had to send some of the construction debris to the landfill, and energy and natural resources were consumed to create the materials we used. However, that view takes the brief remodeling phase out of context, when it should be seen as only a moment in the life of the building. It's said that the greenest building is the one that's already built, because so much energy is embodied in the existing structure. Tearing an old building down to start over would be a tremendous waste of materials and energy and would require vast amounts of new materials and energy to replace. By retrofitting, we retain much of the embodied energy of the original home but also ameliorate the bulk of its ongoing negative effects on the environment. The next 70 years of this home's life will consume a tiny fraction of the energy it did during the first 70 years. During that time, it will contribute less to the environmental damage associated with energy production, from mountaintop removal to extract coal, watershed devastation, mercury pollution, and rising atmospheric carbon dioxide levels to nuclear energy's radioactive waste, to the potential aquifer contamination caused by hydrofracking to extract natural gas. People who are affected by these evils of our fossil fuel consumption will live slightly longer, healthier lives. Small as the effect that this one deep energy retrofitted home may have on the larger world, that effect exists. Oh, and by the way, remember that land we bought so that we could move to the country? We've decided to keep it, continuing to rehabilitate the damaged hills into good Ohio woodland. I consider it an environmental investment, and a good carbon sink.

On the national security front, our individual effect would be extremely difficult to measure. Still, I hope that some of the energy we save can be put to use in plug-in hybrid vehicles here at home, reducing our need for gasoline in the transportation sector. This would mean that America would import that much less foreign oil. And I hold on to the vision that as hundreds of thousands or millions of DERs are completed, the need for expensive, dangerous military intervention in unstable oil-producing regions of the world would lessen. Fewer American soldiers would be put in harm's way just to help slake our thirst for cheap oil, and more American tax dollars could stay here at home to help solve domestic problems. I won't argue that one individual DER will solve that problem, but millions of DERs, along with a bit of creative rethinking of how we use energy to travel from one place to another, just might do the trick.

✺ Little Blue House, Great Big Picture ✺

Many Americans are still stunned by the breadth and depth of the recent Great Recession. We look forward to the day when all Americans who want to work can, and to the day that the real American Dream is restored. But as the world's economy now begins to repeat its Sisyphean climb, those of us in developed nations are being accompanied by many rising from the Third World, who see as their birthright the same high standard of living that we have enjoyed for generations. Those hundreds of millions of people, on the move from debilitating poverty to their version of the middle class, are in danger of drowning us all in a tidal wave of new, American-style consumption. We cannot simply ignore this predicament, nor can we deny a higher standard of living to people who have endured such economic oppression. Our only hope is to dramatically change the model of our standard of living so that we can deliver a comfortable, 21st century lifestyle without destroying it at the same time. Deep energy retrofits set the example for change, by offering a better life at a minor fraction of the economic, environmental, and security costs of the old model.

People rising out of poverty around the world aspire to a better life, just the way our ancestors did, but instead of leaving their homes for a distant land, they're creating their own versions of the American Dream right in their own homes. They are a product of the latest wave of globalization. That's not a word many people want to be reminded of while in our plodding economic recovery. However, globalization has enriched and enfranchised everyone on Earth, including the poorest of Americans. Low wages overseas have meant lower prices on goods here at home, which has served to boost Americans' buying power, making us richer in aggregate, despite a loss of jobs. That wealth is something most of us have experienced: it now costs us less to live at a higher standard of living than it used to. We become wealthier over time, and energy efficiency adds to that wealth with savings every day.

In theory, we would save that wealth and simply work less, giving us more leisure time. Time to learn a new skill or spend with family. More time for our kids, more time to learn to play the guitar, more time to read a good book, or more time to go fishing with a grandparent. Leisure time not your thing? Then we can put that extra energy into volunteering, working to make the world a better place. We can get involved in our communities and help out our

FIGURE 11.10 Winter, me, Sherri, and Sylvie (left to right) and the real star of the show: our deep energy retrofitted home. Photograph by Sherri James.

neighbors. If you take that idea a step further, by opting to work less time at a job, those labor hours could be shared with an American who is jobless. Job sharing can stimulate total employment while allowing us the time to take advantage of our 21st century wealth. As unemployment lessens, the economy becomes healthier, and we're all better off.

Instead, we're squandering our newfound wealth on an ever-increasing pile of shiny electronic gadgets that we soon lose interest in when the next latest version hits the market. This tendency led David Owen, author of *The Conundrum*, to opine that energy efficiency will solve nothing if we simply spend our new wealth on more energy-sucking, carbon-spewing, pollution-producing junk. While his book is light on mathematics on the subject, his basic premise is correct: energy efficiency alone won't get us to the solutions of a sound economy, clean environment, and safe world that we seek. It's also going to take the character, frugality, creativity, imagination, and the sacrifice of every man, woman, and child to make a meaningful, lasting change in our society.

⇟ The R Word: Responsibility ⇞

As Americans, we are the biggest consumers of energy on the planet. Therefore, we're the most responsible, not only for our own energy woes, but also for those that we export around the world.

What does that responsibility entail? For some, it requires sacrifice like that of our brave men and women of the US armed forces. Many of them awake daily in a world where their lives and limbs are put in harm's way because of our energy use at home. Their families suffer the kinds of losses that most of us can't even imagine. Still other Americans, soldiers and civilians alike, die right here on American soil because the rest of us are too absorbed with our own lives to bother conserving energy. Oblivious, we continue wasting energy, and therefore spew more mercury, sulfur, and soot into the air, water, and soil. That means that an unlucky few of our fellow Americans get sick with asthma, cancer, or another malady, and die early, painful deaths.

For most of us, our responsibility comes in the form of facing our own culpability as perpetrators of these crimes. Look: this isn't precisely *your* fault, nor is it precisely *my* fault. It is, however, incrementally both of our faults, in what is known as a "tragedy of the commons." The basic idea is this: when each of us individually overuses a common resource—in this case, energy—eventually, that common resource will be depleted or irreparably damaged through that overuse. This will happen through no real "fault" of the individual, but simply through each of us blindly using what we believe is our fair share. Without knowing, we undermine the overall economy by leaving ourselves open to damage by wide swings in energy prices. Without knowing, we subject our neighbors to the leveling of their mountains and the poisoning of their supplies of air, food, and water. Without knowing, we are collectively putting American soldiers at risk every day.

The tragedy of the commons was originally witnessed and written about by 19th century economist William Forster Lloyd. He saw farmers grazing their cattle in pastures that were owned by all—the common. As farmers added cows to the common, they enriched themselves. At the same time, each cow slightly damaged the pasture by grazing. Eventually, the number of cows reached a point at which the pasture was damaged beyond repair. That meant no cows could be grazed there, and all of the farmers suffered—the tragedy. In the 20th century, ecologist Garrett Hardin applied that idea generally to all things we hold in common, coining the phrase so widely used today. Most importantly, Hardin wrote that regulation—agreements assigning rights equally to all individuals involved in a common—was the solution to the problem. Essentially, science can tell us where the economic and ecological tipping

Operation Free

"Our military has recognized that there are costs beyond the price that we pay for a barrel of oil or a kilowatt-hour of electricity that need to be dealt with." That quote came from Vice Admiral Dennis V. McGinn (Ret.), who recently became president of the American Council on Renewable Energy, as he tried to explain why energy efficiency and renewables are becoming a key part of the military's energy strategy. Does a retired vice admiral seem like an odd fit for a renewable energy group? Hardly. Since the military is one of the largest single energy consuming entities in the world, McGinn is keenly aware of the negative effects of energy inefficiency. Fuel convoys are among the most dangerous details in hostile regions, and lack of energy supplies on the battlefield can be deadly.

He's not the only military official who is aware: Operation Free is a nationwide coalition of veterans who support energy efficiency, renewables, and alternatives to fossil fuels. Its mission states, "America's billion-dollar-a-day dependence on oil from hostile nations directly funds our most dangerous enemies, putting guns and bullets into the hands of our enemies . . . like al Qaeda and the Taliban. With new, clean sources of energy to power our economy and fuel our military, we will no longer be forced to pay and protect regimes that support terrorism." It's a powerful message from the very people who have laid down their lives to protect our access to foreign energy.

On the home front, Operation Free points veterans to companies like Airstreams Renewables, Inc., a school that trains veterans and others for jobs in the wind power industry. One recent Airstreams graduate, veteran Lawrence "Scott" Fuller, explained his interest in renewable power this way: "Due to our country's dependency on foreign energy, climate change, and my brothers and cousins stationed in the Middle East, I decided to help the situation the best way I knew how; by using 12 years of experience in mechanical, electrical, and hydraulics to work in the renewable energy industry."

Learn more at www.operationfree.net.

points are in various commons, and then we can use that information to draft rules that ensure a commonly held resource is used in a responsible, sustainable manner. The idea has been widely and successfully used in threatened fisheries to ensure fish populations thrive while still providing fish for us to eat. It's also been used on ecologically sensitive rangeland to make sure cattle can be grazed without ultimately ruining habitat for wildlife.

In light of our "energy common" in the United States of America, those regulations could take the form of laws governing how much energy a home or vehicle would be allowed to use—rationing that would ensure enough for everyone but encourage efficiency to minimize damage to our economy, environment, and

Different Politics, Same Solutions

In the early 1980s, when I was a teenager, my family started construction on my parents' Cape Cod–style dream home. The forward-thinking, passive solar home was an elegant use of traditional design, proper building orientation, lots of southern glazing, and carefully calculated roof eave length, which let the sun in during the cold Michigan winter months but kept it out during the sweltering summers. Well before its time, it used a geothermal heat pump—technology that wasn't to become widely used until the turn of the 21st century.

My father did much of the design work himself. Dad was a dyed-in-the-wool, government- and God-fearing Republican, who happened to be a bright, considerate, and thoughtful civil engineer. He believed that the house he helped design, and that he mostly built with his own two hands, would save our family from the energy crises we'd lived through in the 1970s. He believed in an energy independence that kept us separated from the evils of the world.

I did say that he helped to design that house. The other half of that team came from my mother's side of the family. Great-Grandpa Murray Goddard was a stung-by-the-Depression, populist progressive Democrat, who also just happened to be a bright, considerate, and thoughtful civil engineer. His various interests included architecture, bread-making, sailing, genealogy, writing, and experimenting with solar energy. I learned later from my mother that Murray had been an early advocate for desegregation, and that his solar experiments were partially aimed at bringing "power to the people." His interest was in energy *interdependence*, which had the power to bring us together through simple, inexpensive, democratizing solutions.

Great-Grandpa Murray and Dad passed the plans for that house back and forth through the US mail for years, editing and reediting until they came up with the final blueprints. During the process, both men supplied ingenious solutions to the same end. When it was built, the house was much more than just a house; it was the embodiment of both men's ideals, from both ends of the political spectrum, but with the same passion for real solutions to tackling energy problems. Two guys, different politics, same solution.

I tell this story here because it's a microcosm of our own, divided culture. Energy efficiency makes sense, whatever your politics. If you're a right wing, redneck, card-carrying member of the National Rifle Association (NRA), we've got a better economy and energy security for you. If you're a left wing, granola crunching, card-carrying member of the American Civil Liberties Union (ACLU), we've got a better economy and environment for you. If you're like me, a pragmatic idealist, take all three, along with all of the other benefits of the Greened House Effect. Here's a patriotism that everyone can participate in: deep energy retrofit patriotism gets you off the couch and away from the television. A positive, actionable solution that walks all talks and lets you spur on the economy, clean up the environment, and contribute to our national security, right from your own home.

security. More likely, we would simply make laws restricting the amounts of specific types of pollution that could be emitted from energy-generating plants, vehicles, factories, and buildings. That would be most easily done in the form of a tax on each pollutant, making it more expensive to pollute, in turn encouraging all of us to use energy more wisely. The revenue from those taxes would then be distributed to fund energy efficiency projects like deep energy retrofits on older homes and buildings. That would come in the form of grants, tax credits, low-interest loans, and other incentives for energy efficiency. Although you would pay more per gallon at the pump and per kilowatt-hour on your electric bill, your overall energy bills would drop because your home and vehicle would be ultra energy efficient.

Any mention of taxes, subsidies, or rising energy prices sends some political ideologues through the roof. What they conveniently ignore are the enormous subsidies we taxpayers already give to the fossil fuel industry in the form of billions of dollars in defense spending, billions more in health care, and billions more still on environmental cleanup of Superfund sites, oil spills, and mountain-top removal coal mines. Which would you rather fund: a fossil fuel industry set up to profit at everyone's expense, or a homegrown energy efficiency initiative that makes life better for everyone? And how can we justify continuing on our current course? Is it more patriotic to wave a flag, which costs us nothing, or sacrifice some of our own treasure to keep American soldiers out of harm's way?

It would be hard to look at history and argue that passive flag-waving has ever gotten us anywhere. America has been and is being built on the rolled-up sleeves, determination, and ingenuity of patriots of all stripes. Remember, it was a revolution, not a parade, that started this country. The common thread of America's great leaps forward is shared sacrifice. During World War II, on top of the incredible sacrifice of soldiers who fought, all Americans contributed to the war effort in buying war bonds, recycling scraps, enduring rationing, and volunteering with support organizations. The race to land a man on the moon cost American taxpayers dearly but at the same time developed technologies like photovoltaics, computing, and the advanced metallic alloys now used in artificial joints. American progress has always required American sacrifice.

At this point in history, energy efficiency deserves the same attention and sacrifice. We Americans should be insisting that our elected leaders work to rectify our energy problems. That should include taxes on pollution that truly reflect its effect on the economy, the environment, and national security. Those taxes should be levied so that we are discouraged from fouling our own nests. But remember, we're not only perpetrators of the tragedy of the commons; we will also be the beneficiaries once investments in restoring the health of the commons begin to pay off. As we pay more for our energy, those extra dollars should be circulated back through the economy as incentives to encourage even more energy saving practices and technology. This investment will stimulate innovation in efficiency and clean energy on a global scale.

Making these kinds of predictions can sound grandiose, I know, but 20 years ago the rise of the cell phone or tablet computer might have seemed just as unlikely. Some of the changes I foresee from the Greened House Effect might come in actual technology, while some of it might come in less tangible ways. We would live longer and certainly healthier lives. Our factories might adopt "cradle to cradle" industrial processes that utilize and recycle every part of an appliance for reuse in a newer, more efficient model. As energy is better democratized, we might have fewer skirmishes on foreign battlefields, saving American blood and treasure for better pursuits. An energy efficiency revolution could potentially transform the landscape, halting the leveling of mountains in Appalachia. Smart grid and smart home technology could transform the way we generate and use energy, creating a true "free market" of electronically traded electrons. What we experience as sacrifice now would eventually be felt as an investment well made, and history would smile upon us.

We can't *buy* our way out of the current and impending crises with the latest and greatest high-tech. We can't *buy* our way out of it by simply replacing our old stuff with newer, "greener" stuff. That approach only assures that we will continue to experience the *vicious circle* of energy waste and dependence. I would argue, though, that we can *save* our way out of these problems. We could sacrifice some of our current wealth, investing it in deep energy efficiency. As that investment pays dividends and interest in the form of savings, we could invest that in low-energy, non-polluting, life-enhancing activities that would continue to pay off in a *virtuous circle* that would have benefits for all of society.

On summer days at the community pool with my family, I like to jump into the water and start walking around the perimeter of the pool. My kids know the trick. Pretty soon, they join me, and a small current starts. Eventually, a few of the other kids catch on, and they become part of the group. Folks sitting at the edge see the current start to swell, and jump in to help in the effort. In time, we've got a genuine whirlpool going, with 20 or 30 people all jogging in the water, going in the same direction. When I give the sign, everybody lifts their feet, and we all enjoy a few laps around the pool, courtesy of our human-powered current. That's what we need now: a human-powered current.

It took me a while, but well into my forties, I've finally jumped into my own life with the spirit of my father and great-grandfather. It was hard to give up the old dreams of a pastoral country life, but the countless benefits of fixing what we have and staying put were inescapable. I would have loved to talk through that dilemma with Dad and Great-Grandpa, but ultimately I think they would have reached the same inevitable conclusion. Fixing energy efficiency at home, with its snowballing of positive effects, would have made sense to both to my conservative father and to my progressive great-grandfather. It would have been one of the things they could have agreed upon.

My mom said once, when I was ranting a standard teenaged invective against the numberless injustices and inequities in the world, "You can't fix it all. Pick one problem, work hard to fix it, and leave the other solutions to other dedicated people." It was good advice. That advice, married to Dad's and Great-Grandpa's ideas, spawned this story. This is the best that I can offer: the hope that we're smart enough and strong enough to mount a revolution, one deep energy retrofit at a time. One DER has a family-changing effect. Fifty DERs have a community-changing effect. A hundred million DERs have a transformational, planet-changing effect.

That's **the Greened House Effect**.

ACKNOWLEDGMENTS

I'm deeply grateful to Fern Marshall Bradley, Ben Watson, Pati Stone, and everyone at Chelsea Green, for their very hard work on this book. Thank you to my wife, Sherri James, for her photography and videography throughout the project. Illustrator Matt Baker came in at just the right time to rescue me from my lack of artistic talent—thank you. Also, thank you to my agents, Nikole Tsabasis and Jonathan Russo at Artists Agency.

Thanks to those who helped with information and images in the book: Nicholas Koch, John Krigger, Marc Porat, Bob and Tobie Johnson, Ted Clifton, Heather Clark, Alden Hathaway, Stacy Hunt, Craig Savage, David Krebs, David Thorpe, Andy Frame, David Connelly Legg, Sarah Cornwell, Eric Stears, and Aaron Lubeck.

Many people worked to help make the deep energy retrofit of our home possible. Thank you to Andrew Frowine; Tommy DeLoach; Ben Stolzfus and crew; Stalwart Construction; Adam from Athens Paint & Drywall; Third Sun Solar; Erik Kiilunen and EcoStud; Janelle at Guardian Energy Technologies; Joe Klink and everyone at Pro Via; Leigh Marie Lunn and everyone at GS&F and LP Building Products; Jim Fry at Seneca Hand Mold; Carl Bleakney, Charlie Taft, and Kelly Meyers at EcoStar; Craig Kinzelman and Jason Morosko at UltimateAir; David French at WeatherBond; Tim Whaley at Glass Recycled; Deb Richter at Kohler; Brice Hereford at Fastenmaster; and many more. Thank you to those I've forgotten to add to this list—I'm sure I missed a few of you. Thank you to Jeremy Tilley and Peter Koeppen at HGTVRemodels.com for their work on the "Energy Answers" package and the crew at Buildipedia.com for the At Home series on our addition.

I'd also like to thank my father, Donn Wilson, and my great-grandfather, Murray Goddard, both no longer with us, for the inspiration and early life lessons that led me to this project. Also, thank you to my mother, Joan Wilson, who taught me to finish what I start.

Thank you to Winter and Sylvie, for your patience, help, and badly needed comic relief along the way. See, we did it before you left home!

And finally, Sherri: From the start, my equal partner, creative spark. This project is just as much yours as mine. For your hard work, love, and even keel—thank you.

OUR HOME RENOVATION AND DEEP ENERGY RETROFIT TIMELINE

MAJOR CHANGES TAKE TIME, AND THAT'S CERTAINLY THE CASE WITH home renovations and retrofitting. Most families have to fit such projects in among the rest of real life: jobs, school, family commitments, community involvement, and everyday home cleaning and maintenance. Sherri and I actually implemented some of our home renovation and retrofitting projects more quickly than the average homeowner would because they became part of our paid work of creating home improvement videos, such as the installation of the outdoor kitchen and the installation of the kitchenette and bathroom in our new addition. But even so, our renovation and deep energy retrofit spanned a full decade—and I still have some home improvement projects up my sleeve for our little blue house!

MARCH 30, 2001	We move into our 1940s Cape Cod–style home in southeast Ohio.
MARCH 31, 2001	Furnace quits
APRIL 1, 2001	**Phase One DIY Remodel Begins—First Floor**
APRIL 2001–JUNE 2002	Kitchen gut remodel to bare studs, includes removal of walls for a new open-plan space including kitchen and half bath.
MAY 2002	I begin work as HGTV and DIY network host.
JUNE 2002	New tankless water heater installed.
SUMMER 2002	We paint the exterior siding (blue).
AUGUST 2002	Loose cellulose insulation installed into empty wall cavities.
SEPTEMBER 2002	**Phase Two DIY Remodel Begins—Main Bath**

September–December 2002	Bathroom gutted to studs and rebuilt.
January–December 2003	Tying up loose ends: bedrooms remodeled and painted; arched dormer windows restored.
November 2003	We purchase 60 acres in the country, begin planning "green dream home."
Fall 2003	Winter starts kindergarten.
June 2005	HVAC system replaced with high-efficiency system.
September 2005	**Phase Three DIY Remodel Begins—Outdoor Living**
Fall 2005–Fall 2007	Deck replaced; screened porch added; outdoor kitchen with hand-built brick bread oven constructed. All windows and doors replaced on the west side of the house.
Fall 2007	Sylvie starts kindergarten.
January–December 2008	Great recession officially underway. We make the decision to stay in the little blue house in town; search for solutions, decide on deep energy retrofit, begin planning phase.
August 2009	Home equity line of credit approved. We hire Stalwart Construction for major framing and roofing tasks.
September 9, 2009	**Phase Four Remodel DER Begins**
September–October 2009	Stalwart Construction frames new replacement garage addition, installs windows, roofing, and housewrap. Stalwart crew also frames the new rear dormer roof, retrofits main roof, and installs new bay window units.
September–December 2009	I retrofit the arched dormers and install spray foam and insulation for roof; I also install curtain wall on remaining exterior walls and install new windows and housewrap.
October 2009	Third Sun Solar installs 4kW solar array on rear dormer roof.
December 31, 2009	Third Sun Solar connects solar array to Wilson home and grid; panels begin generating usable power.
Spring 2010	I install engineered trim and siding to entire exterior. Sherri caulks and paints the new siding (blue).
Fall 2010–Spring 2011	We finish addition interior.
Fall 2011–Spring 2012	Basement is gutted, EcoStud plastic studs installed, spray foam insulation on interior, foam board on floor; finish materials installed.
Summer 2012	Our DER is complete.

DEEP ENERGY RETROFIT RESOURCES

As someone who works in the world of DIY media, I'm constantly amazed by the range of websites, books, videos, and more on green building and remodeling. In the listings below, I've assembled the most valuable sources I know of for homeowners contemplating a deep energy retrofit (DER). I've also included many sources of very specific technical information for contractors who want to learn retrofitting practices. There are also some general links and references, as well as a list of some of the books that have influenced my philosophical views on the economy, environment, national security, and deep energy retrofits.

One place you may want to start, if you haven't visited there already, is the official website of The Greened House Effect: www.thegreenedhouseeffect.com. There you'll find DER videos, my blogs, links, and more. HGTVRemodels.com turned our story into a set of articles and videos as their "Energy Answers" series (http://www.hgtvremodels.com/energy-answers/package/index.html). On the Buildipedia.com website you can see many of the "how-to" videos we shot of the installation of finish materials in our new addition (http://buildipedia.com/at-home/everyday-diy-video-series).

≫ General Deep Energy Retrofit Resources ≪

- Websites -

- www.greenbuildingadvisor.com: Green Building Advisor (GBA) is a source for homeowners and professionals with both detailed technical information and a robust community discussion of all things related to green construction.

- www.bpi.org: Building Performance Institute (BPI) develops standards, trains building science professionals, and helps homeowners find certified professionals.
- www.regreenprogram.org: The remodeling program of the US Green Building Council (USGBC); case studies and great DER information.
- www.buildingscience.com: Building Science Corporation maintains this free online resource of case studies and technical documents for both homeowners and pros.
- www.cchrc.org: Cold Climate Housing Research Center (CCHRC) has been building and testing high performance homes in Alaska for more than 30 years.
- www.energy.gov/energysaver: US Department of Energy's (DOE) online energy efficiency manual.
- www.energystar.gov: A joint project of the US DOE and US Environmental Protection Agency (EPA) rating appliances, building products, and homes; also a good general resource for energy efficiency matters.
- www.eere.energy.gov: US DOE's Office of Energy Efficiency and Renewable Energy (EERE).
- www.affordablecomfort.org: Affordable Comfort, Inc. (ACI) is a non-profit professional association for pros but also runs the "1000 Home Challenge," helping homeowners who sign up for the program through the DER process.
- www.buildingmedia.com: Building Media, Inc. is part of the Building America Retrofit Alliance and provides online training and certification in the building industry.
- www.eeba.org: Energy & Environmental Building Alliance (EEBA); provider of building science education for professionals and homeowners.

Books and Articles

Krigger, John, and Chris Dorsi. *The Homeowner's Handbook to Energy Efficiency: A Guide to Big and Small Improvements.* Helena, MT: Saturn Resource Management, 2008.

Lstiburek, Joseph W. *Builder's Guide to Cold Climates: Details for Design and Construction.* Newtown, CT: Taunton, 2000. Lstiburek has also written excellent builder's guides to hot-humid, mixed-humid, and dry climates.

Lstiburek, Joseph W. *Builder's Guide to Structural Insulated Panels (SIPs) for All Climates*. Somerville, MA: Building Science Corporation, 2008.

Lubeck, Aaron, and Francis Conlin. "Efficiency and Comfort Through Deep Energy Retrofits: Balancing Energy and Moisture Management." *Journal of Green Building* 5.3 (2010): 3–15.

⤮ Home Energy Use Analysis and Testing ⤮

- www.resnet.us: Residential Energy Services Network (RESNET); excellent source for general energy efficiency information, as well as clearinghouse for finding RESNET trained and certified HERS ("Home Energy Rating Systems") raters in your area.
- www.bpi.org: Search for local, certified home energy raters.
- www.energystar.gov: Search "home energy raters" and an interactive map will help you find Energy Star–qualified raters and contractors in your area.
- www.dsireusa.org: Find an energy audit financial incentive here.
- cs.oberlin.edu/~envs/dashboard/index.php: See Oberlin College's dormitory energy competition and the Building Dashboard monitor.
- www.energy.gov: Download the *Energy Savers Booklet; Tips on Saving Energy & Money at Home.*
- www.flir.com: Flir is a leading manufacturer of infrared (IR) cameras.

⤮ Green Building Design ⤮

⊷ Websites ⊷

- www.regreenprogram.org
- www.greenremodeling.org: National Association of the Remodeling Industry; find contractors, learn about green remodeling.
- Find green certification programs for your DER:
  - www.nahbgreen.org
  - www.usgbc.org
  - www.earthcraft.org/renovation
  - www.northwestenergystar.com.

- www.energystar.com: For a good guide on air sealing, download *A Do-It-Yourself Guide to Energy Star Home Sealing*.
- www.castledeepenergy.com: More about the deep energy retrofit of the Castle Square Apartments in Boston.
- www.barateam.org/CEH: Building America Retrofit Alliance and more information on the Cool Energy House in Florida (from sidebar).
- beopt.nrel.gov: Source of information and download of free Building Energy Optimization (BEOpt) Software developed by the National Renewable Energy Laboratory.
- www.egreengroup.com: Nicholas Koch's Equitable Green Group construction company, which focuses on the passive house standard for new construction and renovation.
- www.passivehouse.us: The Passive House Institute US website.
- foundationhandbook.ornl.gov: Oak Ridge National Laboratory's Foundation Handbook is a great source for proper basement, crawl space, and foundation design.
- www.cchrc.org: Developed REMOTE wall system.

◆ Books ◆

Bainbridge, David A., and Kenneth L. Haggard. *Passive Solar Architecture: Heating, Cooling, Ventilation, Daylighting, and More Using Natural Flows*. White River Junction, VT: Chelsea Green Pub., 2011.

Cotterell, Janet, and Adam Dadeby. *Passivhaus Handbook: A Practical Guide to Constructing and Refurbishing Buildings for Ultra-low-energy Performance*. Totnes, UK: Green Books, 2012.

Lubeck, Aaron. *Green Restorations: Sustainable Building and Historic Homes*. Gabriola Island, BC: New Society, 2010.

Meisel, Ari. *LEED Materials: A Resource Guide to Green Building*. New York, NY: Princeton Architectural, 2010.

⇥ Hiring Building Professionals ⇤

- www.energystar.gov/index.cfm?c=heat_cool.pr_contractors_10tips: Help in hiring an HVAC contractor; also, download the *Guide to Energy Efficient Cooling and Heating* while you're there.
- Find certified green remodeling pros in your area:
  www.nari.org/certify
  www.nahb.org

> www.greenadvantage.org
>
> www.bpi.org
>
> www.sips.com: Structural Insulated Panel Association; trade group provides training and certification for builders; find a SIPs builder or manufacturer in your region.

- www.installationmastersusa.com: Find trained, certified window and door installers in your region.
- www.awdi.com: American Window and Door Institute; find trained, certified window and door installers in your region.
- www.natex.org: North American Technician Excellence, Inc. is a leading non-profit certification program for HVAC installers.

❧ Financial Resources and Incentive Programs ❦

- www.dsireusa.org: Federal, state, local, and utility financial incentives for energy efficiency and renewables; updated weekly.
- www.resnet.us: Energy Improvement Mortgage (EIM) information.
- www.energystar.gov: Search for incentives and EIM information.
- www.energytaxincentives.org: Tax Incentives Assistance Program (TIAP).
- www.hud.gov: US Dept. of Housing and Urban Development (HUD) and the Federal Housing Administration (FHA); search "Home Improvement" for more information on FHA 203k renovation loans.
- www.fanniemae.com: Search for the Fannie Mae "HomeStyle" renovation loan.
- www.solsystemscompany.com: Sol Systems is our SREC broker.

❧ Construction Principles and Techniques ❦

Goddard, Murray C., Mike Wolverton, and Ruth Wolverton, *How to Be Your Own Architect*. Blue Ridge Summit, PA: Tab, 1985. This is a book my Great-Grandfather Murray originally wrote.

Holladay, Martin. "'Innie' Windows or 'Outie' Windows?" published on the Green Building Advisor website. http://www.greenbuildingadvisor.com/blogs/dept/musings/innie-windows-or-outie-windows.

Lstiburek, Joseph. "Foam Shrinks, and Other Lessons." *Fine Homebuilding* February/March (2012): 55–59.

Lstiburek, Joseph W., and John Carmody. *Moisture Control Handbook: Principles and Practices for Residential and Small Commercial Buildings*. New York: J. Wiley, 1994.

Susanka, Sarah, and Marc Vassallo. *Not So Big Remodeling: Tailoring Your Home for the Way You Really Live*. Newtown, CT: Taunton, 2009.

Wagner, John D. *Advanced Framing: Techniques, Troubleshooting & Structural Design*. Williston, VT: Journal of Light Construction, 2004.

⤜ DER Materials and Components ⤛

⤙ Walls, Windows, and Doors ⤚

- www.pactool.us: PacTool International makes the Gecko Gauge, the hands-free siding installation clamps I used to side the house by myself.
- www.ecostud.com: Erik Kiilunen's recycled plastic stud system.
- www.quadlock.com: Quadlock manufactures the R-ETRO masonry retrofit system.
- www.lpcorp.com: LP makes the SmartSide trim and siding used on our project.
- www.proviadoor.com: Pro Via makes the windows and doors used on our project.

⤙ Air Sealing and Insulation ⤚

- www.sprayfoamdirect.com: Foam it Green spray foam kits used on our project.

⤙ Roofs and Attics ⤚

- www.coolroofs.org: Information on Solar Reflectance Index (SRI) of roofing materials, links to contractors and products for cool roofs.
- www.olyfast.com: Home of OMG Roofing and good source for information and fasteners used in roof retrofitting applications. Brice Hereford of OMG is an expert on fasteners for DER projects.

- www.lpcorp.com: LP Building Products made the engineered wood rafters (SolidStart) and radiant barrier sheathing (Tech-Shield) used on our roof.
- www.ecostarllc.com: EcoStar made the 80 percent recycled rubber "Majestic" faux slate used on our roof.
- www.weatherbondroofing.com: WeatherBond is the white TPO membrane roofing used on our nearly flat rear roof.
- www.solatube.com: Manufacturer of Solatube skylight tubes.
- www.insulationsolutions.com: Manufacturer of Insullite recessed light covers for buildings.
- www.hpanels.com: Hunter Panels manufactures Cool-Vent vented nailbase for roofs.
- www.guttersupply.com: All types of gutter materials like our half-round faux copper gutters and downspouts.

⬝ Interior Finishes ⬝

- www.bluemoonbottles.com: This is the website of Sherri's art glass business, Blue Moon Bottles.
- www.senecahandmold.com: Seneca Hand Mold makes the locally produced, handmade tile used in our addition.
- glassrecycled.com: Glass Recycled makes the recycled glass countertop material used in our addition.
- www.kohler.com: Kohler makes the low-flow water fixtures used in our addition.
- www.creelighting.com: CREE makes the LED lighting used in our addition.

⬝ Home Systems ⬝

- www.ultimateair.com: Ultimate Air makes the ReCoupAerator, the energy recovery ventilator we installed on our project.
- www.acca.org: Air Conditioning Contractors of America; sets standards for proper HVAC installation (Manual J & Manual D among them).
- www.arzel.com: Arzel manufactures and installs HVAC zoning damper systems.
- www.gothotwater.com: Manufacturer of the D'Mand hot water circulation pump.
- www.retherm.com: Manufactures drain water heat recovery units.
- www.energystar.com: Find Energy Star–rated HVAC, appliances, and electronics.

- www.crestron.com: Crestron home automation and energy monitoring.

⇥ Basements ⇤

- www.certainteed.com: CertainTeed makes Platon drain mats for many applications, including basement wall and floor retrofitting.
- www.dranjer.ca: Source for floor "check-valve" retrofit drains.

⇥ Recycling Construction Materials ⇤

- www.habitat.org: Search for a ReStore in your area to donate used building materials instead of throwing them away.
- www.shinglerecycling.org: Find asphalt shingle recycling in your area.
- www.jacoenvironmental.com: Search for appliance recycling in your region.

⇥ Renewable Energy ⇤

- www.ases.org: American Solar Energy Society.
- www.awea.org: American Wind Energy Association.
- www.eere.energy.gov: Great source for renewable energy information.
- www.third-sun.com: Third Sun installed our 4kW solar array.
- www.cansolair.com: CanSolAir manufactures solar thermal air heating panels.
- www.apricus.com: Manufacturer of evacuated tube solar water heating.
- www.urbangreenenergy.com: UGE manufactures VAWTs.
- www.air-streams.com: Provides technical training in renewable power installation and maintenance to veterans and others.
- apps3.eere.energy.gov/greenpower/: Purchase renewable energy from your utility; listings by state.
- www.operationfree.net: American veterans' group dedicated to reducing United States demand for foreign energy.

⫸ Philosophy ⫷

⫶ Websites ⫶

- www.ilovemountains.org: Organization dedicated to ending mountaintop removal coal mining.
- www.architecture2030: Architecture 2030 is a non-profit founded by Edward Mazria to design buildings to rapidly transform the building sector to reduce greenhouse gas emissions.

⫶ Books ⫶

Berry, Wendell. "Why I Am Not Going to Buy a Computer." *Harper's* September (1988): 112–113.

Friedman, Thomas L. *Hot, Flat, and Crowded: Why We Need a Green Revolution—and How It Can Renew America*. New York: Farrar, Straus and Giroux, 2008.

Goodell, Jeff. *Big Coal: The Dirty Secret behind America's Energy Future*. Boston: Houghton Mifflin, 2006.

Inslee, Jay, and Bracken Hendricks. *Apollo's Fire: Igniting America's Clean-energy Economy*. Washington, DC: Island, 2008.

Maté, Ferenc. *A Reasonable Life: Toward a Simpler, Secure More Humane Existence*. Norton, NY: Albatross Publ. House, 1997.

McDonough, William, and Michael Braungart. *Cradle to Cradle: Remaking the Way We Make Things*. New York: North Point, 2002.

Owen, David. *The Conundrum: How Scientific Innovation, Increased Efficiency, and Good Intentions Can Make Our Energy and Climate Problems Worse*. New York: Riverhead, 2012.

Princen, Thomas. *Treading Softly: Paths to Ecological Order*. Cambridge, MA: MIT, 2010.

Reece, Erik. *Lost Mountain: A Year in the Vanishing Wilderness: Radical Strip Mining and the Devastation of Appalachia*. New York: Riverhead, 2006.

Thoreau, Henry D. *Walden; or, Life in the Woods*. Boston, Ticknor and Fields, 1854.

INDEX

E

F

G

H

J

K

I

U

V

W

ABOUT THE AUTHOR

JEFF WILSON'S TWENTY-FIVE YEARS OF EXPERIENCE in the building industry includes jobs ranging from laborer to carpenter to remodeling contractor to host of home-improvement shows on HGTV and the diy network. He lives with his wife and two daughters in a perpetually half-renovated home in a small college town in Ohio.

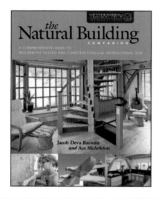

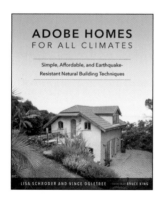
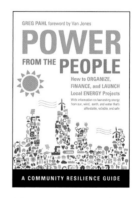

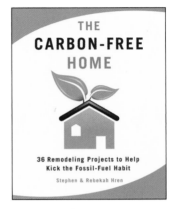
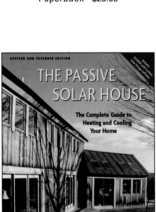
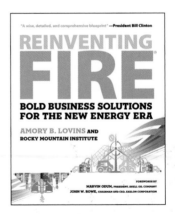